Acclaim for *In the Sha*

"History buffs will fall in love with th[...]
first book in the Darkness to Light ser[...]
tory and captivating characters bring to light a grief-filled perio[...]

—*Romantic Times*

"In an era of castles and kings, of royal decrees and unwavering faith, Golden Keyes Parsons' splendid debut novel pulls taut on the emotions while portraying the heartrending cost of religious freedom in turbulent 17th century France."

—TAMERA ALEXANDER, best-selling author of
Rekindled and *From A Distance*

"Drawing on her own family heritage, Golden Keyes Parsons has given us an absorbing picture of a people who would not bow to the Sun King . . . Dramatic, compelling, challenging."

—GAYLE ROPER, author of *Fatal Deduction*

"[A] captivating story, one you will savor, page after page. *In the Shadow of the Sun King* will resonate in your memory long after you've completed the final page. I was hooked. Don't miss this one!"

—JUDITH MILLER, author of Freedom's Path series
and Postcards from Pullman series

"*In the Shadow of the Sun King* is a story about light fighting against darkness and a woman willing to risk all for her family. The characters drew me in and the historical accuracy of the novel made me feel like I was living in Seventeenth-century France. I loved it! I also appreciated the author's notes that helped me to understand the history behind the novel. I'm eager to see what comes next from Golden Keyes Parsons."

—TRICIA GOYER, author of *A Valley of Betrayal*

"I was immersed into the lives of 17th century Christians who chose to stand courageous in their faith."

—DIANN MILLS, author of *Lightning and Lace*

"Golden Keyes Parsons shows impressive skills as a storyteller, weaving elements of brisk pacing and—even though the book is rich with historical detail—a swift immediacy that carried me along as if I had known this world all my life. A truly fine debut; I eagerly await this author's next work!"

—JAMES E. ROBINSON, author of *The Flower of Grass*

"Let's get a few things out on the table. First, I'm a man. Second, I normally enjoy thrillers and suspense novels. Third, I loved this book. Parsons gives us a fast-paced tale that leads from burned homes to prisons to slave galleys to magnificent Versailles and the intrigues of the royal court. She presents a large cast of characters in an easy-to-follow manner, educating us about history, religion, and the affairs of the heart.

Like Bodie Thoene and Tricia Goyer, Golden Keyes Parsons has breathed new life into stuffy history. She appeals to our souls as much as our minds, guiding [us] through a world that is believable in its old ways and yet so familiar in its human essence."

—ERIC WILSON, *New York Times* best-selling
author of *Fireproof* and *Field of Blood*

"Golden Keyes Parsons weaves a tale with intricate, rich threads, the end a tapestry of life complete with passion, rage, redemption, and deep-in-the-soul faith that spurs her characters ever onward. Turning these pages means being sucked into their world, and I found beauty in every step of their struggle as their faith was made real. Lovers of history, romance, and the fight for faith will not want to miss this stunning debut by Golden Keyes Parsons. I'm eagerly awaiting the next installment of the Darkness to Light series!"

—ROSEANNA WHITE, Christian Review of Books

IN THE SHADOW
OF THE SUN KING

Golden Keyes Parsons

BOOK ONE IN THE
DARKNESS TO LIGHT SERIES

THOMAS NELSON
Since 1798

NASHVILLE   DALLAS   MEXICO CITY   RIO DE JANEIRO   BEIJING

Published in Nashville, Tennessee. Thomas Nelson is a trademark of Thomas Nelson, Inc.

Thomas Nelson books may be purchased in bulk for educational, business, fund-raising, or sales promotional use. For information, please e-mail SpecialMarkets@ThomasNelson.com

Scripture references are taken from the King James Version of the Bible.

Publisher's Note: This novel is a work of fiction. Names, characters, places, and incidents are either products of the author's imagination or used fictitiously. All characters are fictional, and any similarity to people living or dead is purely coincidental.

Library of Congress Cataloging-in-Publication Data

Parsons, Golden Keyes, 1941–
  In the shadow of the Sun King / Golden Keyes Parsons.
    p. cm. — (The darkness to light series ; bk. 1)
  ISBN 978-1-59554-626-5 (softcover)
  1. Huguenots—Fiction. 2. Louis XIV, King of France, 1638–1715—Fiction. 3. Persecution—France—History—17th century—Fiction. I. Title.
  PS3616.A7826I6 2008
  813'.6—dc22   2008024179

Printed in the United States of America

09 10 11 RRD 6 5 4 3 2

Dedicated to the memory of my mother
Lois Clark Keyes
(July 23, 1913 — June 20, 2007)
whose French Huguenot heritage
planted us in a fertile soil of faith

and to my husband
Blaine Parsons
who never doubted that this story would be published.

Brest

Paris
Versailles

LOUIS XIV

Nantes

17TH CENTURY
FRANCE

Lyon

SPA

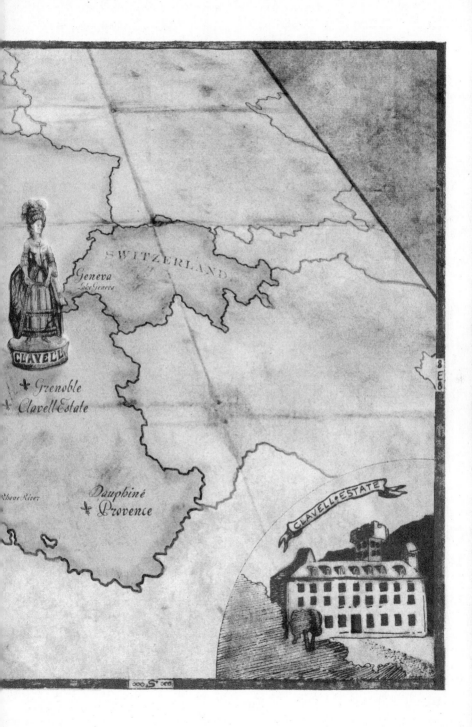

SWITZERLAND

Geneva
Lake Geneva

CLAVELL

✤ Grenoble
✤ Clavell Estate

Rhone River

Dauphiné
✤ Provence

CLAVELL ESTATE

Glossary

Absolument – Absolutely

Ainsí soit-il – So be it, amen

Au revoir – Good-bye

Bal masqué – Costume ball

Bastinado – Beating of the feet with a cane in the galleys

Bête – Idiotic, stupid

Bien – Fine, good

Bonjour – Hello, good morning, good afternoon

Bonsoir – Good evening, good night

Boulle commode – A chest of drawers with elaborate scroll-shaped
  inlay work using tortoise shell, ivory, or brass

Canapé – Settee

C'est bon – That's good

C'est moi – That's me

Chéri, chérie – Sweetheart

Comite/sous-comite – Literally, committee and/or subcommittee.
  In seventeenth-century galley ships, the galley master and second.

Consommation d'huile – Consumption, tuberculosis

Dieu, mon Dieu – God, my God

En titre – Official

Entrée – Entrance, entry

Fiacre – Carriage, hackney

Fleurs-de-lis – The tri-flower symbol of France (plural)

Galère – Galley ship; galères (plural)

Grande Entrée – The royal court who had permission to be present during the king's lever

Grand-mère – Grandmother

Grand-père – Grandfather

Hurluberlu – Fashionable hairstyle of the day

Je t'aime – I love you

Kyrie Eleison – Literally, "Lord, have mercy" in Greek. A chorus sung in many orthodox churches

La Contredanse – A dance performed with couples facing each other, or in a circle

La Courante – A slow waltz

La Pavane – A slow processional dance, which traditionally opened the ball

La Menuet – A dance in three-quarter time

Lever – To get someone out of bed, e.g., the king's morning rising ceremony

Ma bien aimée – Best-beloved

Madame – Mrs., lady

Mademoiselle – Miss

Mais, ce n'est pas possible! – "But, it is not possible!"

Mais non – Of course not

Maman – Mommy

Ma princesse – My princess

Masque – Mask worn at a ball

Méreau(x) – Tokens given to the faithful Huguenots upon entering
worship to be presented to elders before partaking of
Communion; used for identification as well

Merci – Thank you

Mère – Mother

Mesdames – Plural of Madame

Mon amour – My love

Mon petit chéri, petit choux – My sweetie, my sweetheart

Non – No

Oui – Yes

Papa – Daddy

Pardonnez-moi – Pardon me

Pas du tout – Not at all

Patron – Employer

Père – Father

Pirouette – Turn executed in dance

Pourquoi – Why?

Potage – Soup, stew

Robe battante – A loose flowing fashionable style of the day, cut low
in front

Seigneur – Lord of an estate

S'il vous plaît – Please

Toilette – Washing up, grooming

Historical Perspective

The holy halls of church history are splattered with the blood of those from all denominations of the Christian faith who endeavored to worship in freedom the God who came in the flesh to set us free. Something about the fallen nature of man loathes when another desires to praise God differently from one's personal concept of worship. At no time in history was this more pronounced than in the seventeenth-century France of King Louis XIV.

Following Martin Luther's declaration of *Sola Scriptura, Sola Fide* ushering in the Reformation, John Calvin, a Frenchman who eventually was forced to flee to Geneva, had an impact on French Huguenot (Protestant) doctrine in a manner that cannot be overemphasized. Foundational Huguenot belief contained a clear expression of the doctrine of justification by faith and the completed work of Christ on the cross. These tenets contrasted sharply with the Roman Catholic beliefs that the sacraments of the church play a role in salvation.

While Calvin did not support violent insurrection, the Saint Bartholomew's Day Massacre in 1572 of thousands of Huguenots in the streets of Paris during the wedding celebration of Henri of Navarre (Protestant) and Margot de' Medici (Catholic) began to change the thinking of the Huguenots, and the French Reformed theologians allowed more and more room for armed resistance against a tyranni-cal crown. However, in 1598, King Henri IV issued the Edict of Nantes giving the Huguenots legal recognition, and the persecution of the French Protestants waned.

In spite of the official ruling, the Catholic Church never approved the toleration granted by that legal document. The clergy and coun-selors surrounding King Louis XIV urged upon the king that the sta-bility of his government rested on a moral social order that would collapse without the support of a unified state religion. Thus began a steady succession of decrees that moved toward a full revocation of the toleration edict.

In 1660, the assembly of clergy asked King Louis to close all Huguenot colleges and hospitals and exclude Huguenots from public office. In 1670, their assembly recommended that at age seven chil-dren convert to Catholicism and be taken from their Huguenot par-ents to be reeducated in convents and monasteries. In 1675, mixed marriages were declared null and void, and the children illegitimate.

Meanwhile, the dragonnades had begun. Troops took over and lodged in and at the expense of private homes, especially those of the well-to-do. Soon the soldiers were robbing, beating, and raping the Huguenots in whose homes they were billeted, subjecting the occu-pants to forced conversions to the Catholic faith. Terrified, many Huguenots pretended conversion, but thousands abandoned their homes and fled to other countries. The economy of France suffered greatly because of the flight of these skilled tradesmen and artists.

One of the provinces that resisted with particular courage was the southern province of Dauphiné and the family of Vaudois. It is here and in this turbulent time period that our story begins.

ONE

Madeleine paused at the well, her bucket of freshly picked spring flowers teetering on the edge of the stone rim. Barking dogs intruded upon the late afternoon stillness, and birds rose from the trees into the sky. Then she heard the pounding hooves.

The bucket dropped from her grasp and clattered to the cobblestone walkway, scattering the colorful blossoms. She lifted her skirt and ran from the side of the manor toward the entrance of the estate, dispersing quacking ducks and geese as she went. She looked down the road, through the canopy of arching trees, then heard François before she saw him.

Her husband had ridden into Grenoble earlier that morning to oversee the sale of two of their pedigree horses. Now he galloped into view. What could be wrong? His dark hair flew around his shoulders from beneath his hat. His eyes were wild with terror.

"Dragoons! S-saw them from the ridge." He reined in his horse, and chips of dirt and rocks showered in every direction, pelting Madeleine in the face. He jumped to the ground, and his breath came in gulps. "Hurry, they're just a few minutes behind me. Where's Jean? We must get the boys to the cave at once."

Madeleine ran toward the imposing stone manor, crying over her shoulder, "Jean is in the back of the house, in the gardens. I'll get the children. Meet me behind the stable." She swept into the house, grabbing the boys' jackets and caps from the anteroom inside the front door as she called to them.

Her mother, Elisabeth, was sitting beside the huge stone fireplace with three-year-old Evangeline in her lap. "Madeleine, what's wrong?"

"Dragoons! Help me get the boys to the stable. François is getting the horses ready to take them to the cave."

Elisabeth stood, settling the child on her hip. "Come with me, Vangie. Let's go upstairs." She looked to Madeleine. "I'll get their extra clothes together."

"No time for that."

"Maman?" Eight-year-old Charles peered around the corner of a door.

"Where's Philippe?" Madeleine's voice rose.

"He's upstairs. Why? What's wrong?" His innocent eyes widened. In his hand he clasped a tiny wooden soldier.

"I'll get Philippe." Elisabeth, carrying Vangie, rushed past Madeleine up the stairs.

Madeleine took a deep breath and knelt in front of Charles. She took hold of the boy's wrists and concentrated on keeping her rising panic from showing in her voice. "Uncle Jean is going to take you to the hideout for a while. Remember how we practiced?"

Charles nodded.

"Hurry, now. Run to the stable. I'll get Philippe."

"But why, Maman? Why do we have to go to the hideout? Is somebody coming?"

"No time for your questions. Go!" Madeleine ran up the stairs after her mother.

CHARLES DARTED TO THE BACK OF THE HOUSE, OUT THE door, past the turret extension, and down the path to the stable. Henri, their stable master, came out of the barn carrying a saddle and two saddle blankets. François and Jean were bridling two horses.

"No time for saddles," François said. "They'll have to ride bareback."

The older man stopped, holding the blankets in midair. "But—"

"They can do it. Jean, you take the chestnut with Charles. Philippe can ride the mare."

Madeleine and Philippe came down the outside staircase from the second level of the house—Philippe thrusting his arms into the sleeves of his jacket. Madeleine clasped Charles' garments in her hands.

"Don't stop for anyone or anything until you get to the river," François instructed his younger brother. "Go upstream straight to the cave, and stay there until one of us comes for you. If the dragoons follow, they will think you have gone downstream—it would be the easier route."

Jean nodded. "I understand. I'll take good care of the boys."

"The supplies in the cave can last at least a week."

"Don't worry, brother. We will be fine. I'll wait for word." Jean mounted the stallion that pawed the ground, impatient to get underway.

"Here, Charles, you need to wear your cap." Madeleine cuddled his chin with her hand and then tucked his red curls underneath the hat.

Philippe mounted his black mare with twelve-year-old confidence, eager for adventure. "Don't worry, we will be fine. See you soon?"

"Yes, son. This won't be for long."

Jean lifted Charles in front of him. "Hold on tight to the mane, little one."

Charles turned and looked up at his uncle. Jean flashed a reassuring smile to the young lad and patted him on the thigh.

François gave the horses a swat, and Charles, clutching the horse's red mane, turned and waved good-bye.

Jean led the way, quickly urging the horse to a gallop, and Philippe followed, using a small riding whip to drive his mount to keep up.

"Hold on, Charles. Hold on!" Only now did Madeleine sense the lump in her throat. "Hold on, my precious sons." She waved good-bye, then slowly brought her hand down to cover her mouth and stifle a sob.

The two horses followed the low stone wall that ran the length of their property from the chateau until it reached the river. They rode down the slight incline, jumped the wall, and headed toward the line of oak trees along the river sporting the bright, budding green of spring leaves. The mountain peaks in the distance still glistened with the last of the winter snow. A trail of dust arose behind them, but settled quickly in the thick grass.

"Hurry, boys. Get to the trees—get to the trees." François clenched his fists as if the motion would help the young man and two boys reach their destination quicker.

The frightened parents willed themselves to cease staring after their boys and started back toward the three-story chateau. Madeleine glanced up at the gables in the steeply pitched roof and saw the children's governess, Claudine, peeking out from behind a tapestry drapery. Smoke curled from one of the chimneys. The outdoor servants, clearing the formal gardens of the winter debris, stopped their work and watched the masters of the estate return to the path leading to the house. Madeleine looked up to see her mother's plump figure bustling down the path with Vangie in her arms.

Vangie stretched her arms toward the vanishing figures of her brothers. "Vangie go too."

Madeleine took Vangie from Elisabeth, encircling the pouting child in her arms. "*Non, mon petit choux.* Your brothers are going on a trip. They will be back soon. Let's go back to the house now, it's getting late."

Evangeline continued to fuss. She rolled her chubby hand into a fist and rubbed her eyes, squeezing out tears that rolled down her cheeks. "Vangie want to go too."

"*Mère*, take her upstairs and prepare her for bed." Madeleine handed the child back to Elisabeth. "Use the outside stairs. Find Claudine and Suzanne and alert them—but be discreet. The dragoons will be here any moment."

As she hurried to follow François up the path to the house, Madeleine stepped on something. She bent down and picked it up—it was Charles' wooden soldier. Clutching it to her chest, she glanced toward the forest, where the riders were still visible. "Oh, dear *Dieu*, protect them."

For the first time since François came galloping into the estate, Madeleine allowed herself to look into his dark eyes. She saw fear there, but he gathered her into his arms. "Remember our plan. The

boys have gone to visit relatives in Spain. We must remain composed."
The thunder of approaching horses diverted him.

Pulling herself away to look directly at him, Madeleine brushed his hair back with her hand. "This must be a mistake. Louis wouldn't allow the dragoons to harass us."

François gave her a grim nod. "Let's hope so."

The two hastened to meet the regiment at the entrance of the house, François with an arm firmly gripping Madeleine around her waist.

The red-and-blue uniforms of the dragoons came into view, galloping down the entryway François had traveled twenty minutes earlier. The soldiers began to dismount.

François approached the officer heading up the regiment. "Greetings in the name of our glorious Sun King, Louis."

The officer, wearing a scarlet coat with silver buttons, met François' salutation with a cool acknowledgment from astride his magnificent white stallion. "Yes, indeed, we do come in the name of our King Louis. We have orders to billet our soldiers here. As Protestants—Huguenots—you owe our Catholic troops that privilege."

The officer spat the words *Protestants* and *Huguenots* out of his mouth as if they were poison on his lips.

"Of course, sir." François' initial effort to appear gracious melted in the face of the impressive officer.

The commander turned and issued orders for his band of soldiers to take their horses to the barn. "Grain and water for our horses?"

He wasn't asking permission, but giving directions.

"Yes, sir, this way. I'll get our stable master." François led them down the path, flanked by tall shrubbery, toward the barn.

Madeleine knew he was directing the soldiers' attention away from the route Jean and the boys had taken just moments before, moving as slowly as possible to give them opportunity to reach cover. The late afternoon shadows were already beginning to plunge the trees into darkness.

The commander dismounted and gave the reins of his horse to an assistant who looked barely sixteen years old. The young soldier led the stallion toward the barn.

The commander turned and stared at Madeleine, the flag of the dragoon unit, which he was holding, ruffling in the breeze. His muddy gray eyes were encased in a swarthy face, heavily lined from much time in the sun. "I'll have a look at the house now."

Madeleine shuddered and curtsied slightly, embarrassed by her plain brown, rough cotton skirt with the soiled apron. She willed her knees to stop trembling. *I look like a peasant!* She tucked wisps of her thick mahogany hair back under her cap and retied it as they turned to walk toward the house.

A footman stood ready at the ornately carved, arched doorway of the house and bowed from the waist as Madeleine ushered the commander inside.

Entering the foyer, the commander voiced his approval as Madeleine showed him the first floor of the manor. "Um . . . yes."

They moved into an impressive great room with its heavy, burgundy draperies framing sparkling beveled windows. Madeleine was glad that the servants had already done the spring cleaning. She pulled all the draperies back as the commander and his aide entered the room. An elegant sofa and chairs, matching the draperies, formed a sitting area around the fireplace.

"This will do nicely for our headquarters office." The commander walked around the perimeter of the large area, taking off his gloves and slapping them to the palms of his hands as if to punctuate his conversation. He stopped in front of a desk decorated with gold fili-gree, which stood in front of a tall bookcase. "I see you like to read."

"My father valued education." Her father's library of the writings of Calvin, Viret, d'Aubigné, and other Protestant theologians was neatly shelved in the bookcase beside a large fireplace where a fire struggled to stay alive. Madeleine moved toward the hearth and straightened the pewter candlesticks that adorned the massive stone mantel above the fireplace.

"You Huguenots think that the theology of John Calvin is educa-tion?" The officer's ominous voice rumbled through the room. "That is not education—that is heresy."

Then a fake cloak of courtesy covered his ire. His voice, though soft-ened, still held a veiled threat. "Please forgive me, I have failed to intro-duce myself. I am Commander Paul Boveé, of *Régt. des Dragons du Roi.*"

Madeleine curtsied once more. "And we are the Clavells."

"Yes, I know. And *you* are Madeleine de Vaudois-Clavell. A Vaudois—your family is well-known in Dauphiné for your, shall we say, religious heritage."

A familiar shiver fingered Madeleine's spine as she remembered the slaughter of members of her family for their faith when she was but twelve years old. Had they not been nobility at court at the time, she and her parents would have met the same fate.

"You and our king were childhood friends, is that not correct?" Commander Boveé toyed with the cup-shaped handle of the sword hanging by his side and smiled. His lips curved upward, but his eyes remained emotionless.

"Yes, sir, that is correct on both points. King Louis has spoken of me?" She felt a moment of relief. Perhaps they would be spared the atrocities taking place against the Huguenots across the country—the pillaging and burning of homes, the arrests, rapes, murders, and the kidnapping of children to be educated in Catholic monasteries. Did she dare hope that her father's former position at court and her childhood friendship with Louis would protect them?

"King Louis speaks fondly of you." Commander Boveé looked at the bookshelf and followed the lines of the case down to the tiny wooden soldiers Charles had aligned in battle formation in front of the fireplace only minutes ago. "It appears we have a future soldier in the family."

Madeleine began to gather the toy soldiers in her apron. "Actually, the maid was cleaning and took them off the shelf to dust. How careless of her to leave them lying on the floor." She replaced them on the bookcase shelf.

"I see. Interesting formation. Does the maid always line the soldiers up in battle readiness when she dusts?"

"No—well, I don't really know." Madeleine cocked her head demurely. "Grand designs, so perceived, are often the result of chance, are they not?"

"Yes." The commander gave Madeleine another chilling smile. "Perhaps."

She stepped past him. "Let me show you the rooms in the back of the house."

The large cooking area seemed to satisfy the commander. The fragrance of the turnip and cabbage stew, laced with pork, brewing in a large black kettle over the flame in the kitchen fireplace, filled the house. Large rounds of bread, baked earlier in the day, cooled on a heavy wooden table. The rich scent of yeast lingered in the air.

"The granary, buttery, and cheese rooms are there—through the breezeway." Madeleine indicated the utilitarian rooms with a wave of her hand.

Commander Boveé started through the breezeway. "May I?" His red cap with the falling bag and fur turnup followed the movement of his head from side to side as he surveyed the surroundings.

"Of course." Madeleine led him through the chambers where servants performed their duties to keep the manor in running order.

He paused in the granary. "God has blessed you with abundance—and lots of places to store it."

"Yes." Madeleine watched as Commander Boveé poked his sword into some of the large sacks of grain. She knew he was looking for her sons. The more time he spent on this phantom hunt, the more time the boys and Jean would have to reach the hideout.

They walked from the buttery room through the breezeway into the kitchen and back to the front of the house. Madeleine's thoughts were jumping from her sons making their getaway to her daughter upstairs with her mother.

Officer Boveé laid his hand on the railing of the staircase to the second floor. "And upstairs?"

"Bedrooms."

"Is anyone up there at this moment?"

"Yes."

"And that would be . . . ?"

"My mother, the children's governess, and our daughter, Evangeline, who is getting ready for bed."

"I see. And your sons? Where might they be?"

TWO

Jean spurred his horse on, shouting to Charles to hold on tighter. Philippe was doing a masterful job of keeping up, although his mare was not as eager as the young chestnut. They reached the trees and plunged into the forest, but Jean did not stop. "Keep going, Philippe. We need to reach the river."

The branches of the oak, ash, and pine trees slapped against them as they made their way through the woods. None of them spoke as they continued to press their horses. Even the normally talkative Charles remained quiet.

The high bank of the river sprang into view. Jean put up his hand, signaling Philippe to stop at the top of the cliff. The only sound, aside from the water swirling around the rocks in the river, was the horses' heavy breathing.

"Go straight down the embankment to the river," Jean instructed. "Let your horse take the lead. She won't stumble if you let her go at her own pace."

Philippe nodded and started down. He leaned back to keep his balance as the dirt and rocks began to crumble beneath the horse's hooves as she picked her way down the steep slope.

Jean began the descent, holding on to Charles with his broad, muscular arms. "Lean back. I will hold you. Hang on to the mane."

Charles did as he was told. Jean could feel the boy's body shivering—either from fear or from the descending temperature of the crisp evening air. He wrapped his arms tighter around Charles and let the reins rest on the horse's neck as he allowed the chestnut to take his lead.

They reached the river and waded into the shallows.

"Let me in front now." Jean moved ahead of Philippe, and they began to plod single file upstream. The horses slipped and slid over the rocks but managed to maintain their footing.

The water deepened and began to move more swiftly. Jean glanced back at Philippe. The older boy's eyes betrayed his fear, but he presented a brave front. "Don't be frightened. Last week's rain must have swollen the river a bit, but I don't think it will get much deeper."

Philippe nodded.

"I'm scared, Uncle Jean," Charles muttered through chattering teeth.

"I know. We'll be all right." Jean's words exuded confidence, but inside he wasn't as certain. They needed to get to the cave and out of sight.

Philippe's horse stumbled on the slippery rocks. "Uncle Jean!" he cried out.

The mare regained her footing, but then she moved from the shallow side of the river toward the middle and stepped off into a hole and began to swim.

"Stay with her. Hold on to her mane."

The whites of the mare's eyes glared as she trudged smoothly through the water.

"I can't—I can't hold on!"

Philippe's body splashed wildly behind the horse's head as the lad hung on to the black mane. The water purled around him—his head went underwater.

Jean's heart began to thud. He turned his horse around to go after Philippe.

"He's going under!" Charles' voice rose in pitch as he watched his hero vanish into the dark water. "Get him, Uncle Jean—help him!"

Jean knew he needed to stay on the shallow side for fear of losing Charles in the deep water as well. But he couldn't simply watch Philippe get swept away in the current of the river. He lunged for the mare's bridle, but the reins dangled out of reach.

The boy came up sputtering and choking as the mare swam toward Jean and Charles. Philippe's hands were still entangled in the horse's mane as he bent over face forward on her neck.

"My cap. I lost my cap!" Philippe disengaged one hand from the coarse, stringy hair of the mane and stretched his arm out in a fruitless grab for the gray woolen cap caught in the swift current of the river, floating out of his reach. It snagged on a log that jutted out into the water from the bank.

"Forget it, there are clothes in the cave. Are you all right?"

"I-I think so," Philippe said, still coughing.

The horses scrambled out of the deep water as the river again became shallow. Philippe settled himself on the horse and gathered up the reins. The horse whinnied and shuddered, spraying water in every direction.

"Good job." Jean directed the horses to the bank and jumped down. "Charles, hold our horses right there." Seizing the mare's reins, Jean patted Philippe's wet breeches. "Are you sure you are okay?"

"I'm sure—just cold."

Jean ran his hand over the mare's legs. "She seems to be fine too. Someone must be praying. The Lord has surely sent angels to watch over us."

Philippe smiled at his uncle.

Jean motioned with his hand. "Let's keep moving. We must hurry and get to the cave."

Jean instructed Philippe to dismount and walk beside the horses, leading them halfway up the opposite bank to a ledge that ran parallel along the riverbank. Jean followed, using a tree branch to brush the dirt and rocks to cover up their trail. "The dragoons may be able to track us to the river, but after they see we went into the water, they will assume we went downstream. That would be the easier, logical way to go."

They walked for several minutes in silence along the ledge. The sides of the bank rose higher and grew more rugged. "There it is." Jean stopped by a well-hidden indentation in the embankment. A brushy outgrowth cleverly hid a boulder and the entrance to the cave. Anyone riding by would never notice it.

"What about the horses, Uncle Jean? What are we going to do with them?"

"We'll have to let them go. Unbridle your horse—try to brush her down a little and get rid of any bridle or riding marks. Then I'll take them up to the plateau and let them go."

"Won't the dragoons be suspicious?"

"Your mother and father will simply explain that they got away and have been out in the meadow. Now, do as I say." Jean helped Charles down and pushed him toward the entrance of the hideout. "Go on into the cave. See what the supplies look like."

"It-it's too dark in there." The sun lingered low on the horizon. Only a bit of gray dusk hung on the bank of the river.

"There are candles."

"B-but . . ."

Philippe nudged his little brother with his elbow. "Scaredy cat."

"I am not."

"Are too." Philippe chuckled and finished taking the bridle off his horse. Using leaves, he brushed the horse's coat as best he could. She neighed and nuzzled his hand as he petted her. "Good girl. You did a fine job." He buried his face in her neck and gave her a final pat.

Jean handed Philippe the bridle he had removed from the chestnut. "Wait here, boys, while I turn the horses loose. Philippe, stay with your brother. I'll be right back." Jean scrambled up to the top of the ridge, clucking at the horses to follow him.

CHARLES SAT ON A TREE ROOT AND POUTED, RESTING HIS chin in his hands.

Philippe joined him, tossing the wet bridles at their feet. "Aw-w, c'mon, Charles, I was just teasing." Beginning to shake uncontrollably, Philippe wrapped his arms around his shoulders and rubbed them. "I-I'm so cold."

"Me too." Charles forgot his pouting and pulled his cap down tighter over his ears. "Are Maman and Papa going to be all right? Will the dragoons hurt them? Why didn't Vangie come with us?"

"Yes—no, I mean, yes, Maman and Papa will be fine. No, King Louis won't allow the dragoons to hurt any of us. And Vangie didn't come because she's a girl, and she's too young for school."

"If King Louis won't let the dragoons hurt us, why did they come?"

"I don't know. Don't worry. We won't let them take us."

"No dragoon is going to capture me and carry *me* off to Catholic school." Charles' jaw jutted out in little boy bravado. "Do they really hold a gun to your head and force you to revert?"

"*Convert*, Charles, *convert*. I don't know, that's what I've heard." Philippe continued to slap his arms in an effort to warm up. "Shush your chatter now. We'd better be quiet."

JEAN SHOOED THE HORSES THE REST OF THE WAY UP THE steep embankment and stood on the upper rim, watching to make sure they wandered on out into the apple orchard to begin feeding. "Don't go back home too soon," he muttered under his breath. The horses moved into the orchard, and Jean slid back down to the cave entrance.

"All right, boys, let's see what we can do to get warm here." He pushed aside the bush that appeared to be growing over a large boulder, revealing just enough room for the boys to scamper inside the cave. Jean had a harder time slithering his muscular shoulders through the opening. "Hmm, must have gained some weight."

The boys snickered as Jean groaned and finally got through. Then he reached through the crack around the boulder and pulled the bush back over it to hide their tracks.

The remaining light of dusk glimmered through the crack around the boulder that hid the opening, though it was barely bright enough to make out their surroundings. Jean inspected the wood stacked

16

alongside the wall of the tunnel, which led to the inner room of the cave. "This wood is wet. The river must have risen higher than we thought. Philippe, check that box up there on the ledge. See if the supplies and food are wet. We need to get some candles lit so we can see."

Philippe struggled up to a ledge, where he found a wooden box and a small trunk. A musket, bow, and arrows hung on a rock outcropping nearby. "They're dry. The water didn't get this high."

"Good. Hand me the trunk. Let's see if we can find you some dry clothes. Hopefully the candles and tinderbox are in there as well."

Philippe tugged on the heavy trunk, then shoved it to the edge of the craggy shelf. "It's too heavy. I can't lift it."

"Go ahead, tip it over. I can catch it." Jean caught the trunk with a grunt and lowered it to the ground.

Philippe scrambled over the edge as Jean opened the lid. The three peered inside, holding their breath in hopes that what they needed would be there. No candles.

"I'll get that wooden box. They're probably in there." Jean pulled himself up to the ledge and handed the chest down to Philippe. The boy fumbled with the latch, but finally forced the lid open. On top were the candles and tinderbox they hoped for.

Jean started to work, striking the flint to ignite the tinderbox, then the candle from that. He succeeded as the boys searched through the blankets and extra clothing that their father had placed in the trunk. Cooking and eating utensils, soap, and food lay in the bottom of the wooden chest, along with a leather pouch.

"C'mon, boys, let's take the trunk and chest into the interior of the cave. Once we are around that curve in the rock, we won't have to worry about anybody seeing the light from the outside. Charles, you carry the candle—bring the extras. Philippe and I will get the trunk. I'll come back in a minute for the chest."

Charles led the way, one timid step at a time, holding the candle high to give maximum light. Jean and Philippe each took an end of the locker. A large room opened up before them only a few feet through the tunnel and around a curve. Jean and Philippe lowered the trunk onto the flat rock floor of the room.

Jean lit another candle and went back to get the chest.

Philippe found dry garments in the trunk and quickly shed his wet clothes, hanging them on an outcropping of rock. Jean returned, lugging the wooden box.

"What about air, Uncle Jean? Is there enough air in here for us?" Philippe glanced about the cave.

"Air comes in from the back entrance. Look at the candle." The small flame flickered, reaching its finger toward the dark abyss behind them. "We have plenty of air. If we should have to, we can get out that way. It's just a bit tricky in places. No need to worry about that now." Jean wrapped his arms around himself and shuddered. "It appears we are going to have a chilly night. I didn't find any dry wood. I'll have to go out and gather some early tomorrow morning. Did you find any food, Philippe?"

Philippe rummaged through the chest. "Some—there's a round of cheese, hard tack, and dried apples, and something else—I can't tell. Maybe dried pears or apricots? Chestnuts—and wine. Papa put wine in the box." He brought out a bottle for Charles and Jean to see. "Here's something else." Philippe held up a leather pouch with both hands. "This is heavy."

"Let me see that." Jean took the bag from Philippe. "That *is* heavy." Jean untied the leather strips and pulled the top open. "*Mon Dieu!*"

Philippe and Charles crowded around Jean to peer into the bag.

Jean reached in and pulled out a handful of gold coins, glinting in the soft light of the candle. He felt around the inside, fingering the gold pieces, and found a smaller purse. Inside that pouch were several *méreaux*—the tokens that identified them as Huguenots. "Look here, your father thought of everything." Jean let the boys look at the coins, then returned them to the box.

They huddled around the candle, as if the meager light would warm them, and Jean doled out the cheese, hard tack, and fruit. "I don't think we will be here long enough to use up all the food, but just in case, let's be frugal. I can get fresh water from the river when I go out for wood in the morning."

They finished their meal in silence. Unspoken questions hung heavy in the dank air of the cave.

"Let's get the blankets out of the trunk, and you can help me make a pallet. We will stay warmer if we all sleep together on one mat."

Jean's concerns for the boys' welfare, finding firewood the next day, having enough food to last, and the possible pursuit of the dragoons weighed on his mind, but he let them lie unexpressed. The boys mustn't sense his apprehension.

"This will be perfect," he said, trying to bolster the brothers' spirits. "You boys get situated and go to sleep. I'll stay up and keep watch."

"What if the candle . . ." Charles' thin voice pleaded with his uncle.

"I'll make sure the candle doesn't go out during the night. Don't worry."

Philippe shoved his brother and laughed.

PHILIPPE OPENED ONE EYE AND PEERED AT THE FLICKER-ing candle. The tallow lay low and melted around the pewter holder, but it still burned. With the blanket wrapped around his head, Charles had cuddled up to his brother's back. Philippe reached out for Jean. He was gone.

Philippe sat up and whispered, "Uncle Jean?"

No answer.

Charles stirred, but did not wake up.

Philippe pulled himself out of the tangled blankets. He labored to clear away the early morning cobwebs from his head. Why was Jean gone? Then he remembered. His uncle was going to go out early to find firewood.

Philippe got up and looked in the wooden box. Papa had supplied ample candles, plus three more candle stands. Philippe took one of the candles around to where his younger brother was still sleeping and lit it. He found some of the dried fruit and munched on it as he moved through the tunnel. Then he sat down at the entrance of the cave to wait for Jean's return.

A muffled bellow penetrated the stillness of the heavy air in the cave. "Over here!"

Philippe's heart began to pound as he heard shouting down by the river. More shouts and muted exclamations. He sat still for a moment, trying to decipher who it was and what was happening. He peered out through the tiny crack. Through the limbs of the bush he could see down to the river, where the clear water sparkled in the early morning sunlight.

"Philippe? Where are you?" Charles had awakened.

Philippe scurried from the cave entrance to his frightened little brother. "Shhh, I'm right here. Be quiet. I hear voices outside."

He put his arms around Charles in an awkward hug, and they sat motionless as they listened.

"They came this way."

The voices were closer now. The boys could hear footsteps clambering up the cliff, knocking rocks down into the river as they ascended.

"*Non*, come back on this side. They couldn't have gotten up there."

Philippe and Charles looked at each other, wide-eyed. Philippe put his finger up to his mouth. After another moment of listening, he mustered up courage and crawled toward the entrance. Philippe peeked out once more, only to fling himself back against the wall, gasping. All he could see through the crack around the boulder were the black leather gaiters of a dragoon.

THREE

Commands to the horses and the jangling of gear roused Madeleine from her restless dreams. Sleep and wakefulness had played tag with her mind all night long. She leaned up on one elbow and listened to the clamor below. The sun cast thin rays through the early morning gray cloak of fog rising from the dewy meadow.

"Whoa! Steady!"

She turned and shook her husband. "François!"

He mumbled, rolled over, and then sat up in bed. "What? What's the matter?"

"Look outside."

In the barnyard a few dragoons were assembled and some were starting down the hill toward the river. François threw the blanket aside and stood sideways by the window so he could not be seen from the outside. "There's nothing we can do, Madeleine. We just have to trust Jean and the boys to the mighty hand of God."

Madeleine climbed out of bed and joined her husband at the window. Her gaze settled on the trees that lined the banks of the river—the dew on the meadow shimmering in the early dawn. The instincts of a mother reached out to her sons. Were her boys safe and warm? Were they hungry? Were they scared? She knew Jean would take good care of them, but the seriousness of the situation tortured her. "I can't stand this. My heart feels like it is ripping apart."

François led her back to the bed and sat her down. He grasped her slender fingers with both his strong hands and patted them gently. "I'll get dressed and go downstairs to see what I can find out."

"I'll check on Vangie and Claudine."

Madeleine slipped across the hall to Vangie's room to find her sound asleep in her bed. She could hear Claudine stirring in the next room. She heard no movement from her mother's room.

François looked up but didn't speak as Madeleine returned to their bedroom and plopped down on the bed, deep in thought. Why would Louis order the dragoons to come here? If she could just speak with him—face-to-face—she knew she could convince him to recall them. She fingered the quilt on their bed and lay back on her pillow.

No, trying to see him and talk him into calling off his dragoons would be folly. What was she thinking? Her childhood friend was the king of France—no longer the boy with whom she rode horses through the mist of early mornings. Not the young man who laughed at her as she struggled with the dance steps of the *menuet* as he patiently instructed her. She was only one of many loves in his past. What if he didn't remember her?

Even as the thought crossed her mind, she knew it was false. On the other hand, what if he refused to see her? That was a more likely possibility. Or what if he simply swatted her away like a pesky fly? It was a long time ago. Maybe he was glad to be rid of her when she left court with her parents.

She bolted upright. All of this shadowboxing was of no avail. She must go see him. It was their only hope. She would go to Versailles.

"François, I've been thinking. I have a plan."

Her husband tied his belt around his waist and reached for his jacket on a chair beside the armoire. "What is that?"

"I'm going to Versailles to see Louis."

François tossed his jacket on the bed and took Madeleine by the shoulders. He held her, looking her straight in the eyes. "No, it's too dangerous. I won't allow it."

Madeleine pleaded with her husband. "But I know Louis wouldn't harm us. Something has gone terribly awry. If I could just appeal to him . . ."

François' gaze penetrated hers, and he gritted his teeth. "Madeleine, he was a young man the last time you were with him. You were adolescents, going to balls and parties. You don't know how the burdens of being king may have changed him. You don't know the voices that whisper to him now, the influences of his wife—and mistresses. Put it out of your mind." He grabbed his coat and stomped out the door and down the stairs.

Madeleine did not call after her husband but turned again to the window. Commander Boveé stood in the barnyard directing his men. Suddenly the commander looked toward the house and upward to the window where Madeleine stood. He smiled and nodded, touching his hat in acknowledgment.

Madeleine was startled, but she maintained her composure and nodded her response. She moved away from the window, her pulse throbbing in her temples.

"Suzanne!" She rang for her chambermaid to assist her in dressing. She wanted to wear something more representative of a *seigneur's* wife than what she had on yesterday when the soldiers arrived. *Commander Bovée needs to realize he is not dealing with mere peasantry, but a family of nobility.*

Madeleine splashed cold water on her face from the porcelain ewer sitting on an ornate wooden table beside the armoire. She went to the armoire and opened the gold, embellished doors to survey her gowns.

"Madame?" Suzanne's normally quiet confidence was betrayed by a tremor in her soft voice.

"Come help me with one of my gowns. Pick out something noble—simple, but elegant."

"I understand, madame." Suzanne moved to the open doors of the armoire and chose a teal silk dress with champagne colored lace at the neckline and cuffs.

Madeleine smiled. She knew her servant favored the teal because it brought out the blue-green of Madeleine's eyes. She pulled a snarled rope of pearls from her jewelry chest, overflowing with tangled trinkets, and found a corset in one of the drawers.

Suzanne shook her head at her mistress's untidy dresser. "Here, let me help you." She untangled the necklace and looked for the matching earrings.

Madeleine looked at her image in the mirror, tilting her head to one side. She began brushing her hair vigorously. "We don't have time to put my hair in a *hurluberlu*. Just part it in the middle, pile it on top of my head, and get my pearl combs to hold it in place."

Suzanne got to work immediately, expertly assisting Madeleine in her *toilette*.

When they finished, Madeleine stood and surveyed the results in the cheval mirror. "Well, I suppose that will have to do." She looked down at her gown—not exactly everyday wear. She felt a bit ridiculous, but decided she would exercise her rightful role as the madame of the house for the time being.

Madeleine swept down the stairs to find soldiers congregated in the kitchen, finishing their morning meal—some moving to the outside, some going to the main room where Commander Boveé had confiscated a table to use as a desk.

Thérèse, Henri's wife, busied herself between serving the potage and distributing bread to the men. She stole a nervous glance at Madeleine but continued her work.

The morning sunlight streaming into the kitchen through the doorway was suddenly blocked by the shadow of the commander, paused in the entryway of the kitchen. He looked about, then stepped inside.

"Good morning, Madame Clavell. Are you well this morning?"

"Very well, *merci*—and yourself?"

"Quite well indeed. Your manor is more than comfortable. And might I compliment the lady of the manor on your attire this morning?"

"Thank you, sir. Much more fitting to entertain . . . guests."

"It is our pleasure to enjoy your hospitality."

"Please, Commander, won't you come into the dining room to eat your breakfast?" Madeleine led the commander into the adjoining room and motioned him to the more formal table, topped by a fine white cloth that reached to the floor on all sides.

Commander Boveé seated himself at the head of the table and

removed his gloves. "I'll have some of that potage now, and bread. It's not often soldiers have the luxury of meat in the stew."

Madeleine nodded to Thérèse, who hastened to serve the commander. A footman placed a pewter tumbler filled with water on the table before the commander. "Our water is very good, cold and pure." She took a seat opposite him at the other end of the table.

"From the river?"

"Actually, from our well—spring-fed." Madeleine picked up her tumbler of water. "Speaking of the river, I noticed from my window that your men were riding in that direction. *Pourquoi?* We have an ample supply of water from the well."

François had come into the dining room and heard Madeleine's inquiry. He approached the commander.

Henri stood behind François, holding a riding whip in his hand, his large form erect and straight despite his age.

Commander Boveé did not look up or acknowledge Madeleine's question. He slurped the potage with relish.

"Good morning, sir," said François. "I believe my wife asked you a question. She is accustomed to respect in this household."

Without looking at François, Commander Boveé wiped his mouth on a starched linen napkin and stood slowly, his hand on his sword. He turned, squaring off with François.

The master of the manor held his ground. The moment seemed suspended in time as the seconds ticked by—both men glaring at the other.

Madeleine held her breath as Henri moved forward, fingering his riding whip.

"Papa!"

Vangie, still dressed in her nightgown, bounded into the room and between the men, into her father's arms. She planted a kiss on his cheek and wrapped her arms around his neck.

Smiling, François returned the exuberant affection, giving her a lingering hug.

Looking at the dashing commander, Vangie asked, "Who are you?"

The commander's posture relaxed. "Well, now. What a pretty little girl. I'm Commander Boveé. What is your name?"

"I'm Vangie—and I'm three." Vangie held up three dimpled fingers for the commander to see.

"You are only three? Precocious for three years old, I'd say."

Vangie shrank back in her father's arms and began to suck her thumb. She reached for Madeleine. "I'm hungry."

Madeleine gave her daughter a kiss as she took her in her arms, then called for Thérèse. "Get Evangeline's breakfast. I'll go check on Claudine. Vangie should not have come downstairs by herself."

François caught hold of Madeleine's arm. "No, wait, Madeleine. Commander Boveé still has not answered your question."

Claudine burst into the dining room at that moment. "Vangie! Shame on—" Sensing the tension of the moment, she stopped midsentence.

"Officer Boveé?" François folded his arms.

A few more seconds passed, then the commander gave an un-amused laugh. "Yes, of course. Please forgive me. Living on the road with soldiers causes one to forget common courtesies." He gave a slight bow, then sat down to continue his breakfast.

François persisted. "My wife asked you a question."

Madeleine implored her husband with her eyes.

The commander did not look up, but answered, "A simple explor-ing expedition. Some horses seem to be missing from your stable."

"Out of a stable of forty horses, you were able to detect that some were missing?"

"Experience has taught my men to be observant. Two stalls, empty, and obviously vacated not long ago."

"Well, it's easily explained. They are out in the pasture. They got away when Henri was cleaning the stable yesterday. We simply need to go find them."

The commander swiveled in his chair to face Vangie. "Tell me, little girl, do you have any brothers or sisters?"

Vangie wriggled in Claudine's lap as she ate a piece of buttered bread. She looked at her mother.

"Tell the commander, Vangie." Madeleine's voice was soft but firm.

"Uh-huh."

"Uh-huh, what? Brothers or sisters? Or both?"

"Yes, sir," her mother corrected her.

"Yes, suh."

"How many?"

"Two brothers."

"What are their names?"

Vangie again looked at her parents, then down at the bread she was eating. "More butter." She held the bread up to Claudine.

Claudine stood, holding the little girl, and walked to the buffet where a covered bowl of butter sat. She removed the cover, dished out more butter for the child, and spread it on the warm bread.

François, standing by the fireplace, answered the question. "We have two sons. Philippe is twelve and Charles is eight."

"I believe I asked Evangeline the question." Commander Boveé used Vangie's formal name, and the implication was clear.

"Vangie, where are your brothers?"

"They're gone."

"Where did they go?"

Evangeline took another bite of the bread. Her hands were greasy with the melting butter.

"Uh-oh," Claudine fussed. "Let's wipe that off before it drips all over you." She set Evangeline down on the edge of the buffet and pulled a cloth out of a drawer to wipe the child's hands.

Commander Boveé stood and moved to the buffet and took the child in his arms.

She pulled away from him and stretched her arms for her father. "Papa."

"You are frightening her." François moved to take his daughter.

"Where are your brothers, Vangie?"

"Gone." She had the fingers of one hand in her mouth, pushing away on the chest of the commander with the other.

"Gone—where?"

"I dunno."

François took Vangie from the commander. "We have already told you—the boys are visiting relatives in Spain. They will be gone for the rest of the spring and all of the summer."

"Maybe—just maybe. We shall see." He turned to face the family. "Good day, for now. You'll excuse me, as I have work to do." The commander gave a deep bow and with authority strode out of the dining room, banging his sword on the chair as he left.

A collective sigh of relief filled the room. François held up his hand to caution them to keep quiet. "Go about your tasks as normally as possible," he whispered. "Pray God's protection over the boys and Jean."

Elisabeth had joined the family in the dining room. She moved to take Vangie from François, but the little girl clung to her father and pressed her head to his chest.

"She's all right," he said. "Let's all sit down and eat breakfast as we normally do."

The family bowed their heads for their customary blessing of the meal, frighteningly aware of the antagonistic soldiers in the other parts of the house.

"We will not be intimidated into denying our faith." François' hands remained steady and his voice firm as he brought his pewter tumbler to his lips.

Thérèse served the family breakfast, and Henri went outside to the barn. Vangie remained in her father's lap the entire meal.

François finished his breakfast in a hurry and joined Henri in the stable.

Henri's clear blue eyes reflected concern underneath his bushy white eyebrows. "What shall we do about the horses?"

"Go look for them in the pasture. They may be across the river, but don't go that far to look for them. They'll come back on their own eventually. It would perhaps dissuade the commander from believing that the boys took off on them, however, if we could get them back in the barn this morning."

"I'll saddle up CiCi and go out right away." Henri walked to the front stall and got out the faithful dapple-gray that had been François' horse for many years. "She has a sense where the others are."

François concurred. "Go to the meadow and call for them. They probably ended up grazing in the orchard on the other side of the river."

Henri set about saddling and bridling the old mare. She whinnied, and he fed her an apple. She was the stable favorite, although they owned many that were faster, better bred, and more beautiful. But CiCi was strong and dependable and seemed to have an instinct about her master and the family. Henri had taken care of her for a long time. He smiled as he outfitted her, remembering the boys learning to ride on her broad back. Philippe never knew any fear while learning to ride. Charles was a bit more timid, but they both took to it well and were capable in the saddle.

Henri mounted up and called to François, making sure the soldiers remaining in the barnyard heard him. "I'll be back soon. I'm sure I'll find our missing steeds straightaway."

François waved as Henri disappeared over the hill of the rolling meadow, trying to appear unconcerned before returning to the stable boys who were feeding the rest of the stock.

His attention was diverted by shouts coming from the front of the house. Smoke rose above the roof. François dropped the feed bag and ran around the side of the manor, following the smoke and the whoops of the men. There in the circular driveway of the house stood a mound of their treasured books from the library bursting into flames. Soldiers stood by, guffawing and stoking the fire. Thick, black smoke rose from the leather covers.

Madeleine, Elisabeth, Vangie, and Claudine came tumbling out of the front door. Madeleine stopped—her eyes wide with shock, then narrowing with defiance. "Oh no! Not the books! How dare you! You have no right!"

She started toward the fire, but a strong hand grabbed her wrist.

"Surely you wouldn't defy King Louis' orders, now, would you?" Commander Boveé's grip tightened on her wrist, his dark fingers digging into her tender flesh. He brazenly drew her close. "Would you?" he repeated.

Madeleine struggled to free herself from his grip. He pressed his body up against hers, challenging her to continue her resistance.

François bolted toward them. "Take your hands off her!"

Officer Boveé turned a steely gaze on François. "But of course." The commander stepped back and released Madeleine's arm. "I envy you, monsieur. You have a great prize in your wife—fiery temperament, and so beautiful in addition. No wonder she is a favorite of King Louis."

François' face reddened.

"Now, if you will allow me, I must return to my work, Madame Clavell."

Madeleine rubbed her wrist where Commander Boveé had grabbed it. "Work! You call the destruction of valuable books *work?*"

"Be thankful that is all we intend to dispense with at the moment."

"Are you threatening us—a family of nobility?" Madeleine challenged Commander Boveé. "I shall see to it that Louis hears about this."

"Oh, I have no doubt about that, dear lady." The commander put his gloves on. "No, not threatening. Just carrying out direct orders from our king. The latest assembly of clergy has encouraged the king to unify our country in faith as well as politics. Your family is well known for your resistance."

Madeleine continued her objection. "This is a terrible mistake. Someone else must have issued the orders—or you are acting independently. Louis would never have allowed this."

Commander Boveé replied through clenched teeth, his words clipped. "A soldier never acts independent of his commander, madame. Yes, indeed, you are nobility. You are also Protestant, and as such constitute a threat to the sovereignty of our king. We merely intend to assure His Majesty of the loyalty of all of his subjects."

Madeleine struggled to maintain her composure. "You may return to Versailles with a glowing report of our loyalty to King Louis, with fondest regards from me personally."

"Ah, yes. I will do that." Commander Boveé relaxed and flashed a wide smile, making him appear almost handsome. "Ha! That's quite some competition you have, Monsieur Clavell—the king himself."

Madeleine stepped to François' side. "No competition at all. King Louis and I are simply old friends."

The commander wrinkled his forehead and grinned. "That's not what I hear from the whisperings at court. However, if this should be an error in the dispensing of orders, it may take a personal visit from so fair a lady to the king himself to clear it up."

François glared at Commander Boveé as he reached for Madeleine's hand.

Madeleine faced the imposing figure of the commander, pulling her husband with her. "I shall look forward to seeing you at Versailles, Officer Boveé."

FOUR

Jean crouched beneath the tangled underbrush and peered through the brambles toward the river. In his arms he held pieces of wood gathered from the forest in the early light of dawn. Over the plateau on the opposite side of the river, he could see several dragoons swarming down the ridge directly across from the cave. He heard the splashing of water as some of the men led their horses into the river.

A web of panic began to weave sticky fingers around him. *O Dieu, blind their eyes.* Jean's hands trembled uncontrollably, and a piece of wood fell off the top of the pile.

"Uh-h!" He grunted as the wood fell. Jean cringed, his breath coming in short, shallow spurts. He stared at the edge of the cliff. No sign of a dragoon on his side of the river yet.

He carefully and quietly placed the wood on the ground and backed into the thicket for protection. Just as he reached the cover of a log sprayed with the early fronds of spring fern, a dragoon's red-and-blue hat appeared over the edge of the cliff. The soldier pulled himself to the rim and stood rigid, scanning the orchard. In one hand he held his long, flintlock musket loosely in front of him; in the other he held Philippe's cap, still dripping with water from being fished from the river.

Jean flattened his body. Prickly briars and twigs punctured his flesh. Tiny yellow and purple wildflowers nodded their silent heads at him, and the scent of damp earth and moss writhed its way into his nostrils as he buried his face into the earth. He noticed wild mushrooms springing up in the midst of the moldy, natural compost.

The dragoon, kicking rocks and using his musket to part the underbrush, began walking toward the forest's edge directly in front of Jean. Jean held his breath, so the vapor from his exhalation wouldn't reveal his location.

The dragoon came so close that Jean could see the pistol in his holster and hear his axe clicking against his leg. The soldier looked left and right—then turned and walked through the low-lying scrub brush toward the trees on his right. He tucked the cap in his belt and leaned the musket against an oak tree, and commenced to relieve himself.

Shouts from the river summoned him. "Come back down. They wouldn't have gone up there."

Jean heard the soldier swear as he hurried back toward his comrades, sliding down the ridge.

Bile bubbled up in Jean's throat. He swallowed hard and remained motionless until he was sure the dragoon had gone over the side of the cliff. Then he backed under the cover of the brush, but he could still hear the soldiers' voices.

"Let's try downstream. No sign of them here. They must have

gone the other way." The dragoons slid down the cliff, waded into the river, and headed downstream.

Jean lay limp and motionless in his refuge of spring foliage.

PHILIPPE PULLED CHARLES AWAY FROM THE ENTRANCE OF the cave, holding him tight against his body, and covered his brother's mouth with his hand. The cold, jagged rock wall jabbed into his back as he molded himself against it. He dared not even whisper, "Shhh!"

The command—*Come back down. They wouldn't have gone up there*—sounded as if the soldier issuing the mandate were standing at the entrance of their hideout. Then they heard someone slide down the cliff, followed by the splashing of water.

The boys did not speak for several minutes but squatted on the rock floor, looking at each other, weak-kneed and breathless.

"Where's Uncle Jean?" Charles managed a hoarse whisper.

"Don't you remember? He said he would go out and find dry wood for a fire today."

Charles started in with the drilling questions. "But why did he leave us here without telling us where he was going? What if the dragoons found him? What if he can't get back to us? What if we're left in here alone? What are we going to do?"

"Hush. He probably thought he could go out, get the wood, and be back before we woke up. He'll be back soon. Let's get something to eat."

Philippe tried to sound reassuring, but he wondered the same things himself. He knew that if Jean did not return, it was his responsibility to take care of Charles. He pulled himself up to the ledge and removed the flintlock musket from the outcropping of rock. Jumping

back down, he searched through the wooden box for packets of pow-
der and balls.

Charles munched on a piece of cheese as Philippe readied the
musket.

A soft rustling toward the back of the cave startled the boys.
Philippe put out his hand to caution Charles to be quiet. He moved
around the wooden box and in front of Charles with the musket
pointed toward the inky black of the inner cave. The rustling stopped.
Then began again.

It could be an animal. Philippe knew he couldn't fire the musket
for fear the dragoons would hear and return. But what if it was a dragoon who had found the back entrance? Philippe motioned for Charles
to move the candles behind a rock into the shadows. Charles blew one
out, then tripped noisily as he lunged for the second one. The noise
echoed through the cave. The boys remained motionless. The rustling
resumed.

"Philippe? Charles? It's me, Jean."

Philippe exhaled. "You scared us to death."

Jean appeared around the corner of the rock where their sleeping
pallet lay. "The dragoons are out looking for us. I—" He stopped
abruptly as he noticed the musket in Philippe's hands. "Is that loaded?
Put it down before you hurt someone."

Philippe's chin quivered, but he stifled the urge to cry and set the
musket against the wall of the cave. "We heard the dragoons and saw
them through the crack around the boulder at the entrance. We
thought they had found you. I-I didn't know what to do."

Jean embraced the boy. "You did well, son. You did exactly right."
As Jean released Philippe, he looked at Charles sitting in front of the
candle, blinking back tears. "Well now, we still need dry wood. I left

what I had gathered when I heard the dragoons nearby. We shall wait a bit until we are certain they've left the area, and I'll try again."

"Why did the dragoons come upstream looking for us?" Philippe asked. "Papa thought they would go downstream."

Jean looked again at the musket Philippe had put aside. "Is the hammer cocked on that? Uncock it right now. Those things are dangerous."

Philippe uncocked the musket and set it back against the rock. "Sorry." He repeated his question. "Why did the dragoons come this far upstream?"

"Your cap was the culprit. I saw a dragoon holding it. He was so close I could see the buttons on his jacket and smell the sweat of his uniform."

"Weren't you scared?"

Jean rubbed his forehead. "So scared I thought my heart was going to thump out of my chest. If the dragoon hadn't had to take care of personal business, he probably would have found me. A few more steps, and he would have stepped on me. That's when one of his comrades hollered at him to come back. Your maman and papa are going to have some explaining to do regarding that cap when the dragoons get back to the manor."

"I'm sorry, Uncle Jean. I couldn't help it."

"It wasn't your fault. It was just one of those things that happens. Let's wait awhile longer to make sure the dragoons are gone, and then I'm going to take us out the back way. We can survey the area better from there because the back opening comes out in the forest. Plus, you need to know the way just in case . . . well, it'll just be good for you to know how to get out another way.

"When we get to the back entrance, I want you two to stand guard while I go get the dry wood. Then I'll go downstream a ways and get some water out of the river. Didn't I see a pail up on the ledge where we found the trunk?"

Philippe paused a moment. "Yes, but I didn't get it down."

"Would you go get it, please, Philippe, while I get something to eat?"

Charles sidled up to his uncle. "Can I stay here with you, Uncle Jean? Please?"

Jean put a strong arm around Charles. "Certainly. Go on, Philippe."

Philippe picked up a candle and headed toward the tunnel, calling over his shoulder, "Be back before you know it."

As he entered the tunnel leading to the entrance, blackness engulfed him—his lone candle flickering in the gloom. Philippe's momentary bravery flickered like the candle flame. He found the pail and hurried back to Jean and Charles, whistling to bolster his nerve.

The three waited for an hour or so, then Jean stood up. "Let's go. Philippe, get the musket but don't cock it. Pick up another ammunition packet just in case. Charles, get one of the candles and follow me. Philippe, you bring up the rear." Jean hunched down in front of Charles. "It is very important that you keep your candle lifted high so we can see. Do you understand?"

Charles acknowledged Jean's instructions and dutifully took his place. Jean lit another candle and led the way, carrying the small bucket in his other hand.

"The trail out is easy to begin with, but we have to navigate a narrow ledge right before the opening. When I tell you we are coming up to it, turn sideways and back up as close as you can to the wall. It is a fairly steep drop-off from the ledge, and there is water below, so be careful." Jean had the boys' full attention. "Are you ready?"

Both boys nodded and fell in line single file. They were able to stand up most of the way. As they got closer to the narrow ledge, however, they had to stoop to avoid low hanging rock formations.

Jean paused and looked up, holding his candle higher to illuminate the ceiling above them. "These formations are magnificent when one has the time and sufficient light to observe them. Someday we will come back and do that."

Charles and Philippe turned unseeing eyes toward the natural wonders.

Jean chuckled and muttered, "Perhaps it's not such a good time for a natural history lesson, yes?"

Charles managed a weak grin and nodded. Philippe remained stoic.

Jean urged them on. "We're almost there." Then he straightened and whispered, "Here's the ledge. Stand up against the wall and follow me."

The boys stayed close behind him, inching their way toward the light coming from the opening. A rock tumbled from the ledge, ricocheted off the steep incline, and then plunked into the water far below. Charles and Philippe froze as the splash echoed through the cave.

"Don't stop, boys. Keep inching sideways—not much farther."

The ledge widened as they approached the opening, but they had to crawl on their hands and knees to get out.

Jean exited and then pulled Charles out. "Whew! There now, that wasn't so bad, was it?"

Philippe tumbled out on his own and hunkered down with the musket. "Not so bad."

Charles blew out the candle and set it down at the entrance of the passageway. "I wasn't scared at all."

Jean and Philippe grinned at the younger boy, and Jean tousled the lad's hair. "Now, Philippe, I want you to wait here and watch. I don't think the dragoons will come back this way—at least not today. However, if you need to warn us, signal by whistling like a . . . uh . . . like a starling. Can you do that?"

"Sure. Like when we're out hunting?"

"Exactly. Charles, do you think you can carry that bucket if it has water in it?"

Charles had regained his courage. "I can do it. I'm strong."

"Good boy. Philippe, the wood I dropped is right behind those oak trees toward the clearing, before the cliff drops down to the river. You keep watch, and when I whistle, you move to where we are. Then, if it is clear, we will all go to the edge of the cliff. Charles and I will slide down the cliff to the front of the cave while you cover us. I'll stop in front of the entrance and watch from that vantage point while Charles goes on down the rest of the way to get water. Then you can come down, and we will go into the cave. Or, Charles, had you rather carry the wood?"

"No, Uncle Jean, I can get the water. I can do it. I promise I can."

"I believe you can too. Philippe, ready your musket now."

"I'm ready."

"Let's go, boys." Jean and Charles crept through the trees as Philippe shouldered the musket, alert and ready for any sign of danger. The two reached the heap of wood, and Jean signaled Philippe to join them. They moved to the tree line leading to the clearing without incident.

As they paused before advancing to the cliff, Philippe pointed toward the estate. "Look! Smoke! They're burning our house!"

The three Clavells stared in the direction of the manor, shocked into silence. Dark smoke billowed skyward.

Jean whispered, "Dear Jesus, what are we to do now?"

Charles dropped the empty water bucket. "Maman . . . Papa . . . Vangie . . ."

"Hurry. Let's get into the cave. We'll decide what we need to do after we get the firewood and water. Let's go."

The threesome skidded down the embankment to the entrance of the hideout. "Charles, take the musket. Philippe, hold that bush out of the way so I can toss this firewood into the tunnel."

Charles picked up the musket without speaking and turned his head toward the manor. The column of smoke riveted their attention homeward.

"There's nothing we can do right now to help," Jean said as he nodded his head toward the estate. "We need to concentrate on staying safe here. That's what your maman and papa would want us to do-stay safe." He shifted his weight of wood.

Philippe planted one foot on the ledge and one in the rocks and dirt below the entrance and pulled on the bush. As he tugged, the rocks began to crumble and he lost his footing. "Ow! My hand is caught!"

Philippe's hand became entangled in the bush as he struggled to regain his balance. He yanked it out, cutting and scraping the tender skin as he did. Blood oozed from his thumb and ran down his arm onto his shirtsleeve.

Jean looked at the boy. "That looks like a nasty cut. Are you all right?"

Philippe shrugged it off. "It's not as bad as it looks." He scrambled back to the entrance and pulled on the shrub again. "C'mon, I've got it."

Jean tossed the wood into the tunnel, turned, and took the musket and water pail from Charles. He set them down at his feet and gave Charles a boost into the tunnel. "In you go. I'm going to hand you the musket." The young boy scrambled inside and took the weapon.

"Now you, Philippe. I'll hold this open while you get inside."

Philippe let go of the bush. As he did, he took a look at his injured hand.

"Get in the cave. We'll deal with that cut after I get some water. Get the musket and cover me while I fill the water bucket."

Philippe wriggled around the boulder into the tunnel. He stuck the barrel of the musket through the opening and watched as Jean slid down the bank to the river.

A quick sweep of the bucket was all Jean needed. But getting the bucket through the opening without spilling the contents proved more difficult. Finally Philippe managed to pull it through on the other side as Jean pushed, retaining about half of the contents.

Jean squirmed through the entrance and took the bucket. "Let's get out of this tunnel so I can tend that cut."

Jean took another look at the smoke through the slit around the rock. He shook his head and led the way through the tunnel to their sleeping quarters. "Set those candles on the trunk, boys. Philippe, is it painful?"

"The cut doesn't hurt as much as where I caught my fingers in the bush when I started falling."

Indeed, as Jean inspected the hand, the cut was minor. The bleeding had almost ceased. "Um-m, no wonder your little finger is hurting so badly. I think you've broken it." It was beginning to swell, had turned purple, and was splayed out to the side.

Jean turned Philippe's hand over. "The rest is just scrapes. We'll bind the injured finger to the others. It will be painful for a few days, but it will heal. Sit down while I make a fire to heat some water."

Jean built a small fire. He poured water in a black pot that was among the cooking utensils in the wooden box and waited for the water to boil. Phillipe sat down on their pallet, and Charles sat close to his older brother, glancing gingerly at the injured hand. He pulled the blanket over his head, not wanting to watch Jean doctor the injury.

Philippe grimaced. "It's hurting more now."

"I'm sorry. You're just going to have to endure the pain for a while." The water was steaming. Jean held Philippe's hand. "Let me clean it up."

Jean cleaned the wound and tore strips of cloth from a thin blanket and bound Philippe's little finger to the fourth digit.

Charles had fallen asleep on the pallet with the blanket still over his head. Jean instructed Philippe to drink a cup of wine to dull the pain of his broken finger, and soon Philippe dozed off as well.

JEAN LEANED AGAINST THE HARD, COLD SURFACE OF THE rock and rested his elbows on his knees. The imposing crags began to close in on him, forming a prison not only around his body but around his thoughts as well. He pressed on his brow as if by doing so he could extract a solution.

Oh, mon Dieu. *What are we to do?* What a tortured history his people endured because of their faith. Friends and family members slaughtered for refusal to convert to Catholicism, children kidnapped and raised in monasteries. "Night walkers," some called the Huguenots, because they were forced to run and hide like common criminals.

Jean turned his head and looked at his nephews, more like his own sons to him than nephews. Tears came to his eyes as he recalled the birth of his own son three years before. He could hear his Dina's screams as the child was born—then the stillness that was too quiet. No baby's cry. He had stood, frozen, in the corner of the room, afraid to speak. Even now he could see Dina's long blonde braid hanging over the edge of the bed, wet from her perspiration and the labor of childbirth. Her blue eyes were open, although she had stopped breathing. Blood seemed to be everywhere. The midwife wrapped the tiny baby boy in a blanket and looked at Jean with tortured eyes, shaking her head.

"*Mon Dieu*, your Word tells us to listen, and we will hear a voice behind us telling us whether to turn to the left or to the right. I'm listening, Lord. I'm depending on you to show us our next course of action."

Jean wiped his eyes with the back of his sleeve. Glancing back at Philippe and Charles, who were still napping, he walked through the narrow tunnel to the entrance. He wanted to see if the smoke in the direction of the manor had continued to grow or maybe, just maybe, had ceased. Perhaps it wasn't the house? Dare he even hope it was something else?

Jean peered through the opening. He could see no more smoke. Excited, he searched the sky as thoroughly as he could from his hiding place, but he wanted to get a better view. Squirming out through the small entrance, he landed on his hands and knees. He stood up, brushing the dirt from his hands as he surveyed the horizon. The column of smoke was gone. All that remained was a low-lying cloud. It couldn't have been the house.

Jean continued to stare for a few moments in the direction of the estate, then turned and wriggled back into the cave. He had given François his word that he would not leave the cave until someone came for them. But if someone didn't come soon, he would have to go to the manor and see what had happened. What if everyone was gone, had been taken away—or worse? In spite of his promise, and of the risk of leaving the boys, Jean needed to leave the cave to find out what had happened—for their ultimate safety. That trumped all else. He would wait for nightfall and venture out under the cover of darkness.

FIVE

Madeleine's hands shook with rage as she grabbed the ornate handle and opened the front door. François followed her into the entryway.

"Thérèse! Thérèse!" The timbre of Madeleine's voice rose, verging on hysteria. "Where is that woman when I need her?"

François gripped Madeleine's arm. "Calm down. Nothing is going to be accomplished by allowing Commander Boveé to sense our alarm."

"Madame?" The older woman appeared in the archway between the kitchen and the hall.

Madeleine wrenched free of François' grip. "Get Henri and tell him to prepare the coaches. We're going to Versailles."

Thérèse shot a furtive glance at François. "But, madame . . ."

"Are you questioning my orders?" Madeleine's fury spilled over on the servant who had been with the family since Madeleine was a child.

Tears glistened in the creased, gentle eyes that now suffered from failing sight. "No, madame, b-but Henri is not here. Monsieur sent him after the horses."

Her soft answer cooled Madeleine's fury.

Madeleine's eyes darted from Thérèse to François and back to Thérèse. Her shoulders slumped—she buried her face in her hands and exhaled her anguish. "Ah-h-h—Thérèse." She raised her tearstained face, which at this moment looked so much like the little girl's reddened cheeks that Thérèse wiped years ago.

"I-I'm sorry. You've been nothing but loyal to our family." Madeleine leaned against François. "I don't know what came over me. Please forgive me for being so discourteous."

"Thérèse, come upstairs with us, please," François said quietly. He led Madeleine quickly up the staircase, away from any soldiers who might venture into the house.

Madeleine's deflated composure began to rise even as they climbed the stairs. By the time they reached the first landing she was formulating plans for the journey.

"Fetch Suzanne and tell her to get my small trunk out of the attic. Then go outside and give Armond instructions to ready the two small coaches for a trip to Versailles. Tell him I want both him and Henri to accompany us."

Thérèse looked at François with raised eyebrows. Uncertain, she remained standing in her place.

François slowly shook his head. "Madeleine, don't push me on this. I fear for your safety. I'm afraid . . ."

The unspoken memories of Louis and Madeleine's relationship hovered in the air.

"Don't, don't even think that I could betray you."

François looked down, then at Madeleine. She knew he hated the thought of her going to court. Even though as a country nobleman he was expected to make an appearance at least once a year, he never had. He backed away from the two women, then shifted his weight from side to side.

Madeleine watched her husband struggle with his conflicting emotions, but she held her ground.

He turned to the servant. "Go on, Thérèse. Do as she says."

"Yes, sir." Thérèse curtsied and turned to go down the back stairwell leading from the end of the second story hallway to the gardens and the stables. Her rapid steps of yesteryear had slowed to a shuffle.

Nostalgia and tenderness welled up in Madeleine's heart for the aged servant, and she regretted even more her harsh words. "Thérèse."

"Madame?" Thérèse turned and faced her mistress.

"I'm . . ."

"Yes, madame, I understand. I'll see to the details."

The unspoken forgiveness in Thérèse's eyes was all Madeleine needed. "Thank you. Proceed with your duties."

The couple retreated to their bedroom and shut the door. Madeleine faced her husband and put her arms about his waist. "Please, François . . . our sons are shivering out there in a cave, hiding in fear for their lives. How else are we going to resolve this? The soldiers aren't going to leave simply because we have been civil to them. They hate everything we stand for. The Edict promised us protection, but they will never rest until we convert." Madeleine hesitated. "Or do you have a better plan?"

François shook his head and kissed her gently on her cheek, then embraced her. He sat on the bed, pulling her down with him. "I won't oppose you, *mon amour*, but neither can I approve your plan."

Madeleine remained in François' embrace, but her mind was already churning with the details of her trip to the magnificent court at Versailles.

She sat upright. "When Commander Boveé sees the coaches pulling out to go to Versailles, he will abandon his belief that the boys are anywhere near. He would never imagine that I would leave, with my sons close by. That will give you a chance to get the boys out of hiding and take them to a safer place."

François moved to the window and looked toward the river.

"François?"

"I heard you." He turned and faced Madeleine. "Our identities as Huguenots brought us together. I know God destined us for each other and that our children will carry on the faith. But I'm weary. Oh, God, I am so weary . . ." François sat on the window seat and dropped his hands onto his knees, rocking back and forth, almost as if in pain. His head dropped onto his chest, and he heaved a sigh. "Living every moment on the lookout for soldiers or spies sent out at the whim of an increasingly intolerant king. Will the label *Huguenots* forever hound us and threaten our lives?"

Madeleine moved to the window seat, sat next to her husband, and traced her fingers along his shoulders. François had always been brave in the face of the persecution they had suffered for their faith—a faith that followed the teachings of John Calvin and resisted the tentacles of Rome and the pope. Huguenots simply wanted to be free to practice their sacraments of baptism and the Lord's Supper as they understood the Scriptures—an outward sign of the work God had done in their hearts, not to earn salvation. Was her husband at the point of turning his back on their heritage now?

Madeleine's first memory of François remained vivid in her mind. The Vaudois family had only been home from court a few days. Madeleine always hated leaving the extravagance and excitement of court life, but her recent secret rendezvous with Louis made it more difficult than ever to leave this time.

Their country estate, left under the capable supervision of Henri and Thérèse while the Vaudois family remained at court, was known throughout the province as a refuge for Huguenots fleeing the tyranny of the very political system that Madeleine's father served. Madeleine had been given the task of watching from the doorway of the granary of their manor that night for those of their fellowship who would steal out of the darkness of the forest to attend an underground worship service in their home.

François and his brother lurched toward the Vaudois estate, supporting their father and carrying the limp body of their little sister. A story of terror tumbled from François' lips as he described the pillaging and burning of their home in a neighboring province and the rape and murders of his other two sisters and mother. The three men bore on their bodies the bloody marks of their valiant but futile effort to protect their family. Their little sister died during their escape through the woods before they could reach the safety of the Vaudois estate.

The four of them had fled through a secret passage in their wine cellar and barely escaped with their lives. A bloody cloth was tied around François' head, binding an open gash, the result of a slashing dragoon's sword.

Madeleine remembered the desperation on their faces, and the firmness with which François, the oldest son, protected and took charge of his fractured family. She fell in love with him that first night—fell in love with his strength, a strength tempered with a tender vulnerability. His straight, thick, dark hair insisted on falling over his eyes—eyes that squinted almost shut when he smiled and teased with her.

He took little notice of her in the beginning. Although the Clavells were wealthy and respected entrepreneurs, François had not led a pampered life.

Madeleine smiled to herself as she recalled vying for his attentions during those early days. The opulent days of court and Louis' affection began to fade, especially the night she stayed up late to help François care for his ailing father. A multitude of servants were available in the Vaudois household to render aid, but Madeleine insisted upon doing it herself.

She remembered the casual brushing against François' arm and the touch of his hand as they sat his father up to sip a spoon of broth. She recalled the young man's lingering gaze, their first embrace and kiss as the fire died down and his father fell into a fitful slumber. And then her father's outrage when he discovered the two of them together in the early morning hours. François courageously defended her honor. Madeleine almost chuckled out loud now, remembering the confrontation.

She patted her husband's hands as he sat in the window seat, torn between protecting his family and allowing her to go to Versailles. She loved her husband's hands—hands with slender fingers that really should have been the fingers of a musician or a painter. They were not the rough, stodgy digits of a laborer, although François was not above working hard with his hands, even in the role of seigneur of the manor. But the delicacy of the fingers broadened into the back of his hand

and to a wrist and forearm that were wiry and strong. She could still see in her mind's eye the fire flickering across his hands as he wiped his father's brow with a wet cloth to lessen the fever, then tucked a blanket under his chin when the chills descended on his shivering frame.

The affection between the young couple had grown as the days flew by, and the Clavells took up residence with the Vaudois family. François captured Madeleine's mother's heart from the beginning, but had to prove himself to the patron of the estate. Monsieur Vaudois, impressed with François as the young man took on more and more responsibility, before long agreed to the union. When Philippe was born soon after, Monsieur Vaudois could not have been more pleased.

Madeleine stood and looked down at her disheartened spouse. "I know I have been sheltered and have little concept of what others have had to pay for our faith. I have not suffered the way some of our brothers and sisters in the faith have—as you have. But we must not turn back now. This is not the time for weakness." Her accusation pierced the air like a dagger.

François blanched. "But I—"

"I know you are weary, François. I am too. But we must remain strong for our children." Madeleine repeated her argument. "There's no other recourse but to appeal to Louis. I know he will listen to me. I don't believe he's even aware of the havoc the dragoons are heaping on the countryside, much less to us. He has always supported the Edict of Nantes."

François' eyes reflected his sadness, but he stood and faced his wife. "Do what you must. Perhaps it will work. I have no other solution to offer." He started to walk away, and then turned, took his wife into his arms, and kissed her tenderly.

Madeleine flung her arms around his neck and eagerly responded.

Even now, after nearly thirteen years of marriage, François' touch caused her heart to pound.

Suddenly Madeleine pulled away. "Do you think I'm still pretty? Do I look old?"

"Look in the mirror, darling. What do you see?"

Madeleine turned and looked at herself in the gilded mirror that hung above her vanity. She tilted her head and fingered the lace around the neck of her dress. "I don't know. I don't know anymore. What do you see?"

François wrapped his arms around her from behind and looked in the mirror with her. "I see a woman with eyes so dark and deep, one could get lost in them. I see a woman with skin the color of the lilies of the valley in our garden. I see a woman with hair the color of mahogany."

"With a few strands of gray." Madeleine brushed her hair away from her face with her hand.

"Where? I see none."

"Look closely. See, there's one." Madeleine pointed to the hair above her forehead.

François let go of her, and his mood turned cool. "Why this sudden vanity about your appearance? Perhaps you want Louis to admire your beauty once again? To remember you as you were when the two of you were young and in love?"

Madeleine turned from the mirror and faced him. Her reply was measured and firm. "You know I was never truly in love with Louis. It was a youthful infatuation. How many times must I reassure you?"

Madeleine looked down, twirling her wedding ring on her finger. "Yes, I was drawn to him. Who wouldn't be? He was young and charismatic, and a king. But he was also Catholic, and I couldn't betray my heritage. And I didn't want to spend the rest of my life as a mistress, or a wife who had to contend with her husband's other mistresses.

"I wanted someone like you, François. Someone who would love me through abundant times and lean. Who wouldn't toss me aside for the latest beautiful mademoiselle at court. I didn't know what mature love meant until I met you. You are the one I chose—above a king."

Unshed tears filled François' eyes. "I'm sorry, my dear. I do know that you are a faithful and loving wife, but I battle the ghost of Louis that lingers in your heart—a ghost that will remain eternally young and handsome. Commander Boveé was right. Louis is monumental competition."

Madeleine touched François' cheek with the backs of her fingers. "And as I rightly told the commander, there is no competition at all. If Louis came here today in all his pomp and splendor and riches, to carry me away in a gold carriage drawn by six white horses, I would refuse him. I am richer than the king right here with you."

Madeleine laid her head on François' chest. "But yes, I do want him to find me attractive. That will be my leverage. My old ties with Louis may work to our advantage." Taking François' hands in hers and looking directly in his eyes, she questioned him. "Could it be possible that God foreordained my relationship with Louis to provide a way of escape in these perilous times?"

The old scar across François' forehead crinkled as he returned her gaze. "This is a dangerous game. Our God directs us, but we can choose the path that we walk. Be sure you are choosing the right one."

"I know this is right, my dearest. You must trust me. This is our way of escape."

François smoothed her thick hair with his rough hand and managed a meager smile. "I love you unendingly, my stubborn, hardheaded, irresistible wife."

"And might I return the compliment, my sweet, stubborn, protective husband?"

THE CHESTNUT STALLION AND BLACK MARE THE BOYS had ridden away on the day before galloped to the watering trough in front of the stable, with Henri close behind on CiCi. Several dragoons loitering in the stable area cast not so much as a casual glance in their direction. Henri dismounted, unsaddled and unbridled his horse, and let her join the two steeds for their fill of the cool water. He took the saddle and bridle into the interior of the livery and was fetching brushes to curry down the animals when Commander Boveé approached from the back of the barn.

Henri maintained his composure. "Yes, just as we suspected, I found them grazing in the orchard. They like to forage the apples that fell to the ground last fall." He moved to the large door, brandishing the curry brushes in his hands. "May I help you, sir? Were you looking for something in the barn?"

"Simply admiring your equipment. An impressive facility. I applaud your abilities as a stable master."

"Monsieur is generous and recognizes the benefits of investing in good equipment. And I have good help." Henri nodded, indicating the men working in the gardens and with the other horses. "If I may not be of further service, you will excuse me. I need to get these horses taken care of."

A smirk curled the edges of Commander Boveé's lips. "Yes, of course. Their junket to forage apples must have been exhausting for them." He walked out of the barn with Henri. "There *is* one thing I was curious about."

Henri was already busy brushing the horses. "Yes, sir?"

Drawing Philippe's cap from a pocket in his jacket and twirling it on his fingers, the officer baited him. "Might you recognize this? It appears to be a young boy's possession."

Henri continued his chore, glancing at the cap. "Why, I do indeed. Where did you find that? Master Philippe had been looking for that for weeks."

"One of my men found it in the river, snagged on a log. It doesn't look any the worse for wear, for having been missing for weeks."

Henri reached out to take the cap. "Hmm, I don't know, sir, but it *is* wool. Wears well, you know. I'll just take it into the house when I finish here."

Commander Boveé held the cap out of Henri's reach for a moment, then handed it to the servant. "See that his mother knows we found it." He raised his head, mocking the servant with his crinkled eyebrows. "I'm sure she's been concerned about it."

"Yes, I will. Thank you, sir."

Commander Boveé strode up the path to the house, whistling no particular tune, passing Thérèse on her way to the barn. He tipped his hat and proceeded toward the house.

"Henri! Oh, Henri!"

Leaving the horses, Henri approached her. "What is it, Thérèse? You look worried."

"Madame wishes you to get the two small coaches ready. She is going to Versailles. She is determined to see King Louis and try to convince him to call off the dragoons."

"What does the master say? Has he given permission?"

Thérèse twisted her apron in her hands. "He's not in favor of it— but she has made up her mind."

Henri squared his shoulders. "She'll not go without me." Since Madeleine's father passed away, Henri, although a servant, had assumed the mantle of father and grandfather of the estate.

"She wants you and Armond. I don't know what women she is taking. You're to start preparations at once."

SIX

Madeleine heard the *thump, thump, thump* of the small but heavy trunk echoing through the small spiral stairwell as Suzanne struggled down the attic stairs.

"François, that's Suzanne with my trunk. Help her."

He opened the door and assisted the servant in pulling the trunk into the bedroom.

The young girl curtsied. "I'm sorry, sir. Thérèse told me to bring Madame Clavell's small trunk down from the attic."

"*Merci*, Suzanne. I am on my way out to help Armond and Henri while you help your mistress pack some things. It seems you all are going on a trip."

"Sir?"

"To Versailles."

Suzanne's blue eyes danced. "Versailles? I've heard such grand tales. Are we really going, madame?"

Madeleine looked intently at the young girl, flushed with the excitement of a promised adventure. Could she trust her? "That we are. But it is not a pleasure trip. We have grave matters to address—this business of the dragoons seeking the boys and billeting in our home."

François left the two women alone.

Madeleine opened the doors of her ornate armoire and began to search through the gowns. "You know that King Louis and I were childhood friends, when my father was part of his court?"

The servant looked down. "Yes, madame, I've heard that you were."

Madeleine stared at her. She wondered what stories the servant had heard about her days at Versailles, when she and Louis were young. Madeleine ran her fingers through her curls. *Let her think what she likes.*

Madeleine began to give orders to Suzanne as to which dresses, jewelry, and toiletries they needed to pack. The maidservant went about her duties, excitedly asking questions.

"Is King Louis really as handsome as they say?"

"He is indeed very handsome. One of the handsomest men I've ever seen. François being the *most* handsome, you understand."

Suzanne returned her mistress's smile. "Does he really eat as much at each meal as they say?"

Madeleine laughed. "That is not legend. I remember one time at supper he ate four plates of soup, a whole pheasant, a whole partridge, two slices of ham, a salad, some mutton with garlic, pastry, and finished with fruit and hard-boiled eggs."

"Impossible!"

"I was with him at mealtimes too numerous to count, and I can testify that he always ate huge amounts of food. Peas were his favorite, and he would eat them any and all ways—raw, cooked in potage, roasted, boiled. He loves peas."

"Is he a heavy man?"

Madeleine shook her head. "Not at all. It's a mystery to everyone around him. You would think that as short as he is, he would be fat, wouldn't you?"

Suzanne nodded. "Do you think they will perform any ballets while we are there?"

"Perhaps. Louis loves the ballet. He even performs in them at times."

Madeleine sat down at her vanity and opened a small drawer that held the combs and adornments for her hair. Keeping an eye on Suzanne, she watched until the maid turned her back and bent over the trunk. Madeleine slowly reached behind the box of combs to find a small button in the back of the drawer. She pressed the wooden circle, which silently unlatched a hidden compartment. Stealing another glance toward Suzanne, who was busy arranging shoes in the bottom of the trunk, Madeleine pulled a velvet pouch from the compartment and slid the small bag under the box of combs. She removed two ivory combs and a magnificent black glittering tiara, and closed the drawer.

"Here, Suzanne, I want to take these, as well as the pearl ones. And be sure to pack my pearl necklace, brooch, and earrings."

"Oh-h-h, madame, I've never seen that."

Madeleine held the tiara in her hand. "It goes with my black lace veil. I wore it the first time I went to court, before Louis started building Versailles. We were still holding court in Paris, and I was very young." Madeleine's voice became soft, barely audible. "I was only sixteen, and Louis was twenty-one. He taught me how to dance."

Suzanne giggled. "King Louis was your dancing partner? I've heard he is the best dancer in the court."

"What you have heard is true. My father told me it was time for me to go to a court ball, and I went with my parents that night. I was nervous, and beside myself with excitement. As the musicians struck up *La Pavane* to begin the ball, Louis came to me, and we led the procession together. His confidence put me at ease."

"What was your favorite dance?"

"Oh, I don't know. I liked them all." Madeleine began to hum a tune in three-quarter time. "I suppose *La Courante*. It's a slow waltz."

Suzanne clapped her hands like a child. "Oh, it all sounds so romantic!"

"Louis said he would wait for me to grow up—that I had captured his heart with my innocent beauty, and he would never marry until I agreed to be his bride. My father didn't like any of this. He was well acquainted with Louis' wandering affections, and he knew the king was filling my head with the same promises he whispered to every other young girl at court."

Still seated at the vanity, Madeleine handed the tiara to Suzanne, laughing. "Predictably, he didn't wait for me to grow up. He married the queen, Marie Thérèse, shortly after we left court. But I shall always remember those festive days at Versailles. And taking a wife didn't stop Louis from taking mistresses."

Suzanne gasped. Captivated by Madeleine's tales of court, Suzanne had completely ceased her packing.

"A wife, Versailles, and mistresses. And all that didn't stop him from courting other young women. However, I truly believe he loves Versailles as much as he loves any of them. Versailles is his true mistress."

"Did he ever try to . . . win your affections again, madame?"

"Oh, he tried . . ." Madeleine's eyes took on a faraway look. "That was a long time ago, Suzanne."

"What is he like? Tell me what you remember."

"He loves a good joke, and in his own dry way can be most witty. He loves music and is, as I said before, a skilled dancer. He is polite—always tips his hat to the ladies, whether noble or of lower rank. But there is a ruthless side to his nature as well."

Suzanne stared at Madeleine.

"You've heard of the man in the iron mask?"

Suzanne clutched one of Madeleine's gowns. "Is that story true?"

"Nobody knows for sure. Those who pass the tale say there truly is a prisoner of high rank who has been kept in solitary confinement for years. Neither his identity nor his crimes are known. Some say it is Louis' identical twin brother whom he has kept incarcerated, so the throne will remain his alone."

"What do you think?"

Madeleine walked to the window and looked out toward the barn. "Truthfully, I don't know. There were times . . ." Madeleine's voice trailed off. "But enough reminiscing. You'll see for yourself soon. The splendor of his royalty will astound you. People have been known to tremble at the mere sight of the Sun King, as he calls himself."

Madeleine rose and removed a black velvet cape from the armoire. "We'll be in Versailles within the week. Remember, however, Suzanne, for all its grandeur and opulence, life at court is a sinister game that requires shrewd thinking and alertness."

"Madame?"

Madeleine walked to the trunk with the cape and inspected the garments in the luggage thus far. "Pack my blue dressing gown, please." She turned and looked directly at Suzanne.

"All is not as it seems on the surface. Beneath the chivalry and finery, beautiful women and handsome, gallant men, run streams of dirty politics, currents of intrigue, and whirlpools of jealousy. Observe and learn. Don't be swept away by the deceit."

Suzanne nodded solemnly.

Madeleine's voice brightened. "Go up in the attic, Suzanne, and bring me my old court gowns. I'll select what I wish to take."

"Yes, madame." She took a step toward the door, then turned back to her mistress. "Madame, how do you know that Louis will honor the ties you formed when you were young?"

"Honestly, I do not know. But I must try. And I need you to do whatever I ask you to do. Do you understand?"

"Yes, madame. Always. What do you need?"

"I'm not talking about this immediate moment. I'm talking about— never mind. Just remember what I've said, Suzanne. Now hurry along. We have much to do."

Suzanne curtsied and left the room. After the chambermaid's exit, Madeleine reached inside the drawer and pulled out the velvet pouch again. She removed a small, silver poesy ring from the bag and slipped it onto her finger.

Visions of warm summer days and starry moonlit nights with Louis flooded her thoughts. She held it up to the sunlight and admired the ornate carvings of the circle. Taking it off, she turned it so she could read the inscription around the inside: *Toi seule pour toujours . . . Louis.*

Madeleine put the ring back into the pouch and walked to the trunk. Placing the treasure in a side compartment of the luggage, she mused, "'You only, forever,' you said. I hope you still mean that, my dear friend."

SEVEN

François marched down the path to the stables, his hat bunched in his hands, his jaw set. Four stable boys grunted as they pushed one of the coaches out of the enclosure.

Henri's deep voice boomed from the side of the barn, "Bring it around here." Henri stood where he wanted the coach to rest and guided it himself when it got close. "That's good. Go fetch the other one and bring it alongside."

He ran his hand down the leather siding, checking for tears and nicks. "Seems to be in pretty good shape for being in storage so long."

François joined Henri in the inspection of the vehicle. "The wheels appear to be fine, as well." He squatted in the dust and checked the bottom of the carriage.

Henri put his hand on François' shoulder. "I thought you were not in favor of this trip."

"I'm not."

"And that you had not given your permission."

"That's true."

"So why are you down here at the barn checking the carriages?"

François stood with his arms crossed in front of him. "That doesn't mean I won't do all I can to assure my wife's safety. Madeleine is stubborn. She is convinced if she can talk to Louis face-to-face, she can persuade him to call off the dragoons."

Henri leaned against the coach, laboring to catch his breath. He pulled out a large handkerchief and wiped his brow. "But—"

François held up his hand. "You know Madeleine as well as I. There's no use arguing with her. She's made up her mind. I'll stay to take care of things here, and"—François glanced behind him to be sure no dragoons were within hearing distance—"let Jean and the boys know the status of the situation."

"A week going, a week or so there, a week coming home. I estimate we will be gone a month."

François nodded. "Take Armond to drive the other coach and four other footmen. You know every turn in the road—the dangerous places, the secure overnight stops. Madeleine needs your wisdom and experience."

Henri acknowledged François' confidence in him with a down-turned glance.

François continued, "Armond is young, but he is mature beyond his years and shoulders responsibility well, and he holds Madame Clavell in fond regard. Choose footmen who are loyal and quick-witted. I'm fearful not only of what you may encounter on the road but also at court. Dimwitted servants will not serve us well."

"I agree, monsieur. I will see to it all. What about the women?"

François rubbed his chin. "I don't know yet. Suzanne, certainly. Madeleine has not told me who else." He paused. "Would you want Thérèse to go?"

Henri shook his head. "No, monsieur. Her health is not good. I fear she would not fare well on the trip." He chuckled and threw up his hands. "But you know she is going to protest. She will want to go to cluck over her mistress like the mother hen she has always been."

"And a good one at that. You and Thérèse have been like parents to us. We are indebted to you."

Henri brushed the compliment aside. "Madame wishes to take Suzanne?"

Before François could answer, Armond came through the large barn entrance with the other stable boys. The second coach creaked as it rolled to a stop. Armond's authoritative voice rang out, "Over here. Move sharply."

"Sounds like we have a problem with the underperch on this one," Henri said. He peered beneath the vehicle and pulled on one of the metal bands. Suddenly the band snapped and punctured the floor of the coach. The rear axle collapsed, bringing the coach against the fence with a resounding crash.

The stable boys, footmen, and servants in the gardens, startled by the sound, ceased their activities. Two dragoons ran around the side of the corral—a short, stocky man with his sword drawn and a larger soldier bearing a musket. Henri and Armond stepped forward, one on either side of François.

François threw up his hands, pointing to the coaches. "Please, put down your weapons. We simply pulled on a metal band, and the whole thing collapsed."

Scowling, the dragoons scrutinized the grounds. Eyeing the broken axle, they shuffled back toward their duty stations muttering under their breath.

François gestured to his servants. "Go back to work. Everything is fine."

Nervous laughter filtered through the stable area and gardens. Beads of sweat popped out on François' forehead. "I guess we're all a little on edge." He made a feeble attempt to appear assured in front of Henri and Armond.

Armond rubbed his hands together and looked in the direction in which the dragoons had departed. "Who wouldn't be, with those simpletons watching your every move? I'd love to get my hands on one of them."

François saw a younger version of himself in Armond. "Don't be too anxious. You may get your chance soon enough. But for now, we have work to do. We have a coach to repair before tomorrow morning." He turned to Henri. "Is that possible?"

Henri took off his hat and scratched his head. "I believe we have more metal bands in the loft. I may need to switch out wheels to make them suitable for the journey, but with Armond's help, perhaps we can be ready."

Armond gave a mock salute and stalked resolutely into the barn.

THE DOOR TO HER MOTHER'S ROOM WAS CLOSED. "MÈRE?" Madeleine knocked softly. "Mère?"

"Come in."

Madeleine opened the door and peeked in. Gloom permeated the bedchamber. The dark burgundy curtains remained closed against the daylight. Embers from the early morning fire lingered in the fireplace. Smoke had settled in the room.

Her mother, reclining in a chaise lounge by the window, motioned Madeleine to enter.

Madeleine marched to the windows and threw them open, tying them with the matching cords. "It's stuffy in here. Let's get some fresh air circulating."

"I was trying to rest." Elisabeth covered her eyes with the back of her hand. "I close my eyes and see the smoke rising from your father's books and Bibles and journals—destroying any hope of peace." She dabbed at her eyes with a lace handkerchief. "It's such a waste."

Madeleine went to her mother's side and hugged her. "Don't cry, Maman."

"Those journals were the most precious items I had left from your father." The tears started to fall again, and she turned her head away.

Madeleine buried her face in her mother's hair, once so like her own. The scent of jasmine filled her nostrils. She patted her mother's shoulders, cooing assurances, much as her mother had soothed her own little-girl hurts.

"There, there. We are not going to allow these atrocities to continue. We are going to do something about this."

Her mother sat up, blew her nose, and swung her legs over the edge of the divan. "What do you mean? We are powerless against the dragoons and that egotistical Commander Boveé."

"I want you to go with me to see Louis at Versailles."

"What?" Her mother leaned forward. "What are you talking about?"

"I know I can persuade Louis to call off the dragoons from our family."

"And how will you manage that? You have had no contact with him for years."

Madeleine clasped her hands for emphasis. "I am confident he will honor our past relationship. I know I can reason with him."

"Don't be ridiculous, Madeleine. How do you know he is even at Versailles? He could be off on one of his perpetual hunting trips or in Paris. To my knowledge he has yet to move the court permanently to Versailles." Her eyes flashed a warning to Madeleine. "You will be putting yourself in a precarious position to even try."

"Mère, I am going, with or without you, but I desperately need your knowledge of the court and your diplomacy in dealing with the nobility. Your days at father's side have given you experience I don't have. If Louis is not at Versailles, we will simply go on to Paris. But you know as well as I that Louis spends every minute he can there. My chance of meeting him is best by going to Versailles." Madeleine remained quiet for a moment—then pleaded, "Please, Maman. Come with me."

Her mother rose and paced back and forth in front of Madeleine. "Your father would never allow such a thing."

"Father is not here. If he were, the dragoons would never have been allowed to occupy our property in the first place—searching for our sons like common criminals. We must do something." Her voice rose with each sentence. "I cannot sit in my house, watching soldiers hover over our estate like vultures circling until they find a carcass and devour it piece by piece. I cannot exist swirling in this gray twilight realm, blandly smiling and curtsying to that despicable Commander Boveé. Whether it's right or wrong, I must do something."

Her mother turned to face Madeleine. "What exactly do you mean by 'past relationship'?"

"It's no secret. You knew Louis pursued me."

"Of course we knew. Your father and I discussed the implications of that far into many a dark night. But he pursued every attractive girl at court, and still does, I am sure. Why should he honor any request you might make of him? If I'm to go, I must know the truth, Madeleine. What kind of alliance did you have with Louis?"

Madeleine stepped to the window and looked down upon the gardens. She could see François and Henri inspecting the first coach and the stable boys bringing out the second. Her heart swelled with love for her husband. She turned and searched her mother's face.

Her mother cocked her head and waited.

"He declared his undying love for me."

"Pshaw! As he did to every attractive female at court."

Madeleine continued to gaze out the window. It had all happened so long ago, yet the lives of her family were caught in a trap. Only Louis, Madeleine knew, had the power to release it. One slip, one false move, and that trap could snap shut and kill them all.

She gathered her skirt and went to the door. "Come, let me show you something."

The two women walked down the hall to Madeleine and François' bedroom. Madeleine went to the trunk and pulled the velvet pouch from the side compartment. Taking the ring out of the bag, Madeleine extended it to her mother. "This was a gift from Louis."

Elisabeth casually took the ring. "Really, Madeleine. Poesy rings flowed like the water between paramours at court. They meant nothing."

"Read the inscription."

Her mother held the ornate silver circlet at arm's length to accommodate her aging eyesight. She turned the ring, read the inscription, and looked at her daughter with new understanding.

"Well." Elisabeth clutched the ring in the palm of her hand. "This does shed more light on the situation. What were your feelings toward Louis? What is your heart telling you now?"

Madeleine chose her words carefully. "I-I would not trade what I have with François for all the gold in the kingdom, or for the king."

Elisabeth probed no further. She handed the ring back to Madeleine. "Very well. Tell Suzanne to come help me after she finishes here."

The bedchamber door swung open, and Suzanne halted at the threshold, her arms laden with gowns. "Excuse me, madame."

Madeleine stuffed the ring back into the pouch. "Come in, Suzanne. Let's see what you found."

The attention of the women was diverted by a loud crash coming through the open window. They ran to the window and saw two dragoons running around to the front of the stables with drawn weapons.

"François!" Madeleine cried out. The culprit coach lay against the fence amidst rising dust. Madeleine saw her husband throw up his hands and diffuse the predicament.

"Always the peacemaker and protector." Madeleine stifled her alarm. "I love you, my husband."

The dragoons disengaged their weapons and walked away from the scene of the accident back to their posts.

Madeleine, still holding the velvet pouch in her hand, stuffed it into her bodice, then moved from the window and gazed into her mother's dark eyes. "Let's get back to work. We must be ready early tomorrow morning."

Suzanne placed on the bed the gowns she had found in the attic— some of them too young in style for the mature woman Madeleine had become, some too small, some out of style. But Madeleine found a few that would do for her visit to court.

"This red one for sure, Suzanne. I purchased it on my last visit to Paris and wore it at the *patronal* festival last year." Madeleine ran her fingers over the long, multilayered tiers of lace adorning the sleeves, which would provide a graceful, fluid flow when dancing. The frock was elegantly styled in the latest fashion of the court, long-waisted and slender, with an extended V-shaped point at the front. Madeleine did not want her apparel to appear dated. She knew Louis' meticulous taste. He would approve of the low, wide, horizontal neckline.

She stood in front of the mirror and tried to encircle her waist with her two hands. Having three children had expanded her waist. Suzanne would just have to cinch the corset as tightly as she could. Madeleine pictured herself dancing, the liquid flow of the lace swirling about her as she executed the moves. She was young again.

Suzanne lifted the heavy gown. "Ooh, *oui*, madame." A subtle shimmer of black iridescent threads shone as Suzanne maneuvered the gown into the luggage. "This will be perfect for you to wear with the black lace veil and tiara."

"Yes, that one will do nicely. Do you have my black earrings and necklace?"

"I have already packed them."

Madeleine pointed out a champagne-colored gown, and an emerald green one as well. "And, of course, this one." Madeleine returned to the armoire and removed a dress made of brilliant blue flowing chiffon. "This *robe battante* is the height of fashion at Versailles these days."

She held the gown in front of her and looked once again at her reflection in the mirror, swishing from side to side. The garment fell from the shoulders in voluminous folds. Madeleine grinned. "Do you know why it has become so stylish recently?"

Suzanne shook her head.

"From what I hear, Louis' latest mistress, Athénaïs de Montespan, designed the garment to hide her pregnancies. At least Louise de la Vallière, his mistress *en titre*, carries herself with modesty. Athénaïs parades her shame. She makes it stylish. And the ladies of the court follow along like sheep being led to the slaughter." Madeleine hesitated, deep in thought. "The Lord must be grieved."

"Yes, madame."

"Some call Athénaïs the *real* queen of France." Madeleine paused, caressing the fabric of the gown she had draped over her arm. "We shall see how true these rumors are."

She laid the robe on the bed with the others. "That should do. Be sure we include the accessories for each ensemble—shoes, under-garments, combs, and jewelry."

Elisabeth called to Suzanne from her room. Madeleine nodded and shooed the chambermaid down the hall. "Go help Madame Elisabeth now. I can finish here."

Suzanne scurried out the door to Elisabeth's room. Madeleine pulled the pouch from its soft hiding place and stowed it once again in the side pocket of the trunk.

"What precious treasure did you have tucked away in such deli-cious concealment?" François had entered the room. He looked about. "Have you seen my gloves?"

Madeleine's pulse quickened at the unexpected entrance of her husband. "Oh! You startled me. I thought you were outside." She pointed toward the bed. "There—on the bedside table."

François picked up his gloves and looked at Madeleine question-ingly. "Well?"

"Oh, that. Nothing, really. Just a piece of jewelry."

"Um." François motioned toward the window. "I suppose you heard the crash at the stable."

"Yes, and I also observed your bravery in the face of the dragoons." Madeleine hugged François. "I am proud of you."

François returned Madeleine's embrace with a perfunctory pat on the back.

"Can the coach be repaired by morning?" Madeleine looked out the window at the fallen vehicle.

"Henri and Armond are already working on it. If there are no extra metal bands stored in the stable, we will have to make new ones. That will take at least a day to forge and cool properly."

"I *will* leave tomorrow, and with two coaches. The status of two coaches entering Versailles will give our request to see Louis more validity."

"We will do our best, my dear. But if we can't get the other small one repaired, what are your wishes? Do you want to take the large one?"

"Only if I have to." She paused, thinking. "But if I can take two coaches, I want one team of horses all white. The other all black."

"Madeleine, you are not listening to me. I don't know if we can get the repairs done on the second coach. If one coach is all we can get ready, which team of horses do you want?"

"The white team. They are flamboyant and command immediate attention."

"I could have guessed as much." Anger crept into François' voice. "Henri will have his hands full driving that team."

FRANÇOIS WALKED OUT OF THEIR BEDROOM, SHAKING HIS head. In the hall, he bumped into Elisabeth.

"François, I thought you were in the stable."

"I forgot my gloves."

Elisabeth's quiet grace and elegance, once so admired at court, brought a sense of comfort to François. "I'm going with her to Versailles. I don't agree with her decision to go, but she is determined."

"I don't agree either, but, thank you, Elisabeth, for agreeing to accompany her. Between you and Henri, perhaps you can keep her in check?"

Elisabeth smiled, placing her hand on François' arm. "Something I've not been able to do for thirty years—you expect me to accomplish now?"

"Hmm, I suppose I'm dreaming, eh?" François stuffed his gloves into his belt and tramped down the back stairwell.

PAUSING IN FRONT OF THE DOOR TO HER DAUGHTER'S room, Elisabeth mumbled, "I'll follow her into the lions' den, my dear son-in-law." She sighed and shook her head. "Ah, my courageous daughter. It was Daniel's courage and faith that delivered him from the lions' den, but that was also what got him into the lions' den!"

She turned her face heavenward and clasped her hands in prayer. "I implore you, merciful God, that as you closed the lions' mouths and protected Daniel in the enemy's camp, that you will protect us from being devoured as we travel into enemy territory."

EIGHT

A meager evening meal of hard tack, cheese, and chestnuts lay on top of the wooden box next to a flickering candle. Jean, Philippe, and Charles huddled around the makeshift table, pulling their jackets and a blanket around them to keep warm.

Jean bowed his head to offer thanks.

Charles shivered. "I-I-I'm not too thankful for this. Why can't we go home? I'll bet the dragoons are gone by now. Huh, Uncle Jean? Can we?"

Philippe was silent.

Jean's voice was firm, but tender. "We have a safe hiding place from danger, and we have food and water. We must not be ungrateful."

Charles hung his head. "But—"

Philippe joined in to provide big-brother encouragement to his sibling. "Maybe the dragoons won't stay much longer, and we'll be home before you know it."

Jean stood and rubbed the back of his neck. "Boys, here's what I think I need to do. Later tonight I am going to go back to the manor and see what caused that column of smoke."

Philippe and Charles looked at their uncle, but their thoughts remained unspoken.

"I believe I can get into the barn without anybody seeing me. Then I'll signal your father. He'll recognize my whistle and come to the barn. We used to signal each other when we were little boys—when we wanted to slip away in the night and hunt badgers without our parents knowing."

"But what if a dragoon sees you? How will we know what has happened? What will we do if something happens to you?"

"Stay here—no matter what. If something happens to me, someone would eventually come and get you. We need to know what happened at the house today. God forbid, but if the dragoons have done something with the family . . ."

The look of alarm on the two young faces stopped Jean from verbalizing his own fears. "Well, we need to know what course of action to take—whether to flee or remain hidden until the dragoons leave."

Philippe played with his food, setting a piece of cheese on top of a biscuit, then removing it and setting the bread on top of the cheese—back and forth, back and forth. "We would leave Maman and Papa and Vangie and *Grand-mère* behind? Not knowing what happened?" He didn't look up. "I won't do it. I won't go without them." Philippe challenged Jean to defy him.

Jean leaned over the wooden box, the candle casting an eerie shadow over his face. "I understand how you feel." He reached and placed his hand on Philippe's arm. "My heart screams the same pro-tests. But we cannot make life-changing decisions based on our emotions. The fact is, we must do all we can to keep you boys from being kidnapped and taken to be educated in Catholic monasteries. Who knows what God has in store for you two in the future? We must serve God first, then our family."

Jean paused and relaxed. "But we may be borrowing trouble. Everything could be just fine back at the house. The dragoons may even be gone by now."

Philippe still toyed with his food. "If the dragoons were gone, Papa would have come and gotten us," he said softly.

"Yes, well, maybe he hasn't had time to get here yet. Anyway, I will go out after dark, late, when I'm certain that everybody is bedded down and I can get to the house undetected. In the meantime, let's try to get some sleep." Jean stood and brushed the biscuit crumbs off his tunic.

"Philippe, I am proud of you." He turned to Charles. "Both of you."

Tears rolled down Charles' cheeks, and he did not bother to wipe them away. He ducked his head and leaned forward with his elbows on the box, his face in his hands. "I don't care about Catholics and dragoons and soldiers. I just want to go home." He put his head all the way down in his arms and sniffled.

Jean patted his head. "Soon. We'll be home soon. And this will all seem like a bad dream."

The boys settled down for the night, and Jean stoked the embers of the fire. He sat and leaned against the jagged wall of the cave, waiting for the right moment to make his way to the manor. He waited with his arms around his knees, watching the fire, mesmerized by the dazzling dance of the flames.

Scattered across the country of France, thousands of Huguenots suffered in all kinds of prisons and waited to be freed. Their prisons were dirty dungeons, unheated cells, or spartan convents, and exile to a foreign country instead of a cave. What would the fate of the Clavell family prove to be? Imprisonment? Escape? Death?

The cozy warmth of the blaze nestled around him, and he dozed off. The logs snapped and popped as the fire died down to glowing coals.

A few hours later, Jean woke from his fitful nap. He added some logs to the fire and then sorted through the supplies. He found what he was looking for—a short but lethal knife that he could conceal and draw easily.

He checked on the boys as they slept. *Dear Jesus, protect the boys and me this night*—a short and direct prayer before he scurried down the tunnel and out the entrance.

The night was cool and blessedly dark. Jean skidded down the bank to the river. He made his way downstream until he found a shallow place to cross. Icy water nipped around his ankles. He shivered and pulled his hat tighter around his ears. His eyes adjusted to the dark night. No stars appeared in the sky. Clouds covered the quarter moon.

Once across the river, he made for the stone wall that they had followed to their lair just the day before yesterday. It seemed a lifetime ago. He crouched behind it on the opposite side from their pasture, feeling his way along the smooth gray stones. The low wall followed the contour of the land as the gentle hill rose toward the estate. He knew every crook and turn of the wall. He followed the three-foot high enclosure, using it for cover until he came almost directly in line with the stable.

An ancient oak tree stood just ahead with low-lying, sprawling branches reaching over the wall. François and Jean had helped the Clavell children build a tree house in the broad crevices of the old landmark last summer. Jean could see a few stars through the slats in the flimsy structure. Using the gnarls of the tree trunk as handles and steps, Jean slithered over the rock wall and hid in the shadows of the tree. He peered through the leaves toward the estate.

Lights shone from within the barn. *Why would somebody be in there at this hour?* Perhaps some of the dragoons had been assigned to sleep in the hayloft.

He felt a raindrop and looked back toward the river. Lightning sparked the horizon, and he could hear the distant roll of thunder. He could see the outline of the manor now. All seemed to be in order as far as he could see. The rain fell harder, and the lightning and thunder were moving closer. The wind picked up and produced an eerie howl around the gables of the house.

Crouching as low as he could, Jean moved to the barn. Thunder continued to roll closer. Approaching a window, he looked inside. What luck! François, Henri, and Armond were busy working with some metal. One of the estate's smaller coaches sat in the middle of the stable, logs of wood stacked under one side where a wheel was missing.

Jean glanced at the stalls inside the stable and all around the corral. A horse whinnied softly. He could see no one else. Plastering himself close to the side of the barn, he made his way to the front, then peeked around the corner. Leaning against the door, blocking his way, slept a dragoon, his musket lying across his lap.

A bolt of lightning struck close by, and the thunder rattled over the hill, shaking the rafters of the barn and jolting the dragoon awake.

81

He jumped up and grabbed his gun, swinging it around. Jean flung himself back around the corner.

What an idiot—to draw his weapon against the powers of the sky during a rainstorm.

The overhang of the roof of the barn offered the soldier little shelter from the rain that was beginning to come down in sheets now, driven by the wind. He slid open the door and moved inside.

Jean turned again to the window and peered in to see what the dragoon would do once he was out of the rain. The soldier motioned with his musket upward toward the loft. François nodded and pointed to a ladder on the wall. The dragoon took a look around the interior of the stable, stopped and looked at Henri and Armond's work, then climbed the ladder and disappeared into the hay on the upper floor.

Jean heaved a sigh of relief. He decided to wait a few moments to give the dragoon time to go back to sleep. Then he would make his move.

The wind died down, and the cloudburst became a soft, steady spring rain. The display of lightning moved across the hill and on toward the orchard. Rumbles of thunder could be heard in the distance.

Jean peered around the corner once more. Suddenly the door opened, and light from the interior of the barn sliced the darkness. François left the door ajar and ran toward the house, holding his jacket over his head against the rain.

Jean whistled. François stopped and whirled around. Jean stepped briefly into the light from the barn so François could see him, then disappeared again into the cover of darkness.

François ran to Jean's side. The brothers locked in an embrace, pounding each other on their backs.

"What are you doing here? Are the boys all right?"

"The boys are fine. Are *you* okay? We saw smoke. I had to find out what had happened."

François pulled Jean by the arm into the barn. "Let's go inside out of this downpour."

"But the dragoon."

"He's asleep. He was lifting the roof with his snoring when I came out."

The men slipped through the door. Henri and Armond looked up. François held his finger to his mouth, and the two men simply nodded. François motioned for Henri to continue hammering the metal.

Beneath the clang of the hammer and anvil, François and Jean huddled in a stall close to the door, and François explained about the burning of the books and laid out Madeleine's plans to start for Versailles in the morning.

"Ah. That's the reason for the coach."

"Truth be told, I don't think it's going to be ready. We can't seem to make another metal band that fits to replace the one that broke. If we can't repair it tonight, Madeleine will have to take the large coach."

"So you approve of her plan?"

François' lips pressed into a tense slit. "No, I do not approve. But there is no stopping her once she has her mind set. You know that."

Jean nodded.

François continued, "We are hoping that when Madeleine starts for Versailles, Commander Boveé will give up on the notion that the boys are anywhere around here and will call off his unit. I want you to remain in the cave with the boys until one of us comes for you."

"That I can do. We have supplies enough for a few more days. We can fish or hunt for rabbits if we have to."

"You'd better get back to the boys. They will become frightened if you are gone too long."

"We will wait for further instructions." Jean embraced his brother once again. "You would be proud of your sons. They are brave young men."

"I am proud of them—and of you as well, little brother." François' eyes brimmed with tears. "You are in charge of precious cargo, Jean. Don't let anything happen to them."

Jean started toward the door.

"Halt, or I'll shoot!" The dragoon stood at the edge of the loft with his musket pointed straight at Jean.

Jean stopped. His eyes darted between the soldier and François.

Before anyone could speak, Armond bounded up the ladder and lunged at the dragoon. The soldier swung and fired at Armond, missing him as the shot whizzed by his ear. Armond tackled the dragoon at the knees, flinging him to the floor in the hay.

The two wrestled, grunting and rolling to the edge of the loft. François started up the ladder to aid Armond, but the muscular stable boy gained his footing and gave the soldier a shove and pushed him over the edge, sending him plummeting to the ground at the feet of the Jean and Henri.

The dragoon moaned and attempted to get up, but was too dazed.

All eyes were on Jean, knife drawn, standing over the soldier. Jean looked at his brother, then at Armond, looking down from the loft, then at Henri at his side, with the hammer in his hand.

"Kill him, Jean. We have no choice." Henri's voice of experience was the one that broke the silence. "If we don't, he will kill us or sound the alarm."

Jean looked at the man at his feet. "He's so young—younger than I am. Barely a man."

The dragoon's eyes flickered open, and he struggled to get up. He saw the knife in Jean's hands and began to shake uncontrollably. "Please—let me go. I'll leave, and nobody will ever know what happened to me. I won't tell anyone you were here." He put his quivering hands up in front of his face as he cringed at Jean's feet.

Henri spoke again. "If you can't do it, son, I will."

A battle raged in Jean's spirit as he tried in the balances of his conscience the verdict of the dragoon's earthly existence. He had to decide quickly.

He stepped behind the young man, reached down, and grabbed his hair in one hand, pulling him up to a kneeling position. He placed the knife at his throat.

"Make your peace with God quickly." Jean's hoarse whisper raked across the room. He looked upward. "Father, forgive me." Jean pulled the knife across the throat of the soldier.

The flesh parted, and blood spurted out on the hay and onto Jean's boots. The soldier twitched for a moment, gurgled, and then gasped his last breath. The sigh of death permeated the barn.

Jean fell to his knees in the blood as it seeped into the hay. "God forgive me."

Henri knelt beside the dragoon and cradled Jean in his arms. "He already has, my boy." Jean's shoulders heaved against the chest of the older man. "Evil must be dealt with—cruelly at times."

Armond and François stood motionless, staring at the surreal scene.

Henri continued, "King David was a brutal warrior, and he was a man after God's own heart. Don't torture yourself, Jean. We did what we had to do. You showed much courage."

Henri helped Jean stand, and the four men encircled the body of the young dragoon.

It was Armond who spurred them into action. "We need to get rid of this body quickly."

Henri pointed to the back of the barn. "Get a couple of those large horse blankets from the tack room."

Armond was already moving in that direction.

"François, go up in the loft and get his musket. Do you think anybody heard the shot?"

François answered over his shoulder as he climbed the ladder. "Let us hope, if they did, they just thought it was thunder." And, indeed, the low rumble of thunder could still be heard in the distance.

Armond brought two blankets. He placed one on the ground beside the soldier, and Jean and Henri rolled the body onto it. Then they covered the body with the other.

Jean went about the gruesome task dry-eyed.

They wrapped the body with a rope, securing the blanket. Armond straightened up. "There, that ought to be good enough. Now what, Henri?"

"You and François take him as far as you can carry him toward the orchard and bury him. Be sure to hide the grave well. Jean and I will clean up the blood, and then Jean needs to get back to the cave."

"I can do this by myself," Armond interrupted. "He's not very big. I can sling him over my shoulders and get to the orchard and back quicker than if two of us go. Besides, if François is missing in the morning, Commander Boveé will be suspicious. No one will miss me."

Henri and François nodded their agreement.

Armond continued, "Jean can get back to the cave. You and Monsieur can clean up the mess."

"*Bien.* Take a shovel." François still held the soldier's musket. "Bury this with him." He paused a moment. "On second thought, give it to Jean. Perhaps it will prove useful later on."

Armond lifted the body of the young dragoon and loped toward the river and the orchard beyond, while Henri began to throw the blood-soaked hay into the fire.

Jean and François clung to each other in a tight embrace—an embrace of farewell that needed no words. Then Jean tore himself from his brother's arms, hoisted the musket over his shoulder, and ran for the cover of the rock fence. He bolted over it and headed for the river.

JEAN RAN AS HARD AS HE COULD, SWEATING IN SPITE OF the cool night and the rain. He tripped and he stumbled, but he willed himself to keep going until he reached the river.

Silent screams burst from his throat as he ran. *Murderer! Murderer!* He could feel the sticky mess on his hands as the blood dried, and the stench of the gore on his tunic penetrated his nostrils.

When he reached the river, he plunged in headlong. He rubbed and he scoured to dislodge the evidence of his crime, but in the darkness he could not tell whether his efforts were successful. He wiped his hands over and over, rubbing his fingers against each other and against his clothing, then he staggered out of the river on the other side.

Jean clawed his way up the daunting cliff. The violent trembling of his frozen limbs made the moderate ascent an arduous task. He felt faint but willed himself forward. Finally he saw the ledge and the bush guarding the entrance. Anticipating difficulty again at making his way through, he made a forceful thrust the first time and plopped in on the other side.

Lying once more in the safety of the cave, Jean remembered something. *Lord, I asked you for protection before I left this cave last night. And you granted it. You protected all of us. Thank you.*

Then Jean buried his head in his hands and wept—wept for himself, for his family, for the life of the young man he had killed. *Oh, Jesus, I cannot bear this. I took another man's life! How can I live with that knowledge the rest of my life? Cover my sin and my bloodguiltiness. I am almost glad Dina is not here to see what I have become. I am a miserable man.*

Jean fell asleep as he prayed. How long he lay on the floor in front of the entrance, he couldn't tell. But when he opened his eyes, the light of dawn was seeping through the crack around the boulder. Groaning, he sat up. His muscles had grown stiff during his time on the floor of the tunnel in his damp clothes.

He picked up the dead man's musket and made his way to the hideout room. The fire burned low within the coals. He glanced around the corner at the boys. They slept the deep slumber of innocence. Jean stirred the embers and added kindling. He perched in front of the fire in the same spot where he had dozed before his trek to the manor.

As he watched the fire spring to life, Jean brooded over last night's events. This fire was almost gone, but it came back. That young dragoon would never come back. One moment a person is here, and then the next he is gone. Like the smoke rising from this fire. Where does it go? Does it simply disappear like a vapor? And one human being holds within his fleshly hands the very existence of another person?

Jean could have chosen to let the soldier live, but he didn't. He took his life from him. Did he have a family? Would a sweetheart or a wife and children mourn for him? His life was gone forever, snuffed out.

Jean stared at the flames. *My life will never be the same. This night will forever be branded on my soul.*

Philippe yawned, stretched, and sat up. "Uncle Jean, did you go check on the manor last night? Is everything all right there?"

Jean folded his arms over his tunic to cover the telltale splotches of blood.

NINE

Sparkling diamonds of dew glistened atop the manicured shrubbery in the formal gardens of the Clavell estate. Cleansed from the rainstorm the night before, the grounds stood on tiptoe awaiting the lively display of daffodils and tulips, and the heady fragrances of hyacinths and honeysuckle. But the surface beauty of spring concealed an ominous secret—human blood lay hidden by a thin layer of hay on the stable floor.

Early that morning, after a few sleepless hours in their beds, François and Henri made their way back to the barn. Much work remained to complete the preparations on Madeleine's coach, but the two men also wanted to make certain no grizzly evidence remained from the encounter the night before. The damp morning air intensified the pungent odor of animal sweat and manure in the stable, combined with the musty milieu of leather saddles and gear.

Now—more comrades than master and servant—the pair stood in the barn staring at the spot where the young dragoon met his fate. Neither spoke.

François moved the hay with his foot to see if any blood remained visible. He could barely see the red stain. He replaced the hay.

"Henri, are you packed and ready to go?"

"Yes, monsieur."

"Let's move the coach outside. Fetch Armond." François lowered his voice. "I want to know precisely where he—where the—I want to know where he went last night."

Henri started toward the door to get Armond and stopped at the stall nearest the spot where the deadly encounter had taken place only hours before. He pointed at the gate. "Monsieur!"

François followed Henri's pointing finger to the spot. Blood was splattered on the rough wood, soundlessly shrieking of the events of the night before. "Go on. Find Armond. I'll take care of this."

François hurried to the water trough outside the barn door as Henri went to locate Armond. "Move quickly."

On his way out, François had picked up one of the brushes used to curry the horses. He dipped it in the water and returned inside to try to erase the stains. He vigorously scrubbed the dark brown spots, to no avail. The sanguine fluid had already soaked into the porous wood and dried. Verging on panic, he tried to think of a solution to hide the revealing signs from the other soldiers.

He didn't have time to paint over it or sand it. His eyes lit upon bridles, saddles, blankets, and harnesses toward the back of the barn. He ran to the equipment and back to the guilty stall, where he quickly flung a saddle blanket over the stain.

"I'm here to relieve last night's sentry."

91

François turned.

The dragoon's bulk seemed to completely fill the large opening of the barn. He glanced around the dim interior of the stable. "Where'd he go?"

"Who? The guard from last night?" The horse in the stall nickered and poked his head over. François stroked the horse's face. "I haven't seen him this morning." He hoped the soldier wouldn't notice the beads of sweat breaking out on his forehead.

The dragoon cursed under his breath. "He's probably already filling his belly with breakfast." Seeing the obvious preparations for the journey, he guffawed. "Getting your wife's coach ready to go to Versailles, eh?"

François stopped, holding a harness in midair, and stared at the dragoon. The soldier shuffled his feet in the dirt, turned, and went outside, taking up his post at the door.

Henri and Armond, carrying their luggage, passed the relief guard at the door of the barn.

François addressed them. "Well, I see you are ready to go."

Armond's bloodshot eyes glanced around the enclosure for incriminating signs of last night's struggle. "Uh, yes, monsieur. I didn't sleep too well, but I will be fine."

François motioned Armond to the rear of the livery. "Let's you and I get the large coach out here in the middle and freshen it up. Henri, give your footmen orders to get the team harnessed. We'll go in for breakfast while they are doing that."

Armond set his small bag to the side and followed François to the large coach. Magnificent gold scrolls embellished the outside of the vehicle. An ornate "V" on the doors atop the Vaudois family crest announced that a member of the nobility rode inside.

François pulled Armond aside. "Where?"

The young man ducked his head and whispered, "On the backside of the orchard, under the biggest of the apple trees, beside the fence. The soil was soft and mushy because of the rain. I dug it deep and covered it with tree branches."

"Good work. Where is the shovel?"

"In the wheelbarrow with some of the other gardening tools in the back of the barn. I wiped the mud off it and left it soaking in the rainwater standing in the wheelbarrow."

"Very well." François grabbed the young man's shoulder and gave him a reassuring pat. "Let's get this coach ready."

François summoned two other men to help them move the carriage outside in preparation for the team of four white stallions. Henri and his men were busy brushing the horses, braiding their manes, bridling and harnessing them with the gaudy accouterments of court paraphernalia—tassels hanging from the ears, ornate gold straps crisscrossing the backs of the animals and under the tails.

François walked over to the first small coach they had rolled outside yesterday afternoon. Raindrops glistened on the top. It appeared to be in good shape. He looked at it, and then looked back at the large coach. François' pride began to surface. *Madeleine does need to journey to Versailles in two coaches. She's true nobility.* He rubbed his chin. "I know what we can do."

He approached Henri, who was laboring to get the restless white stallions harnessed together. "I have decided to send the other smaller coach as well. Get the black team ready."

Henri looked up at François from his kneeling position, checking the hoof of one of the steeds. He nodded and smiled. "*Oui*, monsieur. I understand." The crow's-feet around his merry blue eyes crinkled.

"And I agree. Madame needs to make her entrance at Versailles in two coaches. Then they will know a noble lady indeed is approaching. I'll take care of it."

Henri stood and patted the rear of the horse. Squinting skyward at the mounting sun, he calculated the work yet to be done—preparing the additional coach and team of horses. "However, we probably can't be ready now until midmorning."

"Do the best you can. I'll go tell Madeleine. Coming in for breakfast?"

"I'd better stay here and keep things moving."

"I'll send Thérèse down with some breakfast for you."

François ran up the path to the manor. His efforts to try to appear casual were wearing on him. Every unexpected movement, each foreign sound caused his heart to race and perspiration to break out on his face. *Lord Jesus, I need your peace—the peace that passes all understanding that you promised your followers. In the face of all this danger, please send your peace upon us.*

He pushed against the back door and took the stairs two at a time to check on Madeleine. He could hear feminine chatter issuing from behind their bedroom door.

François entered the room without knocking and discovered all three women, Elisabeth, Suzanne, and Madeleine, chattering about their trip to Versailles. Vangie played on the floor with a doll beside Madeleine's vanity.

Startled by his quick entrance, the ladies looked up and hushed their gossip.

"Excuse me, ladies. Could I have a word with my wife in private?" He smiled and moved to Madeleine, hugging her and planting a kiss on her cheek—making an effort to lighten his mood. "After all, she's leaving me for a month. Don't know how I'll manage without her." He sat down on the bed.

Elisabeth picked up some jewelry from the vanity. "Of course, dear. We were about to go down to breakfast anyway." She started to pick Vangie up off the floor.

"No, leave Vangie here." Madeleine pulled the little girl up in her lap. "I want to be with her until the minute we leave." Madeleine nuzzled the child on her neck. Vangie squealed and twisted out of her arms.

"Let her go with Grand-mère for just a moment, Madeleine. I need to discuss something with you."

"But—"

"It's important."

"If you are going to continue to argue with me about—"

Elisabeth had already taken Vangie's hand and started for the door. "You'll be joining us for breakfast shortly?"

François held the door open for the two women. "Yes, of course. We will be right behind you." He closed the door and faced his wife, who had her fists planted firmly on her hips.

"There is nothing more for us to discuss about my trip to Versailles. I am going."

"Stop right there." François' frowned and shook his head. "I need to tell you what happened last night. My heart's desire would be not to burden you with it." He shook his head. "Such knowledge is a cruel taskmaster, but you need to know."

"The boys. Something has happened to the boys?"

"No, not the boys, something else—but Jean was involved." François proceeded to pour out the dreadful tale.

"*Mon Dieu!*" The color drained from Madeleine's face. "Jean? How is Jean?"

"He left immediately after—devastated. He will have to come to terms with it on his own." François hung his head. "May God have mercy on him."

Madeleine stood. "What's done is done. We need to go on." She fidgeted with her hairbrush lying on the vanity. "We have not discussed what we will do if Louis won't receive me, or won't listen to me."

The self-assurance and brave declarations of confidence melted away, and Madeleine's eyes pleaded with her husband to give her answers.

François' soft answer was nevertheless firm. "If that should happen, make haste to get back here as quickly as you can. I will have a plan of escape ready for all of us. We will go to Geneva if we have to." He shrugged his shoulders. "I don't know what we will do from there. But let us be positive. Perhaps, as you have insisted, this affair is a huge mistake. And Louis will call off the dragoons because of your former relationship." François gazed intently at his wife.

"You are not concerned about that, are you, François? I must know that you trust me."

François cupped Madeleine's chin in his hand. "You are the love of my life and the mother of my children. I trust you with everything I am." He covered her face with kisses, ending with a gentle embrace. "I love you unendingly."

Madeleine kissed the rough palms of her partner's hands. "I love you, too, above all, above all but God." She took his hand and led him into the hall and down the stairs. "Now, my dear husband, let's go eat breakfast and continue to play the role of the gracious host and hostess, as if nothing out of the ordinary has happened."

"WHAT DOES MADAME HAVE IN HERE—ROCKS?" THE footmen chortled back and forth about the weight of Elisabeth's trunk as they trudged down the stairs with the cumbersome luggage.

Elisabeth followed close behind. "Oh, you know us women. We have to take everything we own to be sure we have what we need to charm the men."

The servants laughed good-naturedly and carried the traveling case outside, where they slung it onto the back of the large coach. Madeleine's trunk went on top of Elisabeth's, and they stowed the other luggage on the back of the smaller coach.

Henri, outfitted in his finest coachman's clothing, stood at attention beside the skittish team of white horses, awaiting Madeleine and Elisabeth's entry into the coach. Armond held the calmer black team at bay. Two footmen for each carriage stood behind the primary drivers of the coaches. One would ride alongside the driver—the other would perch on the backside of the coach.

The ladies emerged from the house, followed by their servants, Suzanne and an additional chambermaid plucked from the servants' pool at the last minute. Judith, who had served alongside Thérèse in the household for many years, was chosen to accompany the women because of her experience. In addition, she had relatives serving at court. Madeleine felt that perhaps the time might come when that connection would prove helpful.

The other servants, François, and Claudine, holding Vangie, gathered around the circular driveway to see the procession off.

François grabbed Madeleine's hands as she started toward her coach and encircled her tightly with his strong arms. "Be alert, my love, and cautious. Be as wise as a serpent and innocent as a dove. And return to me quickly."

"Oh, my love." Madeleine stood back and touched the scar on his forehead. "My strong, brave love. Pray that *Père Dieu* will prepare the way for us."

Suddenly mounted dragoons, led by Commander Boveé, galloped up the path to the barn.

Madeleine paused with one foot on the step as she was entering the coach and greeted the officer. "Good morning, Commander Boveé. It appears as if you are going on a trip as well."

"Yes, indeed, madame." Commander Boveé dismounted, and with a flourish removed his hat and bowed. "King Louis would never forgive me if I allowed one of his favorite ladies to travel all the way to Versailles unescorted."

Madeleine smiled. "How kind of you to be concerned for my safety. I welcome your escort."

The commander replaced his hat and swung back onto his horse. "We seem to have a soldier missing this morning. I'm sending two of my troops out to scout the area. You wouldn't know anything about that, would you, madame?"

"How would I know if you had a soldier missing, Commander? And why would I be concerned about it?"

Commander Boveé grumbled, then smiled at Madeleine. "Of course you would not. It is of no consequence to you, is it, Madame Clavell?"

His menacing tone sent shivers down Madeleine's spine. "None whatsoever, Commander Boveé."

She settled herself on the hard bench inside, and Elisabeth followed. Madeleine was smiling.

"What is going on in that pretty head of yours, daughter?"

"Commander Boveé is playing right into my hands. I'm sure he thinks I am staging this trip to Versailles to spirit the boys out of hiding to a more secure place. But we will actually be leading him away from them. How perfect." Madeleine spread her fan in front of her face and giggled like a little girl. "And in the process, he will be giving us the military protection of the king."

Elisabeth joined her, throwing back her head, and a hearty laugh filled the interior of the coach.

Henri and Armond climbed to their positions and shouted to the horses. The teams sprang into action, and the coaches lurched forward. Madeleine ceased her laughter as she gazed out of the window at her husband and child, standing on the steps of the manor waving as the coaches made the turn to the archway of trees leading out of the estate.

Madeleine whirled around in her seat and peered out the back opening. Around the legs of the footman she could see Vangie jumping up and down and waving to her. Tears sprang into her eyes, and she lost sight of her family as the coaches proceeded down the heavily shaded lane.

Soon the branches of the trees completely blocked her view, and she forced herself to turn around.

"These benches are not any more comfortable than they ever were." Elisabeth shifted her weight and bunched her skirts to try to find a cozier spot.

"No, and we have a long, precarious trip ahead of us." Madeleine looked out of the window at Commander Boveé and his soldiers trotting alongside the carriage. "A very long trip."

TEN

"Stop the carriage." Madeleine peered around the heavy window hangings she had pulled aside earlier to let in the fresh spring air. The midafternoon sun had warmed the interior of the coach, and Elisabeth's fan worked back and forth furiously.

Henri pulled the entourage to a halt.

Commander Boveé, never far behind the coaches on the weeklong trip, reined in beside the carriage. "Is there a problem, madame? We will be in Versailles in just a couple of hours. The horses don't need watering. I would suggest we keep moving."

"That is because you are a man, Commander. My mother and I wish to freshen ourselves, and dress accordingly to make our entrance at Versailles." Madeleine folded her fan and ran her fingers through her curls, flouncing them. A coy smile tugged at her lips.

"Order your men to rein in on that side of the road." Madeleine pointed to the left side of the road for the dragoons, and then with a wave of her hand indicated a stream to her right, with ample trees and low hanging vines. "I am taking my servants over there to bathe and dress. If you will be so kind as to instruct your men to give us some privacy. We won't take long."

Commander Boveé, lulled into complacency through the uneventful excursion, nevertheless perked up his ears at this latest development and began to scrutinize the area. "I don't know if that's a good idea . . . ah . . ." The commander twirled his horse around in a circle.

"Really, Commander. What do you think we are going to do? Pull out hidden weapons and attack your soldiers?" Madeleine spread her fan in front of her face and tittered.

"Hmmpff. Of course not. But one can never be too careful. There might be highwaymen hiding in the brush. Observing such lovely ladies bathing might be too much temptation to resist."

Commander Boveé turned in his saddle. "DuBois! Costeaux! Go down to the bank of that stream and check it out. The ladies want to . . . uh . . . freshen up."

Two dragoons rode up beside him, lecherous grins on across their faces. "Yes, sir! It will be a pleasure."

"I didn't say you are to stand guard. I said to scout out the area. Then return."

Laughing, they turned their horses and started toward the water's edge.

"Barbarians! My apologies, ladies."

Madeleine continued to hide her face behind her fan. Commander Boveé, she suspected, still thought that she planned to meet up with her boys and rescue them. Let them search all they want. *Your zeal, Commander Boveé, has taken you miles away from your target.*

"We'll get Henri and Armond to take our large trunks down to the water's edge, Mère. We need some things out of them."

They had used their small carrying cases when staying at the inns along the way. The large trunks remained strapped on the back of the carriages.

The soldiers returned quickly. "Looks safe enough."

"Very well. Ladies?" Commander Boveé dismounted and executed his elegant bow with hat in hand.

"Thank you, sir. We shan't be long. Henri, pull the carriages as close to the water as you can. We will need the large trunks, please."

"Yes, madame. Armond, follow me to the water's edge."

The two coaches rolled down to the riverbank and formed a barrier for the women.

Henri and Armond alighted, and with the help of the footmen, unloaded the women's trunks at the base of a large, overhanging oak tree. Suzanne and Judith joined them.

"Henri, take your men downstream and get cleaned up yourselves. Give us half an hour or so, then come back. Put on fresh uniforms."

"Yes, madame."

Henri, Armond, and the footmen gathered their personal belongings and trudged downstream.

Elisabeth kept a watch out for intruders and hung their garments on the branches afforded by the large trees lining the river's edge, offering a protective screen from prying eyes. With Suzanne holding a blanket up as a makeshift screen, Madeleine slipped out of her outer garments and into the stream. She shivered and caught her breath, then hurried through her toilette.

"Suzanne, hand me the towel." Madeleine rubbed her arms and stepped out of the water into the large blanket Suzanne held ready for her. "Whooo!" She shook her head, laughing. "Help me get dressed. I'm freezing."

"You'll catch your death of a cold," Elisabeth clucked over her daughter. She assisted Suzanne in tightening Madeleine's corset. Suzanne had placed Madeleine's shoes on the ground ready for her to step into and slipped her gown over her head.

"Would you please fetch the rose toilet water out of my case?"

Suzanne opened the case, pulled out the perfume, and gave it to Madeleine.

Elisabeth beckoned to Judith. "I want you to wire my hair. The wires are in my trunk."

Judith grumbled under her breath.

"I know you don't like them," Elisabeth said, "but these curls are the latest fashion."

"It is so hard to form the curls—and to make them stay in place."

"As much as you detest the wires, you do a remarkable job, Judith. Thank you."

Judith quickly completed the task and stood back to check that the curls were even on both sides of Elisabeth's head. The rest of the hair she wound in a bun.

Madeleine's mahogany locks had been cut in the stylish hurluberlu, downward pointing ringlets all over her head, with the longer part of her hair piled up in the back. She ran her fingers through her hair at the side of her head, attempting to widen the style. "Suzanne, my hair is drooping."

"It must have gotten wet. We have no egg whites with which to stiffen it."

"Hmm—well, this will just have to do until we get to Versailles." She continued to attempt to fluff the curls.

Madeleine started up the incline to the coaches and was startled to observe Commander Boveé lounging against a large tree trunk. "Why, Officer Boveé, have you been spying on me?"

"Simply keeping watch over my charges."

"I see," Madeleine challenged him. "And did your 'charges' meet with your approval?"

"Exceeded my approval." The commander stood, adjusted his hat, and offered his arm. "May I?"

Madeleine, hiding her face with her fan, took his arm and entered the carriage. Elisabeth and the two chambermaids trudged up the hill and observed the exchange between Commander Boveé and Madeleine. Suzanne and Judith glanced at each other sharply but said nothing.

The men had returned and were waiting attentively at their stations, resplendent in their fresh uniforms, ready to make an entrance at Versailles.

"Judith, accompany Madame Elisabeth in the smaller coach." Madeleine snapped her orders. "Suzanne, come with me."

A footman assisted Elisabeth as she entered the coach—the chambermaids waiting until their mistresses were seated. As Suzanne lifted her skirt to proceed into the carriage, Madeleine saw Armond step forward and offered his arm to Suzanne. His eyes glowed with warmth and excitement; his smile spilled over with charm.

How interesting. Do we have a budding romance here?

Suzanne placed their small traveling cases on the floor at their feet and seated herself. Her flushed cheeks betrayed her emotions.

Madeleine teased her. "Are you feeling ill? Your cheeks are flushed."

Suzanne ducked her head. "*Mais non,* madame. I am fine."

"Hyaa!" Henri cracked the whip, and the carriages bolted forward. They rolled directly onto the road and northward toward Versailles.

Madeleine chuckled as Commander Boveé vaulted into his saddle and galloped onto the road to catch up with them. The carriage picked up speed, dust from the wheels enveloping Commander Boveé in the rear. Madeleine stared out the window. "We should be in Versailles within the hour."

Suzanne clasped her hands in front of her in glee. "Oh, madame. Thank you for bringing me with you. I cannot wait to see Versailles."

Madeleine reminded her young chambermaid, "Remember what I said. Keep alert. All is not as it seems at court." Madeleine leaned her head against the back of the carriage and closed her eyes.

Ah-h-h, Versailles. What do you have in store for us? And, Louis, how will I find you? What do you have in store for us?

THE CARRIAGES ENTERED THE TREE-LINED PROMENADE leading to the magnificent chateau of Versailles. Henri slowed the horses to a pompous trot, and the entire party seemed to come to attention. The footmen stood straighter and the women sat more erect as the carriages made their way through the mushrooming crowd of horses, soldiers, coaches, and citizens. Roads converged from every direction, culminating at a holding area for coaches and horses in front of the massive gates to the complex.

Suzanne peered outside the window, her hands fluttering to her face and back to her lap.

"Sit back, Suzanne, and do stop that fidgeting."

"*Oui*, madame, but I'm so excited."

"Well, try to conceal it and act like a lady. Your heart can beat like a drum, but your face mustn't reveal your trepidation."

Suzanne sat back, but her eyes continued to dart back and forth at the activity around her. Commander Boveé raced in front of them and led their coaches into the arena. The dragoons flanked each side of the carriages. The guards at the gates saluted Commander Boveé as he dismounted and gave them instructions.

He approached the carriage, opened the door, and offered Madeleine his arm. "This is where I leave you. I have sent for sedan chairs to carry you to the chateau, and with your permission, I have ordered apartments for your stay."

"How kind of you. I am indebted to you."

"It was my pleasure, madame. I must admit . . ." The commander shifted his weight from foot to foot and twirled his hat in his hands. His usual overconfident manner dissolved for a moment.

"Yes, Commander?" Madeleine smiled. "I do believe I detect a crack in that hard exterior."

"Well, I did not expect the trip to be quite so—shall we say, uneventful?"

"Whatever did you expect?" Madeleine closed her fan with a quick snap.

"Nothing, nothing at all." He bowed once more as servants ran up to them with the sedan chairs. "Until we meet again, madame?"

"Yes, of course. Will you be staying at Versailles for a while?"

"No, unfortunately not—just for the night to rest the horses. And long enough to see my son if he is available."

"Your son? Why, Commander Boveé, I had no idea you were a family man."

"I'm not." The commander flashed one of his dazzling smiles. "I will get my orders and then return to your manor to gather my troops. Perhaps we will maintain our headquarters at your place, or perhaps we shall move on. I'm sure our paths will cross again."

"Um, I'm sure." Madeleine offered her hand to the commander. If she had her way, Commander Boveé and his dragoons would never cross her path again.

"By the way, you are in luck. There is a *bal masqué* tonight. If you make haste, you could perhaps attend." Commander Boveé took Madeleine's hand and kissed it. He executed his lavish bow once again, mounted his horse, and left with his dragoons following dutifully behind him toward the stables.

Henri, Armond, and the footmen loaded luggage onto a *fiacre* and followed behind with the rest of the baggage as the hackneys carried the ladies swiftly to their quarters.

"Oooh, madame!" Suzanne's naïve enthusiasm bubbled over as they entered the elaborate flat. She ran her fingers over the gold molding on the wall. A marble fireplace with brass andirons and a bust of King Louis on the mantel flanked the wall on the left. Rising to the vaulted ceiling, a gilded mirror gave the room enormous dimension.

"Suzanne." Madeleine's firm voice refocused the young girl. "Put my traveling case in the front bedroom, please. Judith, Madame Elisabeth's things will go in the second bedroom."

The footmen deposited the trunks in the respective bedrooms and then went outside to the hallway. Henri and Armond took a servant's stance at the doorway.

"Madame, may we assist you further at this time?" Henri bowed slightly at the waist.

"No, thank you for your service. Take the footmen and find a place to bunk in the stables. See to the horses, then you and Armond come back. I wish for you two to accompany my mother and me to the bal masqué tonight."

"Very well." Henri bowed and backed out of the room. "We shall return shortly."

HENRI MADE NOTE OF THEIR ROUTE THROUGH THE MAZE of hallways and staircases as they left the chateau. The men chatted casually about the remarkable surroundings as they made their way to the stables.

The grandeur of the gardens surrounding the chateau exceeded anything Henri had ever seen before. He marveled at the design. Thousands of clipped, sculptured yew lined the walkways. Elegant statues, urns, fountains, and pools punctuated the landscape. Henri's practical mind jumped from one structure to another, analyzing the complexity of the operation of the grounds. Where are they pumping the water from? How much manpower did it take to keep the shrubbery trimmed? How many different kinds of flowers must there be—thousands?

Yellow daffodils and early spring tulips in reds, oranges, and purples announced the fact that warmer weather was around the corner. Trees of hundreds of varieties aligned themselves along the roads and pools like soldiers standing at attention. The fragrance of flowers and trees mingled and permeated the air.

Travelers and foreign diplomats, easily recognizable by their strange clothes, wandered aimlessly in the arena where coaches arrived. Courtiers stood chatting amongst themselves or bumped into each other as they hurried from one appointment to another.

As they made their way to the stables through the myriad of noblemen and soldiers and servants bustling about performing their duties, Henri issued orders to his men. "We'll take the coaches and horses into the livery. Armond, take your team and get them fed and watered and bedded down."

"There must be two thousand horses in these stables." Armond's awe at the magnificence of Versailles showed on his face. "We can just bed down with our teams. Those stalls are nicer than most accommodations I've had at roadside inns."

The rest of the men mumbled their agreement.

Henri smiled and continued, "I'll take care of my team. Then meet me at the entrance, dressed and ready to escort *mesdames* tonight."

MADELEINE REMOVED HER GLOVES AND PLACED THEM ON a boulle commode standing adjacent to the entryway, scrolled with ornate gold and an inlaid top. "Judith, I assume you would like to find your cousin and stay with her in the servants quarters?"

"Yes, madame, if that would meet with your approval."

"Maman? What is your pleasure?"

Madeleine's mother had seated herself in a chair, attempting to catch her breath. Perspiration beaded up on her face from the exertion of the trek into the apartment, and she fanned herself vigorously. "Do you plan to attend the masqué tonight?"

"Absolutely."

"Then, Judith, would you mind staying to help me dress? After we go to the ball, you may be dismissed to go find your cousin and stay with her."

"*Oui*, madame." Judith curtsied and went to Elisabeth's room to begin preparations.

"Suzanne, I wish for you to stay here with me," Madeleine said. Suzanne nodded.

"Start unpacking my things, and get the red dress ready."

Madeleine walked to the window and peered at the teeming activity below. Scaffoldings teetered beside several buildings. "I wonder when Louis will be satisfied with his creation here. Will he ever finish it?"

Her mother joined her at the window, shaking her head. "I don't know, dear. But isn't it magnificent?"

The view from their corner room overlooked the orangery and manicured gardens and fountains. The variegated colors of green shrubbery, lawns, ponds, and the early blossoms on the trees produced a springtime kaleidoscopic view in the setting sun.

Memories of earlier days flooded Madeleine's mind. "The strangest emotions are tugging at my heart. This world is most foreign to me now, but, in a peculiar way, I feel as if I've come home."

Concern flitted across her mother's face. "I suppose that would be natural, as you spent your growing up years here—but, I must warn you, guard your heart. Versailles is a Jezebel. She will seduce you. Don't be swept away by the lure of high society and the court. This is an unreal world, Madeleine, populated by characters playing a part on a stage. But the end of the play will be very real."

"Yes, Maman, I do know that. I will be cautious. I am simply surprised at my feelings." She turned from the window and started for her bedroom. "Hurry, now. We must get ready."

Whirling around suddenly, Madeleine said, "I wonder why we rated such exquisite quarters. Many of the flats are not nearly as well furnished and are tucked away with no windows. Do you suppose Louis was expecting us?"

"I was wondering the same thing."

Madeleine waved her hand. "Well, whether he is expecting us or not, we can enjoy our comfortable quarters, can we not?"

"Of course. I must ready myself now." Her mother moved toward her room. "Judith, is there water in the basin?"

Madeleine walked through the entryway and opened the door. She glanced down the hall. Servants scurried up and down the massive staircase and into the hall lighting candles. The glow from the candles illuminated the night and glinted off the gold railing, turning the staircase into a cascade of moving lights as the servants performed their evening ritual. The trail of candlelight was beautiful, but Madeleine shuddered.

"Madame?" A chambermaid holding a large brass candlestick holder stopped in front of Madeleine. "May I be of assistance?"

"No, thank you. I just, well . . . on second thought, yes. Could you light the fire for us—and some warm water would be welcome."

"Of course, right away." The dutiful servant started toward the stairs.

"In which ballroom is the masqué being held tonight?"

"Would Madame like an escort to the ballroom?"

"That would be lovely. Yes, I would like that very much." Madeleine turned to go into the apartment. "Oh, and one more thing."

"Madame?"

"Um, could you—would it be possible to bring me some egg whites from the kitchen?"

ELEVEN

A sudden urge to flee seized Madeleine. Her heart thudded wildly, and she struggled to catch her breath as the small cortege made its way through the maze of halls and rooms to the ballroom. Magnificent pieces of art and tapestry graced the walls of the corridors. Portraits by Mignard and battle scenes by Parrocel appeared around every corner. The flickering candlelight from the golden candle stands lining the hallway gave the paintings an eerie lifelike quality. Louis' image invaded every corner. A thousand silent eyes watched their trek.

Madeleine clutched her masque at her side. She forced herself to take a deep breath and keep walking. The poesy ring encircled her finger, and she twirled it nervously with her thumb. She touched the glittery black comb and straightened her black lace veil. Her mother walked silently beside her—head held erect, trained by years of proper etiquette.

The strains of *La Menuet* reached their ears as they drew near the ballroom, Henri and Armond striding protectively behind them.

As they approached the entrance, the servants of the chateau, who had escorted them, bowed and left. Madeleine nodded and indicated to Henri and Armond to take their places alongside the wall with the other servants. Without a word, the two women raised their masques in unison and stepped into the throng of dancers and onlookers.

Madeleine fluttered her fan in front of her face, while holding the gold masque with the other. The majesty of the scene overwhelmed her, and she stood frozen on the spot for a moment. Her mother caught her by the elbow and maneuvered her to the side of the room.

Dancers executed perfect pirouettes and swayed in rhythm back and forth, stepping toward their partners, then retreating. Massive crystal chandeliers, glowing with lighted candles, brilliantly illuminated the ballroom. The elegance of the choreography was matched only by the lavish costumes—reds, golds, burgundies, greens, purples, and blues, every hue in the rainbow, combining to create an undulating canvas of color.

The dancers unashamedly flirted with their partners from behind their masques. The subtleties of the choreography extended sensual invitations to participate in the perpetual game at court of *yes, no, maybe,* or *try-and-see.* And then the instigator would twirl away to approach another and begin the game over once more.

The dais, its royal blue curtained background sprinkled with gold fleurs-de-lis, was empty. The royal party obviously had not yet made their entrance. Madeleine watched the footwork of the couples and searched the dancers for the familiar figure of the king, but he was not to be seen.

Suddenly, even as Madeleine was looking for him, the crowd

parted in front of her, and the king, with the queen on his arm, entered the ballroom. His loyal subjects bowed low to the ground as the music faltered and then halted. Madeleine's knees trembled.

Approaching the dais, the king turned and with a wave of his hand, spoke a soft "Continue."

Madeleine peeked over her fan and saw the gentle curve of a smile that she had known so well in years gone by. He had aged, but remained the dashing, handsome regent she remembered. His voluminous dark wig fell around his shoulders over a resplendent red-and-gold brocade jacket, with gold epaulets and an ecru lace collar and cuffs. He surveyed the crowd, seating himself slowly on the throne, nodding to the crowd. His gold breeches, red tights, and gold shoes with their fashionable red soles and heels glinted in the candlelight as he settled himself on the royal seat.

The queen appeared to be uncomfortable with the grandeur of the court. Her gown was a charcoal gray with scarlet accents, dark and rather plain. Nothing about her was radiant or appealing. Louis treated her with distant respect, but otherwise ignored her.

The musicians resumed playing, and the dancers rose from their positions of humility and picked up the rhythm as if they had never been interrupted.

Madeleine motioned to her mother. "Come with me. Keep your masque up and your face covered."

Madeleine took her mother's hand and wove in and out through the merrymakers along the wall. She motioned to an alcove carved out behind a pillar. "Stay here."

Madeleine made her way to the dancers in front of the dais and positioned herself behind a large woman, bending in time with the music. Then at precisely the right moment, when the woman twirled to meet her partner, Madeleine faced the throne and lowered her mask, smiling impishly at the king. She then pivoted away quickly and lost herself in the crowd.

Louis stood abruptly, knocking over his gold-handled walking stick. He scrutinized the crowd, then sat down, but remained on the edge of his chair. The queen looked at her husband, her face registering shock. He bent toward her and whispered in her ear. The queen searched the room, shaking her head.

Madeleine spun lightly to the alcove where her mother awaited her. "Let's go to the other side."

"You tease the king? You are playing with fire. Why don't you just let him know you are here and want to see him?"

"Louis loves a chase, and I want to challenge him. Come, I know what I am doing."

The pair made their way to the back of the room, then to the front on the opposite side. Madeleine motioned to Henri and Armond to follow them as well. They watched the prancing procedures of the ball for a moment, entranced by the production.

A courtier approached Madeleine. "Such a lovely lady, seemingly unescorted?" The young man glanced around. "May I have the pleasure for *La Contredanse?*"

He wore a black masque rather than carrying the façade.

Madeleine tilted her head and smiled coyly. She held her fan in front of her mouth. "How might one determine that I am such a lovely lady? Perhaps the face of a dog conceals itself behind this disguise." She chuckled. "Or perchance I have teeth missing, or a wart on my nose."

The entendres of court conversation, long since left behind, fell effortlessly from her lips.

The courtier flushed at the intrigue. "Oh, madame—or, if this is my lucky night, possibly mademoiselle—the sweetness of that voice could never come from the face of a dog."

Madeleine could see intense gray eyes staring at her from behind the masque above a square jaw. *His is no dog face*, she thought.

He extended his hand to her and bowed.

Madeleine lowered her fan and flashed a brilliant smile. She placed her smooth white hand in his tanned one, stepped onto the dance floor, and whispered as she strode past him to join the other dancers, "It is *madame*."

"*Mais, ce n'est pas possible!* Such misfortune! I find the fairest flower at the ball, and she is already plucked." He looked over his shoulder toward Armond, Henri, and her mother. "Is the fortuitous victor of your affections in attendance?"

"Not tonight. Just my mother is with me." Madeleine swept onto the dance floor and took her position in the circle.

The musicians struck up the music, and Madeleine's partner faced her—taking advantage of the dance to move much too close for her comfort.

As they moved back and forth in front of the throne, Madeleine waited for her chance. Her unsuspecting partner gave her the right opening as the dance was coming to an end. He whispered in her ear as he drew her to his side for the final twirl of the dance. "Won't you let me see your face? It would be torture if you should choose to keep yourself concealed all night from me."

Madeleine simply flitted her fan.

She maneuvered herself so that she was facing the king as the dance ended. At the final bow, she slowly lowered her masque, looked at her partner, then stepped aside to look at the king. Her partner, expressing his delight at her beauty, escorted her back to her mother. But not before Madeleine observed the king mouthing her name.

The strains of *La Courante* began, and King Louis rose, extended his arm to his wife, and moved to the dance floor. The subdued three-quarter time slowed the tempo of the crowd. The king expertly executed a few steps with his wife, then, without fanfare, the queen curtsied and left the room.

Once again the dancing ceased, and a hush settled over the room. Even as the queen made her way toward the door, Louis began searching the room. Upon spying Madeleine, he began making his way toward her. However, the queen had scarcely made her exit when an extraordinarily beautiful woman, commanding attention simply by her presence, entered.

The king's focus swung to her, and he went to her side, again waving the musicians to resume. The woman curtsied, offered her hand, and they began to dance. The king's countenance shone with adoration, and it was returned in kind. He did not take his eyes from her face.

Madeleine turned to her mother. "Madame de Montespan? Athénaïs?"

Her mother nodded. "That is she."

The beauty of the king's current mistress stunned Madeleine. Her blond curls were anchored with fresh spring flowers. Gemstones of jade studded the front and hemline of her low-cut, ivory-toned gown. She held a blue velvet, ermine-lined robe loosely around her shoulders. Her pale complexion was accented by a sensual rosebud mouth, which burst into laughter easily as the couple danced.

Madeleine stared at the twosome as they affected the intricate moves of the dance. "I had no idea."

"What did you expect, dear? That Louis' mistress would be as homely as his wife? She is quite an extraordinary woman. And not one to be taken lightly."

Madeleine kept her masque over her face and stared at the couple as they took command of the dance floor. Louis' expertise in the dance was matched by Athénaïs' grace and skill. A more stunning couple could not be found anywhere in France, Madeleine was sure.

The king did not so much as glance Madeleine's way the rest of the evening. The young courtier, whose name Madeleine learned was Pierre, returned for several more dances. She agreed to his invitations so she could get on the floor—perchance to encounter the king, but the room proved to be much too crowded, and the king too evasive.

Now who was challenging whom? Madeleine couldn't discern whether the king was avoiding her, teasing her, or simply didn't care to see her.

The masqué ended in the wee hours of the morning. King Louis and Madame de Montespan stayed late and enjoyed the festivities, but as soon as they departed, the others began to exit the ballroom, winding their way through the rooms and halls of the chateau.

Monsieur Pierre reappeared and offered to escort Madeleine and her party to their apartment, but Madeleine declined his offer. He departed with crestfallen face.

Upon leaving the ballroom, a blue boy, one of the court attendants, approached Madeleine. He handed her an envelope, bowed, and stood aside.

"You need a reply now?"

"*Oui*, madame."

Madeleine turned the correspondence over and ripped through the king's seal.

Meet me at the Porcelain Trianon tomorrow evening at eleven o'clock. At ten o'clock a courtier will arrive to escort you.

As ever, Louis

Madeleine held the note in her hand, tapping it with the handle of her masque. "Tell the king I would be honored."

The blue boy bowed and left.

"What did it say, dear?" Her mother probed for information as they started for their apartment.

Henri and Armond walked a respectful distance behind them.

"Louis has asked me to meet him tomorrow evening at the Porcelain Trianon." Madeleine smiled. "And, of course, I shall."

Her mother smiled. "Of course you shall, dear."

Madeleine motioned Henri in front of her. "Take the lead, Henri. I'm not sure I remember the way back to our apartment."

"*Oui*, madame." Henri moved quickly to take charge of their walk back through the halls, the only sounds the rustling of the women's skirts and clicking of their shoes on the black-and-white tile floors.

Armond remained in the rear.

Madeleine wondered as they walked the darkened hallways how welcome they would be if those they encountered knew they were Huguenots, not Catholics. Would the weapons carried by the Swiss guards be turned on them at any moment, demanding conversion? How long would her deceased father's former status at court protect them? How tolerant would Louis remain if she refused his advances at this stage in their lives?

She was no longer a young girl flirting with a young king for favor at court. She was vying for the lives of her family and her home. How far was she willing to go to ransom her family? And if she obtained

Louis' word to protect them, how long would that last? Until the next wave of hatred against the Huguenots swept like a wildfire through the country, destroying everything in its path, including the Vaudois and Clavell family and estate?

The gravity of the situation began to break like waves upon her. As their apartment came into view, she ran through the door, bolted into her room, and retched into the bowl on her washstand.

Suzanne, sleeping on the chaise by the window in Madeleine's room, leapt up, awakened by the sound of her mistress gagging.

"Madame! Are you ill? What's wrong?" She grabbed a towel from the washstand and offered it to Madeleine.

Elisabeth followed close behind. "Are you all right, dear?"

Madeleine sat on the bed—her face ashen. Her hands shook as she wiped her mouth and face with the towel. "I'm fine, Maman. I took for granted that Louis would be delighted to see me. We are in the middle of a national upheaval, and the destiny of our family is held in the balance on the delicate scales of my youthful obsession with the regent of France."

Her mother sat on the bed and patted Madeleine's hand.

"A slight tilt of the head or a word misspoken could plunge us all into prison or even cause our death." She held the towel up in front of her face as tears began to roll down her face. "I don't know if I can do this. I'm frightened." She looked at her mother, her eyes bright with tears. "I'm sure Louis recognized me. But he seemed oblivious. Like someone I didn't know."

"Listen to me. We are here now." Elisabeth took Madeleine by the shoulders. "You are a Vaudois. You are strong. You can do this." Her mother held Madeleine tightly in her arms until her daughter's tears subsided.

After a few moments passed, Madeleine stood. "Well, let's get some sleep. Daylight is not too far off. Maman, get this corset off me. It's too tight. I feel like I am suffocating."

Madeleine tossed and turned the remainder of the night in the massive bed. The events of the evening played over and over in the nether land between wakefulness and sleep. The early morning sky had begun to lighten into a milky soup over the gardens of the chateau when she finally drifted into troubled slumber, the faces of her loved ones floating in and out of her dreams.

FRANÇOIS STOOD AT THE BEDROOM WINDOW WATCHING the sunrise over an early morning mist rising from the river bottom. He whispered to himself, "Jean and my brave boys, are you faring well? And my beloved Madeleine, are you meeting with success? Is our king looking upon you with favor—or perhaps too much favor?"

He paced the floor. "I won't torture myself with possibilities. Dear God, I stand here a helpless man, a helpless father and husband—helpless to protect my family from an enemy who wants to destroy us because of our differing beliefs in the way of salvation. Cover us with your divine protection. Protect Madeleine from the schemes of the king. Give her discernment and wise words. We fall on your mercy and strength. You are mighty to save."

François went to his empty bed and lay down with his hands behind his head. Disjointed thoughts flickered through his mind, and he dozed off for a moment, then awoke with a start, got up, and dressed for the day. Another day with dragoons watching every move of the Clavell family. This must end soon.

JEAN OPENED HIS EYES TO A SLIGHT LIGHTENING OF THE darkness of the cave. He glanced at Philippe and Charles sleeping soundly and tiptoed past them and into the tunnel leading to the entrance. He peeked through the crack around the rock and saw fog rising from the river.

How long, O Lord, how long do we have to stay hidden in this miserable cave? Show us what to do. Give us strength for this day. Help us. Jean sank to his knees, tears spilling down his tanned cheeks. *O Dieu, where are you? Why are you silent when we so desperately need some answers? Why do you hide Yourself from us? The heavens are cold, unhearing brass. Jesus! Help us!*

He pounded his fist against the rock wall of the cave, until his knuckles were scratched and bleeding. *Help us!* The cries of the discouraged young man echoed through the yawning tunnels and bounced off deaf granite, mocking his faith by the silence.

TWELVE

Suzanne pushed open the tall, gold-embellished shutters, and shafts of afternoon sunlight streamed across the room onto the weighty tapestry comforter.

Madeleine stirred and covered her eyes with the back of her hand. "What time is it? Have I slept all morning?"

"*Oui*, madame. It is nearly two o'clock." Suzanne fussed over Madeleine, plumping her pillows. "Madame needed to sleep."

A dressing gown lay at the foot of the bed, and the tantalizing aroma of a bowl of potage sitting on a tray atop the nearby vanity coaxed Madeleine from the warmth of the bed. She threw the dressing gown around her shoulders, picked up a piece of bread, and walked to the window. The courtyard of the chateau and gardens teemed with activity.

Madeleine gazed down at the Grand Canal. Crystal bangles of

light sparkled across the surface of the reservoir. Gondolas floated lazily in the water, one of which would transport her tonight to the king. "Is my mother awake yet?"

"*Oui*, she's been up for some time now."

"What about Judith? Has she returned from the servants' quarters?"

"*Oui*, madame." Suzanne paused in her fidgeting with the breakfast tray. "Would you like me to summon her?"

"Yes, please, both of them. Leave the tray on the vanity."

Suzanne grumbled about the meal getting cold, but obediently went into the living area to fetch the two older women.

Elisabeth, still in her dressing gown, bustled in, bringing her usual cheeriness and a hug. "Good morning, dear, or should I say afternoon? Didn't we have a grand time last night? And that handsome young man who kept returning to dance with you, what was his name? Isn't it a gorgeous day? Are you feeling better?"

Her mother's questions amused Madeleine. Charles is so like his Grand-mère—with their incessant questions and no waiting for an answer. "Yes, I have been admiring the gondolas on the Grand Canal."

Judith, holding one of her mistress's gowns, followed Elisabeth into the room. She stood unsmiling against the wall, next to the door.

Madeleine probed for information. "Did you find your cousin last night, Judith?"

"*Oui*."

"And is she well? Did you enjoy your visit?"

"*Oui*, madame."

Judith's terse answers annoyed Madeleine, as did as the domestic's grim countenance. "What is her name?"

"Madame?"

"Her name, Judith. She does have a name, *non?*"

"Her name is Francina."

"How old is she?"

"Madame?"

"Her age? How old is she?" Madeleine was losing her patience.

"Why, I think she is about ten years younger than I—around forty, I guess. Maybe younger."

"Protestant?"

"*Non*, madame, Catholic."

"I see. I'd like to speak with her. Do you think you could bring her here?"

"Right now?"

"Yes, right now. I would like to speak to her before the evening."

"*Oui*, madame. She works in the kitchen. I think I can find her."

"Good. Now we are getting somewhere. You're excused, Judith. Go find Francina and bring her here as soon as you can."

Judith left quickly, snapping her skirt first in a brisk curtsy.

Elisabeth waited for the door leading from the apartment to be fully closed. "What was that all about?"

Madeleine sat on the vanity stool and began to toy with her breakfast. "I want to probe someone for information who knows the procedure of the evenings at the Trianon, someone who might have a bit of fealty for our family. I was hoping, however, that she would be Protestant. I'll just have to trust my instincts." She tasted a spoonful of the potage. "This is good. What's in it?"

"Peas." Her mother laughed.

"Ahh, yes! Louis' great fondness for peas. Have you had your breakfast yet?"

"Oh my, yes. I've been up for hours." Elisabeth moved to Madeleine's gowns, which Suzanne had hung up the night before, going through them one by one. "What sticky web does my little spider plan to weave tonight? And with what alluring gown?"

"Maman!"

Elisabeth's switch from a concerned mother to a comrade in conspiracy shocked Madeleine.

Her mother's dark-rimmed eyes turned icy. "Listen to me, Madeleine. I maneuvered and manipulated and schemed at this court for years to keep us alive and integrated into the politics of the governing council. As Huguenots, that was not easy. But we did it, and we maintained Louis' confidence, and, ultimately, his protection. At times, we had to participate in alliances and plots that we did not believe in, did not approve of, nor did we wish to be involved in. But for the sake of the safety of our family, we went along with the schemes."

Madeleine stared at her mother. "You?"

Elisabeth turned from her daughter and sat on the bed. "God will direct you through the maze of intrigue. You must listen to his voice. You must trust that voice. He will tell you what to do and where to go."

NEARLY TWO HOURS PASSED BEFORE JUDITH REENTERED the apartment with her cousin. Unlike her dour cousin, the plump, middle-aged woman bore a pleasant countenance.

"Francina?" Madeleine rose from the settee.

"*Oui*, madame." She curtsied politely and smiled.

"Did Judith tell you why I wished to see you?"

"*Non*, madame."

"I need details concerning the protocol of the king's dinners at the Trianon. Can you help me?"

"I think so. I work the meals there frequently. In fact . . ." Francina paused and looked around the room for permission to proceed.

Madeleine nodded.

"I am to serve the king's dinner tonight at the Trianon."

"Excellent! You are exactly the person I need. What luck!"

Her mother, seated by the fireplace reading a book, chided her, "This is not luck, Madeleine. This is God's guidance."

"Hmm, of course." Madeleine paced as she questioned Francina. "Who are the guests at such a dinner?"

"The king's family, mistress, courtiers, specially invited guests." The domestic ducked her head. "And . . ."

"And . . . ?"

"Sometimes the king arranges for beautiful women with whom he desires a secret rendezvous to join him for dinner."

"I see." Madeleine felt herself blushing. "And how does he manage that with his wife and mistress looking on?"

"They are discreet."

"I can't imagine Madame de Montespan being that discreet—looking the other way long enough for Louis to meet with another woman."

"When our king invites a 'special guest,' Madame de Montespan usually does not attend."

"And Maria Thérèse excuses herself early?"

"*Oui*, madame."

"What can I expect when I arrive?"

"Will Madame have an escort?"

"Yes."

Elisabeth looked up quickly from her book. "Really? Did I miss something?"

Madeleine continued her pacing and tapped her fingers together as she schemed. "Armond could pass for a courtier, in the right clothes. He certainly can't wear a footman's uniform. Yes, he will do nicely. He's young and handsome, and Louis would wonder who he might be." She paused, then continued, as if talking to herself.

"What if Louis saw him last night at the masqué with us? No, I don't think he did. Armond and Henri were against the wall with the other servants. He wouldn't have noticed him." Her ponderings, half-whispered, began to set her plans in motion, even as she gave birth to the thoughts. "Suzanne, you will go with us."

Suzanne managed to maintain her decorum in front of the other servants, but her smile revealed her pleasure.

"Francina, could you manage to find some men's clothing suitable for my young footman to wear this evening? He's rather muscular and stocky. Has Judith explained my mission to you?"

Francina nodded vigorously. "*Oui*, madame. May I speak freely?"

At Madeleine's nod, Francina continued, "Although I am Catholic, I do not agree with the persecution of the Huguenots." The servant crossed herself. "God forgive me for defying my king, but I have many family members who are not Catholic, and I have seen their suffering. Some have been killed and some are, at this very moment, in prison." She hung her head. "Forgive me for speaking so frankly. I myself lost my husband and only child to the dragoons."

"I am sorry. Please, go on."

"He was only five years old, a beautiful child. He was one of those delightful children everybody loved and who brightened any room he entered."

Madeleine's heart quickened as she thought of her own children, in jeopardy even as they spoke.

Francina continued, "The dragoons raided a community celebration outside of Paris. Our families, mixed in our religions but not in our love for each other, had gathered from all parts of France for the occasion. I had to remain at court in Paris but encouraged my husband and son to go. My parents were to be there and had not seen our son since he was three. The dragoons swept down on the assembly, assuming all were Huguenots. They demanded a mass conversion to Catholicism. Some converted on the spot, but when my husband tried to tell them that they were already Catholics, the dragoons, convinced they were lying, became enraged. My husband and son were butchered."

A momentary malaise of grief plunged the room into silence.

Francina's voice dropped as she proceeded with her story. "When the news reached me, I was inconsolable. It was my Huguenot relatives who surrounded me with love and compassion. They understood the agony of being pursued and persecuted for their faith." Francina pulled the corner of her apron to her face to wipe a tear, which had escaped down her right cheek.

Judith moved to comfort her cousin, and Francina patted her hand. "Judith was one who came to me in my sorrow."

"I remember that," Elisabeth exclaimed. "I recall allowing you, Judith, to leave the manor and travel to Paris to be with your cousin after a family tragedy." Elisabeth turned to Francina. "That cousin was you."

Francina stared past Elisabeth, unseeing, as if watching a play being acted out on a faraway stage. Her bottom lip quivered as she fought to maintain control of her emotions.

Madeleine watched the wounded woman, realizing Francina's fate could be her own. She questioned the servant gently. "With the way they destroyed your family, why have you stayed at court? And why remain Catholic?"

Francina drew a deep breath. "Where am I to go? And how am I to support myself? If I converted to Protestantism, my job would be gone. I would be subject to persecution. With no husband, what am I to do?"

Francina's countenance brightened. "Besides, who knows, but what I might have come to the kingdom for such a time as this."

The quote from the book of Esther pleasantly surprised Madeleine.

"I would be honored to help in any way I can." Francina curtsied and rose from her stance with her chin lifted and her face resolute as a flint.

ARMOND STOOD AT ATTENTION IN THE ENTRANCE, AWK-ward in the role he was to play in the charade. Suzanne flitted about, fussing over Madeleine's hair, shoes, and jewelry, although all were perfectly in place. Madeleine and her mother sat on chairs in the room, awaiting the promised escort.

The soft proper scratching on the door, instead of an improper knock, came promptly at ten o'clock. Madeleine chuckled. Elisabeth instructed Judith to open the door.

"Pierre." Madeleine stood abruptly, her fan clattering to the floor. She gathered her composure quickly. "I was expecting a servant." She moved toward her newfound admirer from the evening before and offered her hand, as Suzanne bent to pick up the fan.

Madeleine realized Louis must have been watching her after all. Her old suitor was a clever player. "Well, what a delightful surprise."

"For me, as well." Pierre took Madeleine's hand and bowed, lingering over the kiss to her hand. Rising from his bow, his gray eyes bore into Madeleine's above a crooked, impish grin.

That smile—why does it look so familiar? The thought fluttered through Madeleine's head, but like a fickle butterfly, refused to light.

"Madame," he greeted Elisabeth with impeccable manners, then turned back to Madeleine, indicating the door. "Are you ready to experience one of the most privileged occasions at Versailles? Dinner with the king at the Porcelain Trianon?"

"Yes, we are ready." Madeleine kissed her mother, whispering in her ear, "Pray," and swept past her. To the elaborately coiffed and adorned party, she merrily ordered, "Let's be on our way."

A grim vision of lambs being led to the slaughter flashed through Madeleine's mind.

PIERRE PROVED TO BE AN EXCELLENT ESCORT. HE LED Madeleine through the complex castle to the Grand Canal, where a graceful gondola awaited them. Armond fell into step with Suzanne behind them, slipping comfortably back into the role of servant, rather than escort for his mistress.

After they were seated in the lilting vessel—Suzanne and Armond taking their places discreetly in the rear, Madeleine and Pierre in an enclosed portico, the gondolier maneuvering the craft slowly down the canal—Madeleine turned to Pierre. "To what do I owe this honor of winning you as my escort?"

"Random chance?"

"That would be difficult for me to believe."

"Being in the right place at the right time to make a request of the king?"

"That I might consider more plausible."

Catholic or Protestant? she wanted to ask, but didn't dare. Instead of playing the coquette with just the king, now she would have to maintain a façade with a courtier as well.

Pierre carried on a proper conversation, peppered nevertheless with the usual court innuendoes, as the gondola made the short trek to the Porcelain Trianon.

"I understand you are an old friend of the king's."

"I see that gossip still gallops across the court at lightning speed."

"The appetite of man is always alert to juicy bits of scandal."

"Scandal?"

"Hmm-mmm."

"And?"

"You realize, I must be circumspect with my comments."

Madeleine nodded. "Go on."

"The rumor is King Louis still maintains a guarded place in his heart for the mysterious young girl who fled his court in the face of the Huguenot persecution years ago," Pierre continued, his face becoming solemn. "And that through the years he has shrewdly protected her family from the court politics of the growing hatred toward those who refuse to convert."

"Who *are* you?" Madeleine pulled back, turned, and searched the face of her escort. "You do not have your masque of last night over your eyes, but I detect an even thicker disguise covers your face tonight."

Pierre laughed and smoothed his moustache and goatee. "I am your escort for the evening, assigned by the king. Look, here we are."

The gondola pulled up to the dock, and the gondolier assisted the small party in stepping out of the launch. Madeleine rearranged her skirt, took Pierre's arm, and followed his lead to the banquet hall.

The atmosphere, subdued as compared to the night before, nevertheless sparkled. Beautifully attired men and women stood in groups conversing softly while awaiting the arrival of the king. Simply to be in the presence of the king as he took a meal was considered a great privilege. Madeleine knew that all too well. She covertly glanced around the room to see if perchance there might be anyone whom she recognized. She wished her mother were with her, whispering clues in her ear.

Some of the women were seated in elaborate brocade chairs forming a loose aisle toward the banquet table. Servants were busy bringing the first course to the extensive table of the king with the legendary appetite. This would not be a short evening.

"Pierre," Madeleine spoke softly. "Where should we place ourselves? My court manners are a bit rusty."

Madeleine immediately scolded herself. She knew she must be more cautious.

"Come. I have specific instructions." Leaving Suzanne and Armond with the other servants along the wall, Pierre guided Madeleine to a position of honor in the line of women. He seated her and moved behind her chair. The other women, awaiting the arrival of the king, glanced at Madeleine from behind their fans—some whispering to their partners, others simply observing her.

Presently the king entered, and as he passed by the women, who had stood and were now bowing before their monarch, he spoke a salutation here and there. Neither his wife nor Madame de Montespan was in attendance. While the ambience was more informal than the night before, Madeleine waited in obeisance as the king drew closer. Her knees began to tremble, and she feared she would not be able to maintain her balance.

Madeleine watched his feet through her lowered eyelids. They were delicate for a man's feet, encased in elaborate gold shoes, his gold cane tapping alongside them as he drew near to her. The rustling of skirts and murmuring of greetings before the king replaced the noisy conversations, which had filled the air before the king's arrival.

The tapping stopped in front of Madeleine. "Madeleine! My dear, sweet Madeleine. It *is* you, isn't it?"

She looked up into the eyes of her old friend and paramour.

Madeleine curtsied even deeper. "*Oui*, Your Majesty."

"How delightful to see you! Last night, when I saw you at the masqué, I could scarcely believe my eyes." He offered his hand and gently raised her from her curtsy. She gave him the hand on which the poesy ring conspicuously rested. His thumb brushed over it briefly.

"You are as breathtakingly beautiful as ever." He paused as he scrutinized her unashamedly from her face to the bottom of her skirt. "You would honor me if you would consent to join me at my side for dinner."

An undertone of surprise swirled through the room like ripples on a pond. An awkward hush silenced the crowd as they parted and allowed the king to pass with Madeleine at his side.

Louis looked over the crowd, then at Pierre. "Thank you, Pierre. Please join us as well."

A lavish meal lay before them. Pierre seated Madeleine beside the king, then sat on her opposite side. Madeleine's mind whirled with the implications of the king's welcome. She expected him to casually acknowledge her publicly, then perhaps send for her later, privately and discreetly. But to brazenly receive her in front of the entire company and invite her to dine at his side! Everyone must be wondering who she was, and why she had suddenly appeared, and for what reason the king would receive and accept her in this manner. Such public acknowledgement would only complicate the request she had come to make.

Louis chatted easily with her, recalling their adolescent days, erasing in an instant the years that had gone by. "Tell me about your family. How is your mother?"

"She is well, Your Majesty. As elegant as ever. She is here with me."

"Oh? Was she at the masqué last night?"

"*Oui*, but she was not on the dance floor. She remained with our servants."

"I imagine she still can execute the intricacies of the dance as well as she could when she and your father were at court." The king paused. "I owe a great debt to the service your father rendered our country during his tenure at court. I miss him immensely." He dabbled at his food. "I knew I could trust him."

Madeleine nodded. "I miss him, too, Your Majesty."

Louis placed his hand over hers under the table. "Please, Madeleine, no need for such formality here. Please use my name."

Madeleine blushed and cleared her throat. "Yes, of course, Your . . . um, Louis." She smiled and laughed, and the tension of the moment lifted.

Louis kept his hand on hers and laughed as well. "That's better." He pulled her hand toward him, and she felt him twist the poesy ring on her finger. "Is that . . . ?"

"So, you remember?" Her eyes searched his for affirmation.

"Remember? How could I ever forget? *Toi seule pour toujours.*"

He leaned close to her, and his eyes held her captive. Madeleine noticed the creases of time around his eyes that betrayed his aging but did not diminish his comeliness. Without thinking, Madeleine touched her own face, realizing the passage of time had also left its etchings on her skin.

"To what do I owe the pleasure of beholding your lovely face once again?"

A huge tureen of vegetables was placed before them, interrupting their conversation. Madeleine looked around to see Francina scurrying away from the table as she performed her duties. Madeleine experienced a sudden rush of security, knowing the kitchen servant was in attendance.

Louis gave her hand a squeeze, released it, and turned his attention to the meal.

Course after course of the king's favorites pushed the late evening event into the early morning hours.

Madeleine teased with her childhood friend. "I see the king's appetite is as hearty as ever."

Louis did not respond to her comment but pushed back from the table, holding a strawberry between his thumb and bejeweled index finger. He turned it around, inspecting it as he spoke. "Is this not one of the most beautiful fruits you can imagine? The color is startling. The curvature of the body is enticing." He stared longingly at Madeleine as he took a small bite out of it.

"But you never know until you taste it whether your palate will enjoy a treat—sweet and delectable . . . or sour and tart. You cannot discern by the perfect structure and hue what it holds in the heart for the one salivating over what might be." He finished the ruby red fruit and wiped his fingers on a white linen napkin. "That one happened to be incredibly sweet."

Madeleine tossed the verbal challenge back to the king. "That is true. One never knows. One never knows as well, what storms or drought the fruit has endured to bring it to harvest—how much rain has fallen on it, how diligently the weeds of corruption have been removed, and the loving care the husbandman has given to the crop." Her coy smile challenged the monarch. "All those factors determine the sweetness of the yield."

Louis inclined close to her once more and whispered for her ears alone, "Precisely, and everyone knows that severe pruning produces the sweetest fruit."

The king rose, indicating that the meal was over. The company of fellow diners stood, bowing and curtsying in one fluid motion. Louis again took Madeleine's hand. "Come, Madeleine. I want to show you something."

"What of my servants?" Madeleine motioned to Suzanne and Armond, still hovering in the background.

"They may assist my staff in cleaning up, then wait for you at the canal." Louis was already making his way down the path toward the interior of the delicate blue and white Trianon. "Monsieur Boveé, come with us."

Madeleine gasped as her head snapped in Pierre's direction. "Boveé?"

Pierre beamed at Madeleine. His father's likeness painted itself across his countenance like an artist sketching a portrait. "At your service, madame."

Madeleine's heart raced. *I'm trapped! My web has spun around and caught me in it.* Mon Dieu, *help me!*

And thine ears shall hear a word behind thee, saying, This is the way, walk ye in it . . .

Madeleine muttered a silent *Merci, Père Dieu.* She turned and allowed herself to be led by the king away from the banquet table, with Pierre following close behind.

THIRTEEN

Louis led Madeleine to a small pavilion, walled with the same delicate blue-and-white tiles as the larger structure where they had dined. Fragrant flowers embowered the structure. Pierre followed closely behind. Darting figures of the king's valets discreetly performed their duties.

Louis pranced around the enclosure proudly, then stood in the center with his head thrown back. "How do you like my little retreat from the pressures of running the kingdom?"

"It is beautiful. Your taste, as always, is exquisite." Out of the corner of her eye, Madeleine noticed Pierre slipping away into the darkness.

Louis indicated a large couch, covered in pillows. "Come. Sit here and let us reminisce of more pleasant days gone by, when we were young and were the envy of the court. You are a breath of fresh air to me."

Madeleine sat on the end of the overstuffed couch.

Louis rested his walking stick at the end and sat in the middle. He patted the cushion beside him. "No, no, no. Here, next to me, my dear, dear friend."

He kissed her hand, and when he raised his head, Madeleine saw tears glistening in his eyes. Compassion for her old friend caught her by surprise and clutched her heart. Louis continued to hold her hand as she sat next to him. She covered their grasp with her other hand, patting the back of his awkwardly.

Louis shook his head. "Ahhh, my dear. Indeed, how does a king know who his true friends are? Courtiers and ambassadors and diplomats surround me daily, catering to my every whim, plying me with flattery, manipulating their way into my good graces, advancing their political schemes to further their own status."

"And does that include your wife and mistresses?"

He pulled his hand away, laid his arm on the back of the couch, and began to finger the lace collar on the back of her gown. "Same old Madeleine—right to the point." He laughed softly. "Yes, any woman in the kingdom that I might desire, except the one I truly wanted. She escaped me, and I heard she married a Protestant commoner."

Madeleine chose her words carefully. "Forbidden fruit ofttimes appears on the surface to be the sweetest."

Louis didn't answer immediately, but continued to look directly into her eyes as if attempting to discern her motives. He continu toy with the lace on her dress, then gently caressed her shoul have you made this sudden appearance in my court, Ma

Rising from a repository long forgotten, powerf

across Madeleine's heart. She dared not offend the king by removing his hand, but she knew she could not allow this game of cat and mouse to continue. She feared her emotions would take her down a road that she did not want to travel.

She had no choice but to be forthright. "I look into your eyes, and I see the boy that I loved—the boy that I loved even before he noticed this shy, naïve little girl in court. The boy who rode horseback with me through the forests here at Versailles when this grand chateau was but a dream in your heart, and whose laughter I still remember as the wind whipped through our hair. Those were some of my happiest times, when we met early in the mornings. I still remember the smell of the grounds still wet with dew."

Louis smiled as Madeleine spoke of their youthful carefree days.

Madeleine continued, "I recall the boy who taught me the language of court—how to tiptoe around the advances of the dashing courtiers. The boy who rescued me from an overzealous admirer when I teased and flirted a bit too ardently."

Louis laughed out loud and slapped his knee as Madeleine recollected the embarrassing incident.

"Louis, the boy who was the most elegant dancer of all and taught me the steps." Madeleine paused. "The boy who gave me my first kiss and endeared himself to me when he whispered, '*Toi seule pour toujours.*'" Madeleine looked at her hand. "And then presented me with this permanent token of his affection." She stopped short of using the word *love*.

"With everything that is dear to me, I swear I meant it, Madeleine. I truly loved you. But I was trapped by the position to which I was born. I could not choose for myself to whom I would be joined."

Louis removed his hand from Madeleine's shoulder and moved closer to her. "When I saw you at the bal masqué last night, all those feelings for you returned in an instant. I realized that even to this day, I am still in love with you. I have simply pushed those longings away. The piece of my heart that belongs to you languishes in a prison cell—waiting only for you to unlock the door."

He pulled Madeleine to him and enfolded her in his arms and whispered in her ear, "You alone have the key. I will do anything it takes to have you as my own. To hold you in my arms like this once again is right. It is as it should be."

Madeleine broke the embrace and, breathless, sat back to look at him. His profession of lingering love touched her. She twisted the poesy ring on her finger. *O Dieu*, she prayed, *be my strength in my weakness.*

And thine ears shall hear a word behind thee, saying, This is the way, walk ye in it . . .

"I have come to ask a favor of you, on behalf of my family."

"And what favor might that be?" Louis' voice hardened. "You are no longer a child. What favor would propel you to my side at such risk to your personal convictions?" He leaned forward, resting his crossed arms on his knees, and looked Madeleine squarely in the eyes. "And what persuasion do you think you could possibly offer to me as the king, accustomed to having my every desire met at the wave of my hand—if not to come to me? What price would you be willing to pay, Madeleine, for your family? What are they worth to you?"

Madeleine saw his eyes light with passion for her. Fright swept over her, but she plunged ahead. "No, Louis, my life is not my own. I am pledged to another now, as you were then. The days of our youth are bittersweet, only there for the remembering. There can never be anything between us."

"There could be, if you would but consent and convert. I would give you anything you wish. You know I cannot make you my wife—politics of the kingdom prevent that—but I will make you my official mistress in a moment. Just say the word."

He took her hand and kissed it again. "Our children will be princes and princesses. Your blood and my royal blood." He took hold of the poesy ring and twisted it around on her finger. "Children of our own. If only . . ."

He reached for her and drew her close to him. His familiar scent and touch still moved her after all the years. She felt surprisingly comfortable in his arms. He kissed her gently. Flashes of trysts in the early days of Versailles romped through her mind—stolen moments, awkward adventures exploring each other's bodies, promises made that could never be kept.

Suddenly she pulled away, holding him at arm's length. "Oh, Louis, we cannot live on *if only*. What happened in the past happened. We were forced to go on with our lives. You had to fulfill your destiny as the king of France, and I chose to live my life as a seigneur's wife in the countryside. The bends and turns in the rivers of our lives were predestined by a much higher power than our own. Now I am here to ask you, my friend, to exercise your power as king of France to help my family."

Louis' countenance darkened. "Just like that?" He snapped his fingers. "Louis, help my family, because we once were in love?" His voice mocked her. "And you expect that to happen with no favor in return?"

"Because of all my father was to you, because of our love for each other when we were young, because of—"

"Because of what, Madeleine?" Louis glowered at her, the tenor of his voice rising. "Why did you flee from my side so suddenly? Why did you turn my messengers away?" He grabbed her by the shoulders. "Why did you marry without a word to me? How could you have chosen the dowdy life of a country Huguenot over the life of a pampered, adored companion of the king?"

Madeleine buried her face in his chest and began to weep. "Oh, Louis. Don't you see? I had to leave. I couldn't stay. You were about to marry Marie Thérèse, and I loved you too much to merely be your mistress."

Louis' tone softened. "Don't cry." He gently tilted her face toward him. "I never could bear it when you cried."

Madeleine smiled weakly, dabbing at her nose with a handkerchief. "And how long would it have been before you required me to convert? How long would I, a Protestant, have been tolerated by the court?"

"You would have been protected by the Edict of Nantes, as are all the Huguenots."

Madeleine straightened her shoulders and courageously faced her king. A few seconds passed before she dared to proceed. She knew she was walking on dangerous ground. She took a deep breath. "If we are still protected by the Edict, then why are you allowing the dragoons to ravage the countryside, demanding that we convert? Then when we don't—burning our homes, raping the women, looting and murdering?" Despite Madeleine's bravado, her voice broke with a sob. "And carrying our children away to be imprisoned in monasteries?"

Louis looked at her sharply. "*Our* children?"

"*My* children."

He stood and shook his finger at her. "These children are not being imprisoned. They are being given a true education. Something you Huguenots could never give them."

"Especially since you have closed our colleges."

"How dare you talk to your king in such a manner!" His voice took on a threatening tone. "How dare you question my authority!" The majesty of the Sun King descended on Louis like a cloak. He paced back and forth in front of Madeleine, ignoring her tears. "Pierre!"

The handsome courtier appeared immediately from the shadows.

"You may escort Madame Clavell back to her apartment. She will be leaving Versailles in the morning."

"Yes, Your Majesty." Pierre bowed low in front of his sovereign.

"Louis, please. Have mercy on my family." Madeleine fell to her knees as the tears coursed down her cheeks. "Because of what we were, what we meant to each other."

Louis looked at her as if he had never known her. "You have made your choice, madame." He turned his back on her and walked away. "You are dismissed."

"Louis! Louis!" Madeleine rose and started after him, but Pierre caught hold of her arm in a vise grip.

"If you value your life, madame, we must go. Now."

Madeleine wheeled around to face Pierre. "What? What does that mean?"

"It means that Louis is king, and his obligations to his country and his church far surpass any feelings he ever had for you." He nudged Madeleine toward the exit of the portico. "Come, we must hurry. I will see you back to your quarters. You need to make preparations to leave first thing tomorrow. Don't delay, Madame Clavell."

THE KING STRODE THROUGH THE OPEN HALLWAY BACK into the dining area, which had been vacated of most of the guests. His walking stick struck an ominous clunk against the marble floor with every other step. The ever-present courtiers scurried behind him, attempting to remain unobtrusive, but hurrying to keep up with him.

As the entourage moved past the long dining table, Francina, gathering platters of food from the expansive spread, overheard the king: "I'll teach these upstart Huguenots to defy me. There will be nothing left of the Clavells' estate by the time she returns."

Francina lowered her head and acted as if she had not heard the king's remarks. She balanced several plates on her arm and carried them into the kitchen as the king exited.

A young scullery maid stood at the counter scraping food from the plates. Francina set her load down next to the girl. "Here, take these. Forgive me. I have to go."

The domestic blinked at Francina. "Is there something I can do?"

"No. If anyone asks where I am, just say I felt ill." Francina slipped out the kitchen door and jumped on one of the servants' carts returning to the chateau.

MADELEINE EASED HERSELF THROUGH THE ENTRY OF THE apartment after Pierre escorted her to the door. A candle flickered low in its brass holder on a table beside the fading fire in the fireplace, the flames of both casting moving shadows across her mother's nodding head.

The floor creaked, rousing Elisabeth as Madeleine approached. "Oh, I guess I dozed off." Her mother stood and clasped Madeleine tightly to her in a long embrace. "Madeleine, you're trembling. Come, sit down. How did you find Louis? Did he receive you? Did you have a chance to make your appeal? What did he say?"

Questions. Always questions. "Please, Mère. Give me a moment." Weary both in body and soul from the whirlwind of the last week, Madeleine sat on the sofa, covered her face with her hands, and began to sob.

Her mother sat beside her and cradled her in her arms as if Madeleine were a little girl. "Oh, *chérie*. Everything's going to be fine. Don't worry." She smoothed Madeleine's hair out of her eyes. "Tell me what happened."

In the glow of the rekindled fire, Madeleine began a condensed version of her evening. "Louis received me publicly."

Her mother gasped. "He asked you to dine with him at his side? What of Marie Thérèse and—"

"They were not in attendance. The whispers from the courtiers resonated like shouts as he escorted me to my seat. Pierre stayed close by. As she had said, Francina was among the servants serving the food. Strange, I found some sort of assurance that she was there." Madeleine began removing her jewelry. "I wish you had been with me."

"Why?"

"It did not go well. He claims that he is still in love with me, but his favors will not come without a price."

"And that price?"

"To abandon my family and come to Versailles as his mistress. Only then would he spare the estate and the children."

"What did you expect?" Elisabeth's eyes searched her daughter's. "Given your past history, how could he demand anything less?"

A tear hung on Madeleine's eyelid and escaped, cascading down her cheek. It dropped onto her hand next to the poesy ring. "I was unforgivably naïve." Madeleine slowly removed the ring and laid it on the table. "François was right. The king is a different person from the adolescent I knew. I have failed our family."

She sighed and wiped her eyes. "I am alarmed at what Louis might do. He f-frightened me." Madeleine shook her head and began to cry again. "I simply cannot believe he turned me away." She got up and started toward her room. "We must leave first thing in the morning. But right now I am exhausted."

"Yes, dear. Do try to get some rest."

Madeleine had not reached the threshold of her bedroom before a scratching at the door startled the two women.

"It's Francina. Let me in."

Elisabeth reached the door first and admitted the frantic servant. Francina's hair had escaped from beneath her cap and hung in strings, wet from perspiration, and she wrung her hands in her soiled apron. Her breath came in short gasps. "You must leave at once, madame. The king is in a rage. I fear he is making plans to harm you and your family."

Madeleine's face paled, and her heart tightened within her chest. "I know what Louis is capable of when his authority has been questioned. We must reach home before his spite is carried out. *Dieu* help us." She walked to the poesy ring that was on the table, then turned her back. The door to that part of her life had now slammed shut for good.

MADELEINE AND HER LITTLE PARTY CREPT DOWN THE massive stairs of the chateau at Versailles and out into the cold air of the dark night. They scurried across the open courtyard and into the waiting carriages. The coaches creaked as they moved toward the gates.

They listened to Henri's volley to the guard informing him who they were. "Ho, there! Madame Clavell's party—personal guests of King Louis. Just getting a head start to beat the heat of the day."

Elisabeth and Madeleine held their breath as they listened for the guard's reply.

The guard stepped toward the coach with his musket pointing in the air. He took a cursory look at the coaches. "Personal guests, eh? Do you have far to travel?"

"South of Grenoble."

"Long way. I'd be getting an early start myself, if I had that far to go. Very well, proceed." He waved them forward. "*Adieu*, and good travels."

"Thank you, monsieur." Henri cracked the whip, and the horses sprang into action.

"Oh, hurry, Henri. We must get home before the dragoons."

Madeleine prayed as the night enveloped them. *Dieu, we are in a race for our lives—and the lives of my children. Make our horses swift. Show us the way to go. Protect us from physical harm.*

Madeleine looked out from the curtains at the stars above. The sky shone bright from the luminous light of a three-quarter moon. Every joint in Madeleine's body ached from weariness. She didn't think she had ever been so tired. She wrapped her arms around herself and massaged her shoulders. She ached for François' arms around her, rubbing the soreness out of her neck and back. Instead, the hard, unyielding back of a carriage bench jolted her at every bump in the road. *Nightwalkers. Will we forever be running for our lives as nightwalkers?* The galloping hooves of the horses lulled Madeleine to an erratic sleep.

"Commander Boveé, Your Majesty." The commander's arrival was announced, and he bowed before his king as he was escorted into the king's quarters the next morning.

The king sat at his desk, caressing one of his hounds. One fortunate courtier had already been appointed to hold the candlestick for the remainder of the daily ceremonies. Others stood around the room awaiting their turn, having been given *entrée* to speak confidentially to the king.

King Louis beckoned to the commander. "Forgive my presuming on you so soon after your return. I realize you are just back from your mission in the south of the country."

"It's never too soon to serve my king."

The king continued to pet the dog. "Fine animals, aren't they? Born to hunt. Skilled to fearlessly and mercilessly track down the victim. If they cannot find a deer to satisfy their primeval urge, they will hunt down a rabbit with the same fervor." Louis ceased petting the hound. The animal nuzzled against the king's knee. "He simply awaits my order and will go after anything I designate."

"Yes, Your Majesty."

The king stood sending the dog scurrying. "I need you to return to the Clavell estate tonight and burn it to the ground. Take the residents captive." His face grew dark with anger. "I want François Clavell taken to the Bastille, and the children—" The king hesitated. "I want the oldest boy brought to me. Take the little girl to a convent."

"Sire, as I understand, there are two boys, but we were unable to locate them. They were not at the estate when we arrived. Supposedly they are visiting relatives in Spain."

"And the daughter?"

"She was there—three years old."

In spite of his rage against Madeleine, Louis felt a tug at his heart. So young to be snatched from her mother. But it would be for her good in the long run.

"Yes, take her to a convent. The nuns will take good care of her.

But I want that oldest boy. If you find the boys, bring the older one to me."

"And if they are still absent?"

"Search the area again, but do as I have ordered. Destroy the estate, throw Monsieur Clavell into the Bastille."

Louis sat down, and with a snap of his fingers beckoned the hound back to him. He began to stroke the dog's head once again. "Yes, I want to meet this François Clavell. This country gentleman who never comes to court to pay homage to his king. I shall see him in Paris. We shall see how he enjoys serving his king from the Bastille."

FOURTEEN

François finished looping his belt around his waist and startled to hear the heavy wooden front door bang against the stone wall in the entryway amidst coarse shouting and stamping of feet. Dashing into the hallway, he paused at the top of the stairs and watched dragoons storm into the wide foyer below him, their swords drawn. François turned and ran back into the bedroom, yanked his musket from the corner, and returned to the stairs.

Vangie and Claudine appeared at the door of their room. "What's happening?"

"Get back! Take Vangie and run. Dragoons!"

Claudine whisked the child up in her arms and started for the stairwell leading out the back of the house. François raced to the middle of the front staircase with his musket drawn. "Stop right there! Who gives you permission to invade our home in this manner?"

Commander Boveé strode through the front door with his sword drawn as well. "The time for negotiations is over, Monsieur Clavell. We have returned with direct orders from King Louis to appropriate your estate for His Majesty and take custody of all inhabitants."

François descended the stairs, firmly planting one foot after another on each step. He paused at the bottom, keeping his musket trained on Commander Boveé. "You will accomplish that mission only by killing me first."

The soldiers, who had preceded their commander, continued to overrun the house, toppling furniture and creating havoc. François could hear the exclamations of astonishment and screams of terror from the servants.

"Believe me, I would take considerable pleasure in performing that act myself. Unfortunately, King Louis has given orders to take you—" The commander halted, his attention diverted by Vangie appearing at the head of the stairs, shivering in her nightgown.

"Papa!" She began to run down the stairs.

"Vangie, go back!"

But the child scuttled down the stairs toward her father and leapt into his arms, knocking François off balance and the musket off-site. Claudine peered over the banister, her face pale with fear. François, seeing the governess out of the corner of his eye, jerked his head, signaling her to flee. He stepped backward through the archway opening into the dining room, still holding Vangie and repositioning the musket. "Stay back. I will not hesitate to fire."

"Surely you want no harm to come to that lovely daughter of yours." Commander Boveé's deep, sultry voice curled around François' head like evil itself. "Hand yourselves over and make things simple for all of us. You have been summoned to a private audience with the king."

"I said, 'Stay back.'" François pointed his musket directly at the commander, who had invaded the lives of the Clavells one too many times now. Madeleine's words echoed in his head: *This is no time for weakness.*

François trembled with fury. How dare these barbaric pigs come into their home again, this time threatening his family with their lives? He lowered Vangie to the floor and maneuvered her behind him, keeping himself between her and the intimidating commander.

It seemed to François as if the activity slowed to the pace of the gray, slimy slugs in their garden. The clamor of the soldiers sounded to him like they were underwater, garbled and indiscernible. As they turned toward their commander, the heads of the dragoons appeared as unmanageable marionettes, dangling at the end of the strings of a madman's decree, undecided which way they should turn. The bright reds and blues of the dragoons' uniforms meshed together in a distorted surge. As the soldiers awaited their commander's reply, the silent room pulsated with tension.

François detected movement behind him, and the scene came back into sharp focus. He whirled around to see the snarling face of a dragoon lunge toward him. The butt of the dragoon's musket struck the side of François' head, as at the same time the soldier reached for Vangie and swooped her up in his arms. Swirling black and yellow specks exploded in his head, and he fell to the ground. He remembered hearing his musket clatter to the floor and the sinister laughter of Commander Boveé floating above him—and the screams of his daughter piercing through the fog in his head.

But the brave father was unable to move.

FRANÇOIS FELT HIMSELF BEING LIFTED UP AND DRAGGED across the floor, through the front door of their house. He tried to stand, but his legs would not hold his weight. The soldiers dropped him in a heap beside the shrubbery along the front walkway and bound his hands. Someone doused his head with cold water from the well, and he began to come around.

A chaotic scene assaulted his eyes as he dragged himself into consciousness—dragoons firing randomly at servants escaping into the woods; domestics screaming at being brutally manhandled by the savage soldiers; the pampered gardens being trampled underfoot by the livestock, panicked and fleeing. The pandemonium created by the frightened bleating and screeches and grunts of the animals, coupled with the anguished cries of the Clavell household, tore at François' sensibilities.

The dragoons gathered up the horses and tied them behind their own mounts. François surmised that the Clavell stable of fine-bred steeds was now being conscripted into the king's stables.

Commander Boveé sat astride his magnificent white stallion, with Vangie encased in his arms in front of him. The sight of his daughter in the custody of the bestial commander filled François with a furor he had never experienced before—not even as a youth when his family fought with the dragoons, and he watched his mother and sisters slaughtered. This was his innocent, vulnerable child. And he could do nothing to help her.

François groaned and pushed himself to his feet, pulling at the ropes that constrained him. The guttural voice that emerged from his throat sounded like something from an animal. "Boveé!"

The officer whirled his horse around and pranced over to François, parading in front of the stricken father. "Ah, the hero and protector of the family comes to. Not exactly the knight in shining armor, are we?"

François yanked at his bindings and lunged toward his antagonizer. "Ha! Some fight still left in you."

The stallion pawed and skitted in front of François. Vangie remained strangely quiet, but her eyes begged her papa to rescue her. A small whimper escaped her lips.

"There, there, little one. No harm is going to come to you." Commander Boveé stroked Vangie's hair. "We will take good care of your daughter, Monsieur Clavell. In fact, she will receive much better tutelage where I am taking her than she would under your guidance."

François knew what that meant—a convent.

"You may rest easy about her welfare."

Vangie reached for her papa and began to cry. "Papa, I'm scared." Her bottom lip quivered uncontrollably, and she struggled to catch her breath as tears coursed down her cheeks.

"Say good-bye to your papa. We must leave now." Commander Boveé allowed Vangie to lean over to embrace her father.

"Vangie, your papa loves you more than you will ever know. Don't be afraid, and don't give up. Someone will come for you."

The commander pulled the child back into the saddle and sneered at François.

"I doubt that." Turning his mount around, he ordered his soldiers, "Torch the place. Make sure it will not be of any use to the Huguenots ever again." He clucked at his horse. "*Au revoir*. I doubt that we will see each other again." He spurred his horse into action and headed out of the estate.

François watched helplessly as his daughter was snatched out of his life, riding in the clutches of a cruel commander, twisting and arching her back to try to break free. The soldiers began to throw lighted torches into the house. A crusty older soldier yanked François toward the soldiers gathering into platoons and motioned him to mount one of the Clavells' own horses. The soldier fettered the deposed seigneur to the saddle, and with curses and the rancid smell of liquor on his breath, ordered him to give them no trouble.

The soldiers formed ranks and rode out of the estate soon after Commander Boveé left with Vangie. François turned and watched his house disintegrating in flames. Then he faced forward and did not turn around again. As his mind searched for a way of escape, he cried out to the God that he followed.

O Dieu! Make a way for us. Protect Vangie from the schemes of the enemy.

Slumped in the saddle, but not defeated, François Clavell fell into the rhythmic pattern of the horses' canter and waited.

THE FIRE IN THE HOUSE RAGED, BUT THE TORCHES TOSSED toward the barn fell harmless on the ground. Thérèse staggered from the rear of the house to the barn, her pummeled and swollen face barely recognizable. Reaching the welcome shelter of the barn, she lay down in the hay.

With the other remaining servants, Claudine fled to the woods and hid trembling in the underbrush. In disbelief, she watched the only home she had ever known crumble as the flames licked around the stones that had been a shelter to the persecuted Huguenots for generations.

FIFTEEN

Henri halted the coaches, leapt down with the vigor of a younger man, and approached Madeleine's side of the carriage.

"Why have we stopped?"

"The horses, madame. We will kill them if we continue to drive at this pace."

Madeleine vigorously shook her head. "No, we must keep going." She gripped the window ledge of the carriage.

Henri patted her hand. He opened the door and rested his foot on the running board. "I have a plan."

"Go on."

"I think the white team could make faster time if you took them pulling the smaller coach and rode on ahead, after they rest. They are younger and stronger. Take Armond with you. I'll follow with your mother and the other servants."

Madeleine reluctantly consented. "Very well." She fingered the drooping curls in her hair. "How long do the horses need to rest?"

"A few hours. We can unload all of the luggage onto the other coach in the meantime." Henri smiled at Madeleine. "You need to travel as light as possible."

"Move quickly." Madeleine knew she would not be able to rest until she got home and had her family around her once again.

FROTH FROM THE HORSES' MOUTHS SPLATTERED ON THE sides of the coach as they gnawed on the bits, and their bobbing heads pulled against the bridles. The team sensed they were nearing home, as did Madeleine. Her heart echoed the beat of their hooves, willing the rhythm to hold a few more minutes.

"Smoke! I see smoke!" Armond careened the horses into the lane a frenzied François had ridden down only a few weeks before, shouting warning of the approaching dragoons.

The team of stallions, eager to return to their own stable, surged ahead with renewed energy, jolting Madeleine against the back of the bench inside the carriage. She pulled herself up and tore the curtain back from the window to peer through the arched canopy of trees.

"Whoa—whoa!" Armond's muscular arms rippled as he strained to halt the team.

The still-burning remains of the estate assaulted their visage. Madeleine tumbled out of the carriage. She grabbed hold of the brass handle on the door to steady herself.

Armond sat in stunned silence, still struggling to hold the horses at bay. For an eternal moment of disbelief, only the sound of the horses pawing and snorting broke through the morning stillness.

Then a scream Madeleine heard, but did not recognize as her own, exploded from her—a scream that had been denied and stuffed in the recesses of her consciousness through the years of impending threat of imprisonment, persecution, and death. Now at last it broke free. It echoed over the burned shell of her home—the roof and wooden doors gone, the stone walls still standing, macabre fingers of black soot climbing up the walls.

Madeleine ran to the smoldering front door as Armond looked on, helpless to aid his mistress. Frantic, without thought for her own safety, Madeleine clambered into the rubble. "François! Vangie! Are you here? François!"

The sharp odor of the still-active smoke assaulted her. She began to pull aside charred embers of what was once elegant furniture, oblivious to the hazard of the blistering heat.

Armond ran after her and pulled her back outside. "Madame, it will do no good to injure yourself. Get back. I'll look for them."

He plunged into the interior of the smoking house. Everything stood in heaps. The once fine furnishings had been pulled to the center of the rooms and set afire. The huge overhead beams had caved into the center of the rooms, smashing everything they encountered on the way down.

Armond emerged from the house shaking his head. They started down the path to the barn, which stood unscathed. "François!"

No answer. Armond ran into the barn.

Madeleine stopped and listened and realized there were no animals, no workers, no horses to be seen. It was too quiet. They must have taken the horses and let the stable boys and servants escape.

Armond exited the barn carrying a body. Tears were streaming down his face.

Madeleine stumbled her way toward him. "Who? Oh, no—Thérèse. Oh, dear Jesus."

Armond gently laid the old woman down on the ground. "She's been—they violated her and then shot her. She must have tried to get away."

Madeleine knelt beside the body of her faithful servant and brushed the long, salt-and-pepper hair out of her eyes.

"I don't think I ever saw her without her cap. All those years, and I never knew what beautiful hair she had." Madeleine cradled the older woman in her arms and rocked back and forth. "Oh, Thérèse, Thérèse. I'm sorry. I'm so sorry."

After a moment, Armond spoke, "Madame?"

Madeleine ignored him, consumed by grief.

He cleared his throat. "The dragoons couldn't have been gone very long. Th-they might come back to see if we have returned."

Madeleine looked up at the young man, her cheeks streaked with tears and smudges of smoke. "We-we need to give Thérèse a decent burial, don't we? What shall we do?" Her thoughts bounced from one concern to another. Still holding on to Thérèse as if she could will life back into the cold body, Madeleine rose on her knees as she spoke. "What of François and Vangie? Perhaps they escaped. Yes, that's it, they escaped. The boys, *mon Dieu*, the boys. We must get to the cave to see if the boys are there."

Madeleine took Thérèse's apron off, rolled it into a makeshift pillow, and laid Thérèse's head upon it. She stood up slowly and willed herself to steely calmness as she wiped her eyes and began to issue orders to Armond.

"Unhitch the horses and leave the carriage. After we bury Thérèse, you take one of them and ride back to Henri and my mother." She paused. "Break it to him gently."

Armond, tears lingering in his eyes, hung his head and nodded.

Madeleine continued, "I'll take the other two horses and go to the cave for the boys. Hopefully, François, Vangie, and Claudine will be there as well. We will wait for you."

Madeleine sighed and closed her eyes. "We are going to have to flee to Geneva. If you don't make it back to us by tonight, we will have to go on." She opened her eyes and held Armond's attention with them. "Do you understand? If something happens, and you don't come to the cave by nightfall, we are going on to Geneva. We will meet you there."

"I understand." Armond shifted his feet. "Madame?"

"Yes? What is it?"

"I mean no disrespect to Thérèse, but we-we don't have time to dig a grave."

"What would you suggest?"

"Something quick, but something that will keep the animals away."

Madeleine's tone turned sharp. "Well, what?"

Armond glanced around the grounds as if expecting an answer to pop out of the shrubbery. He spotted the rock fence, and, at the same time, Madeleine cried, "Rocks. Carry her body over beside the fence and cover it with rocks. I'll unhitch the horses while you are doing that."

Madeleine bent over and tenderly touched Thérèse's face. "Forgive us, dear one. All your years of faithful service, and I can't even give you a decent burial. Perhaps when the danger is past."

But Madeleine knew the danger would never be past—not as long as Catholics were in control of France and Protestants were seen as a threat. Danger had become their constant companion, a tangible, palpitating presence that lay like a sleeping dog before a crackling evening fire, deceptively amiable until crossed. Then the teeth would bare, and the seemingly benign bundle would rise and strike with bloodthirsty vengeance.

CRADLING THE MUSKET AND KEEPING GUARD THROUGH the crack around the boulder at the entrance to the cave, Jean watched helplessly as smoke rose once again from the estate. Dragoons had infiltrated the forest even before dawn, making it impossible for him to emerge. The forest was quiet now, as if every living creature had escaped to avoid the coming disaster.

Did he dare try to go back to the house? Jean heard the boys stirring. He turned to move through the tunnel to check on the two brave young men, when he heard a scratching on the boulder. Jean froze in his tracks. *They've found us!* He moved cautiously back to where he could peer outside once more.

He heard a voice calling softly, "Jean. Philippe. Somebody! It's me, Claudine. Are you still here?"

"Claudine! Yes, we're here. Stand back. I'll help you in."

Jean pushed aside the shrubbery and pulled the young woman into the hiding place. She collapsed upon him, grabbing his knees and sobbing hysterically. "Everything's gone. They've destroyed it all. I'm the only one, the on-on-ly o-one."

Jean pulled Claudine to a standing position by her shoulders, shaking her. "What do you mean? The only one? Where are François and Vangie?" His voice rose to a frenetic shout. "Where are they?"

Claudine's sobs punctuated every sentence. "Th-Th-They t-t-ook them. They're g-g-gone. Oh, *mon Dieu*, they took them." She pulled her apron up around her face and whimpered into it. "E-ev-everything's gone—the house, the horses. They let the field hands and the stable boys go."

"What of Thérèse?"

"I don't know. We tried to hide with Vangie upstairs while François held the dragoons down in the hallway, b-but they found us. They-they didn't see me, but they got Vangie. She ran down the stairs to her papa, and-and they knocked him out and got her. I ran down the back stairs and out into the woods. The last I saw, Commander Boveé had Vangie in the saddle with him, and François was tied up by the well. Those monsters were helping themselves to whatever they wanted from the house."

Claudine wiped her face with her apron and took a deep breath. "I guess they didn't see me in all the confusion. I don't know what happened to the rest of the household—some may still be in the woods. The dragoons took the horses. I hid by the riverbank under a cliff until the dragoons left, and th-then I came here."

"Commander Boveé? The same man who was here before?"

Claudine nodded.

"How many dragoons?"

"I don't know, maybe six or so."

Jean pounded his leg with his fist. "Are you sure you weren't followed?"

She sniffled and looked at Jean. "I-I don't think so. I waited a long time. I didn't see anybody."

"What of Madeleine? Has she returned from Versailles?"

"No, monsieur." Her eyes filled once more with tears.

Had Madeleine failed? Had she been too late to stop this nightmare? Jean put his arm around Claudine's shoulders. "Come with me. The boys will be glad to see you."

Philippe, holding the musket, was standing in front of Charles, who was stoking the morning fire. The fragrance of a pot of stew coaxed from roots and a rabbit Jean had killed filled the inner chamber of the hideout.

The two boys scrambled to Claudine to embrace her, the musket clattering against the stony floor. She gathered them in her arms and began to sob once again.

The concern of the older brother voiced itself first. "What's happened?" He looked at Jean. "Uncle Jean, what's happened?"

Jean shushed Claudine with a slight wag of his head, sat her down in front of the fire, and turned to face the brothers. A tug-of-war waged within him. How much should he tell them? What could they accept at their young age? He looked at the two young men, and love and admiration for them welled up within him. They were courageous boys. Jean saw no benefit in keeping the truth from them. They would know soon enough anyway. Plans had to be made.

"Boys, I need you to be very grown-up. I need you to be brave."

The brothers nodded, their faces solemn.

"The dragoons returned last night and destroyed the house. They took the horses and let the stable workers go. Claudine escaped with them into the forest."

Charles moved to Philippe's side, and the older brother put his arm clumsily around him.

Philippe voiced their fears. "What of Papa and Vangie? And Thérèse?"

"We don't know. Perhaps they escaped as well." Jean paused for a moment.

"And Maman and Grand-mère?"

Claudine regained her voice and broke in, "They have not yet returned from Versailles." She smiled weakly. "I'm sure they are fine."

"Uncle Jean, I'd like to pray." Young Charles uncharacteristically took the lead.

A tear escaped and rolled down his cheek, and Philippe's chin began to quiver.

"Yes, of course, by all means, Charles. Go ahead."

They bowed their heads, and in a fragile voice, Charles prayed, "Dear Jesus, please keep our maman and papa safe from the dragoons. And Grand-mère, and Henri and Thérèse too. And keep us safe, and help us have enough food until we can get out of this cave." The boy wiped his nose with his sleeve. "Amen."

Claudine echoed, "*Ainsi soit-il.*"

Jean breathed a heavy sigh. "Yes, so be it, Father. Hear this simple prayer of an innocent child."

MADELEINE WATCHED ARMOND GALLOP OUT OF THE estate. The team had been watered and fed, but not given time to rest. Madeleine gathered the skirts of her traveling clothes about her and swung herself expertly on top of one of the remaining horses, clasping the reins of the other two in her hand. All the saddles had either been stolen or burned. She would have to ride bareback. The massive steed danced sideways, confused and skittish because of the persistent flames.

She started down the hill along the rock fence, vaguely aware that wildflowers had begun to carpet the landscape in brilliant magentas, yellows, purples, and golds. Searching for a low place in the stone wall, she led the horses to jump over and start down the hill to the river. It took all the strength she had to keep the team reined in.

Madeleine glanced nervously around her. She was too visible crossing this meadow. She began to run the horses. The cliffs overseeing the river came into view. She urged the horses on toward the covering of the trees.

The damp odor of the wet grass and a faint whiff of pine greeted Madeleine as she entered the forest. She peered down at the river, relieved to find the water had returned to its normal shallow level. She rode through it, crossing to a ledge on the other side. Letting go of the reins of the two horses she was leading, she called to them to follow her. She watched the horses pick their way behind her along the narrow rim.

As they climbed higher, one of the horses stumbled, and, with rocks crashing into the water below, skidded halfway down the embankment before he regained his footing. Madeleine halted her horse, watching helplessly. "C'mon, boy. Catch hold. You can do it."

The horse came to a stop beside the roots of a tree and regained his footing. Madeleine whistled for him to rejoin them. He lunged up the steep slope and fell into line behind them, his legs twitching. The other two horses snorted and backed up, churning the rocks and dirt on the precarious ledge.

"Whoa, whoa. Calm down." Madeleine's mount reacted to the nervousness of the other two horses. She dared not dismount on the narrow ledge to soothe them. Instead she used her voice as Henri had taught her. "Good boy, good boy. We're almost there. Good boy." She patted her stallion on the neck, and he began to calm, as did the others.

They continued along the ridge until the path widened and the entrance to the cave came into view. Madeleine detected footprints made recently outside the cave. She halted the horses and glanced about. Dragoons could be hiding in the forest watching her. She mustn't give away the hiding place.

With a click of her tongue, Madeleine spurred the horses up to the plateau. "Let's take a look around." The horses lurched up the sheer embankment, their bodies nearly perpendicular with the earth, Madeleine's hands clutching the reins and entangled in the harness for grip.

The ground leveled as they topped the bank, and Madeleine dismounted. She held the horses still and listened. Again, only quiet. No birds chirped their merry spring greetings. No breeze rustled through the trees. Not even the gurgling of the river broke the stillness.

Death hung in the air. She could feel it. Madeleine's ears rang with the morning silence, and her hands shook, whether from fright or from her grip on the harness, she could not tell. She led the horses to a clump of trees and secured them under the cover of the thickening bower.

Giving another hasty look around and seeing only trees, wildflowers, and the tips of the snow-covered mountains in the distance, Madeleine slipped down the steep incline to the hidden entrance to the cave. She attempted to pry the shrubbery apart so she could push herself into the cave, but it proved too tangled. As much as she struggled, she could not pull the limbs back far enough to wriggle through.

Frustrated, tired, and frightened, Madeleine leaned against the embankment and began to cry. "*O Dieu*, help me. All we've been through the past month, and some *bête* bush is standing in the way of finding my sons. I can't stand this!"

Crazed with rage and grief and concern for her children that only a parent at the end of her resources can experience, Madeleine began to tear at the bush with her bare hands. Throwing all caution aside, she began to call, "Jean! Philippe! Charles! Can you hear me? Are you in there? Are you still alive?" Her frenetic tearing at the tangled branches resulted in a small opening that only snapped back before she could scramble inside.

Madeleine backed away, stared at the taunting outgrowth and jabbed the air with a bleeding finger. "You will not defeat me." She turned her eyes toward heaven. "*Dieu*, I'm desperate. You have told us we must come to you as a little child. And that's how I feel right now. I am as helpless as a newborn baby. You know where my boys are. If they are still in that cave, help me get in there!" She shook her fist at the deafening silence of the Almighty.

"Madeleine?"

Madeleine gasped and peered through the maze of undergrowth into the dark eyes of her brother-in-law.

SIXTEEN

"Jean, thank God, you're alive. Are the boys safe? Are my children unharmed?" Madeleine's voice rose in pitch as her fears, unspoken, stuffed and buried over the years, assumed a form of their own and poured out.

"Hold on a minute." Jean squirmed through the crack around the boulder and gave Madeleine a suffocating hug. "Madeleine, we are all well, and I'm relieved you are here, safe and whole."

Madeleine paused. "So, the boys are safe?"

A broad smile broke across his handsome face, so like François'. "We are safe. It has not been easy, but we are well." He glanced from side to side, surveying the woods. "No dragoons around?"

Madeleine wiped her eyes with the back of her hand. "No, they seem to be gone. But the house . . ."

"I know. Claudine's here. She told us what happened, and I had been watching the smoke."

"Claudine is here in the cave with you? What of François and Vangie?"

Jean shook his head. "We don't know about them. Claudine and Thérèse tried to hide Vangie while François held off the dragoons, but Vangie ran to him. Claudine escaped down the back stairs and ran into the woods with the other servants. The last she saw, Commander Boveé had Vangie with him in the saddle, and François was tied up at the well. She doesn't know what happened to Thérèse."

Madeleine dropped her head, shaking it in disbelief. "They've taken Vangie and François? Oh, Jesus." She fell into Jean's arms once again, and he held her as she wept.

After a few moments, Madeleine willed herself to be calm and exhaled a heavy sigh.

"What happened in Versailles?" Jean asked.

Madeleine stared into space, remembering. "Louis was furious with me after I pled with him to spare us. We left immediately that night. His temper is well-known. *Mon Dieu, mon Dieu,* we are destroyed."

Jean held Madeleine as she continued her story. "The house is in ruins." She wiped her nose on her sleeve. "Thérèse is dead. We found her body in the barn and buried her by the fence. Armond has ridden back to meet Henri and the others and bring them here." Madeleine stifled another sob.

"Maybe if I had not been so stubborn and insisted on appealing to Louis, this wouldn't have happened. Maybe if we'd simply endured the billeting of the soldiers, they would have eventually left us alone.

François tried to talk me out of it, and I w-wouldn't listen." Sobs punctuated her outburst. "O God! I-I am such a fool!"

Jean interrupted her. "There's no need to torment yourself. You did what you thought was the best at the time. We need to decide what to do from this juncture."

Madeleine fell silent. Finally, she pushed away from Jean and took a deep breath. "Y-yes, of course, you're right. There's nothing we can do for Vangie and François at this point. François would want me to get the boys to safety. We will start for Geneva as soon as it is dark." Madeleine motioned to the top of the ridge. "I have three horses tethered in a grove of trees on the plateau."

"Very well." Jean forced the branches apart, speaking as he assisted Madeleine through the entrance. "Come, I'll take you to the boys." He squeezed through after her. "Where do you think they are taking François and Vangie?"

"François to Paris—to King Louis." Madeleine stood and brushed the debris from her skirt. "To mock our family and make a spectacle of those who would dare to question his authority over the Protestants in the land." Even in the dim light, Jean observed the grim constriction of her jaw. "Vangie?" A bitter laugh boiled to the surface. "No doubt to a convent to be 'properly educated,' according to Louis."

"So he wouldn't listen to you at all?"

"Only for a price far too dear."

Jean ushered Madeleine down the tunnel, but she paused and turned back to him. "Jean, the night before I left. In the barn. François told me what happened." Madeleine's heart grieved for her brother-in-law. "How are you with, with . . . with what you had to do?"

"In agony." Jean's curt answer spoke volumes.

"Do the boys know?"

"No, I didn't feel it necessary to tell them."

Madeleine nodded, and they proceeded around the corner into view of the fire and the little group circled around it.

"Maman!" Both boys sprang forward, knocking Madeleine back into Jean with their boisterous welcome.

She knelt, folding them in her embrace and rocking them back and forth as she soothed the ache of her empty arms. "Oh, boys. What brave boys you are. I am proud of you. I missed you so much." She smoothed their hair and caressed each of their dirty faces.

Brushing Charles' thick red curls out of his eyes, she laughed. "You need a haircut, *mon petit chéri*." She gathered their hands in hers and noticed Philippe's splinted fingers. "What happened here?"

"It's nothing. I caught it in the bush at the entrance." He wiggled the injured digits. "See, they're almost all well."

"Ooooh, poor thing." Madeleine kissed the bandaged fingers.

"Really, they are fine."

Madeleine reached out her arms to Claudine, who stood by watching the reunited family. "Claudine, I'm glad you are safe."

The servant accepted the display of affection from her mistress but pulled away quickly, years of custom compelling her to render the obligatory curtsy. "Thank you, madame."

Madeleine smiled and patted Claudine's shoulder. "We are all family here."

"Yes, madame." Claudine brought a bowl of rabbit stew to Madeleine as the five sat on the cold rocks to eat.

Madeleine thought of her meal with the king at the Porcelain Trianon—a stark contrast with the simple dish she now spooned to her lips. She looked at her loved ones surrounding her and realized she much preferred this. But had she made the right choice? Her husband and daughter were somewhere at the mercy of ruthless dragoons. Should she have given in to Louis' demands? Could she perhaps have saved them all?

She couldn't spend time on hindsight. She must move ahead.

Madeleine looked around the circle at her courageous company. "I need to tell you what has happened and what we must do now."

ARMOND SIGHTED THE COACH A COUPLE OF HOURS AWAY from the manor. Observing Henri's erect posture on the driver's bench as the older man urged the horses on brought a lump to Armond's throat. How was he going to tell him that his wife of over thirty years was gone? He pulled up beside the coach as Henri brought the horses to an abrupt stop. *Lord, give me the words to say.*

Elisabeth and Suzanne poked their heads out of a window.

"Whoa, there!" Henri pulled the brake on the carriage, but remained atop his perch. "Armond! What news do you bring? Did you find all well at the estate?"

Armond dismounted, shaking his head. He stumbled over his words. "No. No. All is not well."

Elisabeth opened her door, and Armond sprang to help her.

"What is it? Madeleine? Is she—?"

Suzanne followed her out of the coach. The footmen remained at their station.

"Madame is fine. B-but . . ."

By this time Henri had jumped from the driver's seat. "Well, spit it out, man. What did you find? Where is Madame Clavell?"

The footmen descended from their perch and took the reins of the team, staring at Armond and listening to the news.

"She went to the cave to get the boys. The manor is gone, burned to the ground. Only the walls remain."

Elisabeth dropped her fan. "What of the family? François? Vangie? The servants?"

Armond hesitated, not wanting to continue. "Everyone is gone. Everything but the barn destroyed."

Henri looked at Armond, his eyes reflecting what he already suspected. "Thérèse? What of Thérèse?"

"I'm sorry, Henri. I'm terribly sorry." The younger man fidgeted with the reins in his hands.

A whisper escaped Elisabeth's lips. "Oh no."

Henri stared at Armond, saying nothing. Judith eased quietly out of the coach. The group stood in silence.

Henri turned and walked from the road into a nearby field. He pulled his hat from his head and held it in his hands as he knelt in the dirt of the field. He made no sound. His shoulders shook as he prostrated himself before his Maker.

The band of observers shuffled their feet, each one grieving along with Henri.

A few moments passed, and then Henri rose, put his hat on, and walked slowly back to the coach. "Come, we have work to do." He assisted the women into the coach.

Elisabeth patted his hand. "Henri, I hurt so for you. I have no words."

"No need for words, madame." Tears glistened in the wrinkled face of the old man, whose age now seemed to settle on him like a heavy cloak. "If we truly believe what we have professed through the years, my Thérèse now rests in the arms of Jesus. We do not grieve as the heathen grieve." A weak smile spread across his mouth under the bushy white moustache. "I will see her again."

Elisabeth gave her devoted servant a quick hug.

Henri closed the carriage door and turned to Armond. "Where did you bury her?"

"We did the best we could—fearing that the dragoons were still nearby. We covered her body with rocks near the fence."

Fighting for composure, Henri nodded. "I understand. I would have done the same." Climbing onto his post, he asked, "Did you see any dragoons on the way?"

"None, but I'm concerned they may be lurking nearby. They must have come, burned, killed, and destroyed, then disappeared as stealthily as demons." Armond swung back onto his horse. "As soon as we get back to the estate, we are to go to the cave. Madame plans for us to flee to Geneva at nightfall."

BY LATE AFTERNOON THE COACH PULLED INTO THE LANE leading to the smoldering ruins of the manor. Henri stopped the horses for a moment, and then guided the coach slowly to the barn, which was surprisingly intact. He climbed down from his station and motioned to Armond.

"Go to the cave and tell Madame we are safe. We will wait for you to bring them back, and we will meet you here beside the coach. We should have darkness in a couple of hours."

The women descended from the coach, staring at what was once their home. The footmen stood motionless, gaping at the destruction.

"Get busy, men! We have no time to dally." Henri slipped back into his familiar role. "Horses need to be fed and watered. Turn them loose for a bit."

Armond mounted his horse and loped toward the river. Henri took off his gloves and started toward the rock fence. Elisabeth followed Henri at a distance. Suzanne and Judith remained beside the coach.

Dusky shadows had begun to envelop the manor before Henri and Elisabeth returned. Henri directed orders to the footmen. "Hitch up the horses. Let's be ready and waiting. We have a heritage to protect."

ARMOND, WITH CLAUDINE RIDING BEHIND HIM, CLENCHing his waist, led the weary company through the twilight across the river. Philippe followed, then Madeleine with Charles, and Jean bringing up the rear. Jean carried the murdered dragoon's musket; Armond cradled the musket from the cave; Philippe shouldered the bow with its quiver of arrows. Madeleine had a knapsack, sagging because of the weight, slung across her back. They had thrown the blankets from the cave over the horses as makeshift saddles.

Cresting the top of the hill, they could see the silhouette of the house, a yawning mockery of their previous life. No one spoke—not even Charles. The biting odor of smoke lingered in the evening air. Gray vapors continued to rise into the sky, and in the growing darkness the slight glow of embers flickered, licking up the last of the Clavell family's possessions.

The horses nickered to each other as they approached the coach where Henri and Elisabeth and the others waited. Henri moved forward to help Madeleine and Charles from their horses.

Madeleine took both of the old man's hands in hers and shook her head. "I am so sorry."

Henri patted her hands. "There, there, child. Don't you worry about me."

"I cannot help but do so."

"I will miss Thérèse sorely, but we all have a destiny with our Maker. It was her time."

Charles and Philippe stared at their mother and their longtime servant, who had been so much like a grandfather to them. They waited in silence until Henri broke away from Madeleine.

"We need to get on the road," Henri said. "I know a guide who will take us over the mountains and on into Geneva."

"Yes. Good." Madeleine looked around her modest entourage. "I would like us to pray first."

Echoes of confirmation came from around the circle, and they all bowed their heads. The men and boys removed their hats.

Madeleine began softly. "*Père*, we are beginning a perilous journey tonight, and I don't know exactly what we are to do. Please give us your mind. Help us to make right decisions. Protect our family. You have assured us that you would guide us with your eye, that you would tell us when to turn to the left, or to the right."

Her voice began to mount in confidence. "*O Dieu*, I need that direction now more than ever. Show us literally where to turn, what to do, whom to trust. And I ask you to send your angels to watch over our Vangie and François." She hesitated and took a deep breath. "Wherever they are."

Madeleine could hear sniffles around the circle. She proceeded with a stronger voice. "Set up an angelic force around them, and do not let the enemy penetrate those ramparts." Madeleine looked up at her family and servants, then raised her gaze toward the sky. She lifted her hands to the heavens. "Whom have we in heaven but you?

We declare that we trust you, and we look to you for our direction. Amen."

Whispers of agreement filtered through the air. "Amen."

"Amen."

"Yes."

Madeleine turned. "Armond, assist Henri in hitching the horses back up to the coach. Use only two to pull it. Jean will ride ahead on one of the horses and scout the route. And I want you to take the other horse and ride rear guard."

"*Oui*, madame. But who will drive the second coach?"

"Can one of the footmen handle it?"

Henri answered, "Of course." He signaled to a tall, slender young man. "Daniel, come."

The youth bounded from the coach and pulled off his hat, revealing a shock of unruly blond hair. "*Oui*, monsieur?"

"Madame would like you to drive the small coach. Can you handle that with only two of the white stallions?"

"*Absolument.*"

"Good. Monsieur Jean will ride ahead to scout the area. The large coach will be next, and you will follow it. Armond will bring up the rear."

The men went to their tasks at once and were ready to leave in a matter of minutes. Elisabeth would ride with Madeleine and the boys, while Suzanne, Judith, and Claudine would ride in the second coach.

Madeleine finished her instructions. "If we should get separated for any reason, get to Geneva any way you can. I have given money and méreaux to all who might need it for passage. If that should happen, go to a Protestant church, show whoever is there a méreau, and they will give you shelter. We will find one another, God willing."

The Clavell clan boarded the carriages. Jean spurred his horse and soon rode out of sight. Inside the lead coach, Madeleine and her boys sat huddled together. Lulled by the swaying rhythm of the carriage, Charles and Philippe were both soon asleep. Madeleine and Elisabeth talked and cried softly together. Cried over the trauma of the last month and over the unknown yet ahead, over the loss of loved ones— one to death and others to a fate yet undisclosed.

JEAN RODE AT A CAUTIOUS TROT HALF A MILE OR SO AHEAD of the carriages, straining to hear any noise foreign to the forest. The jarring rhythm of the horse began to annoy him, and he slowed to a walk. Although completely dark by now, it was still early in the evening. Suddenly his horse spooked. Jean stopped and listened. Silence. But something wasn't right.

He moved to the side of the road in the brush and moved ahead. The horse spooked again and started backing up. "Whoa—hold it now." Jean spoke softly and stopped the horse once more. Then he heard it. Coarse laughter—then crying and pleading. He dismounted and moved toward the sounds.

Just over a ridge and down in a gully, he detected a soft glow. He crouched below the ridge, and his heart thumped wildly at the scene that appeared before him in the dim light of a campfire.

SEVENTEEN

A sudden halt of the coach startled Madeleine awake. She heard Jean's voice as he reined his horse in beside the carriage.

"A handful of dragoons are ahead." He stuck his head inside the window. "Philippe!"

Philippe sat up, rubbing his eyes.

"Get your bow and quiver and come with me."

Madeleine put her hand on her son's shoulder to protest, but Jean cut her off.

"No time to explain." His voice carried a sharp edge. "I need Armond and Philippe to come with me. The dragoons have a family tied up—preparing to hang them. You stay here until we return."

Philippe pulled away from his mother, grabbed the bow and quiver of arrows, and jumped out of the carriage and onto the back of Jean's horse before Madeleine could stop him. Armond rode up, and they galloped down the road.

Madeleine looked at her mother and buried her head in her hands. "Oh, *Dieu, mon Dieu*, will this never end?"

JEAN HELD UP HIS HAND TO HALT ARMOND, SIGNALING them to silence as they approached the ravine. Flames from the dragoons' campfire cast eerie shadows upon a hangman's noose dangling from the limb of an ancient oak. Huddled together on the opposite side of the campfire from the soldiers sat a young man and woman and a boy who looked to be about eight or nine. Three dragoons squatted around the fire. A fourth dragoon stood guard nearby, gazing outward from the fire.

Jean whispered orders. "Armond, go to the other end of the ravine. Listen, and when I signal—the hoot of an owl—you shoot the guard."

Armond nodded.

"As soon as you shoot, start reloading, and I will shoot the one on the left stoking the fire." Jean tapped Philippe on the shoulder. "At the same time, Philippe, you shoot the one next to him with your arrow. Armond, you should be reloaded by then and ready to take another shot and get the last one." Jean looked at his tiny army. "Do you understand the instructions?"

"Yes, Uncle."

"Good boy. Armond?"

"*Oui*, monsieur."

Jean touched the knife in his belt and hoisted the musket in his hand. "Go," he whispered.

Armond hunched low behind the brush and made his way to the end of the ravine.

"Philippe, get your arrow ready. Aim well, son."

"I'm scared. My hands are shaking."

"Mine too." Jean held out his trembling hand for Philippe to see. "Know this, my brave little man: True courage is not the absence of fear. True courage is when one does what is right in spite of being afraid." He patted the young boy's shoulder. "Ask the Lord to steady your aim."

Philippe knelt on one knee, cautiously pulled an arrow out of his quiver, and took aim.

Jean watched the guard. Armond should be at his station by now, his gun ready. Eventually the unwary dragoon leaned his flintlock against a tree, and Jean gave the signal.

The forest exploded with the blast of Armond's musket, slamming the guard against the tree.

"Now!"

Before the other soldiers could spring into action, Jean and Philippe fired their weapons as one—Jean hitting his target in the stomach, Philippe's arrow piercing the neck of his assigned dragoon. The dragoons, confounded at the different directions from which the attacks came, swirled around in confusion.

Armond got off a second shot, but missed. The remaining soldier scrambled for the cover of the trees. Armond lunged after him, swinging his musket like a club. He caught up with him before the man even left the circle of the campfire and knocked him out, splitting his skull open with the butt of his musket.

Jean and Philippe jumped into the ravine and turned their attention to the terror-stricken family. "It's all right. You're safe now." Jean glanced around the area surrounding the campfire. "Are there any other dragoons with this party?"

"*Non*, monsieur." All three members of the family shook their heads as the father answered. "You got them all."

Jean drew a deep breath and put his musket down by his side. "Protestant or Catholic?"

"Huguenot."

"As are we." Jean set about untying them. "Where are you from?"

The father picked up his son and pulled his wife to his side with the other arm. "Grenoble, monsieur. And you?"

"We are part of the Clavell family." Jean pulled the hangman's noose from the tree and began to wind it up. "The dragoons have burned down our estate and captured part of our family. We are making our way to Geneva."

"Oh-h-h, *oui*. Monsieur Clavell is our siegneur. A good man." The young father shifted the weight of his son and set him down. "I am David L'Atrec. This is my wife, Angelina, and our son, Eugene." Indicating the slain soldiers with a jerk of his head, he explained, "They must have been some of the soldiers who were at your place. We heard them laughing about it." He looked down at his hands.

Jean stopped winding the rope. "What else did you hear? Did they say where they were taking Monsieur Clavell?"

"*Oui*, monsieur. To Paris."

"And the child? Did you hear them say anything about where they were taking the child?"

"*Non*. Only that their commander took her."

"Commander Boveé, no doubt." Jean muttered the hated name under his breath.

He looked around at the bodies of the dragoons. He had murdered once again, taken a human life, and had found the deed much easier this time. Is that how it was? The most horrible violence became

183

easier the more often one committed it, until a man's sensitivity grew so seared that the crime no longer bothered him?

He addressed the group gathered around him. "I suppose we should give these miserable examples of manhood some kind of burial."

At that moment the dragoon Armond had hit with his musket groaned.

Armond raised his weapon to strike him again. "What's this? We have left one alive?"

"No, wait!" Jean knelt beside the soldier and pulled him up by his coat, the blood from his head wound forming a red ribbon down his neck and onto the red-and-blue uniform. "Perhaps you would like to tell us where your Commander Boveé has taken our little girl." He shook the dazed soldier by the lapels. "Well?"

The soldier skewed up his mouth and spit in Jean's face.

Jean stood, shaking with rage, yanking the man up with him. The white, foamy spittle trickled down his cheek. Jean released the soldier and let him fall to the ground, then wiped his face with the back of his hand. The dragoon lay in the dirt holding his head, moaning.

Jean stepped over the wounded soldier, who had once again lapsed into semiconsciousness, his wound bleeding profusely. "Let's bury his comrades. Leave this one here to bleed to death—and think about his fate."

The three men and Philippe went to work clearing away leaves and dirt to form a shallow grave.

"I have a shovel in my wagon." David ushered his wife and son to their wagon near the edge of the campsite and settled them onto the bench. He pulled some tools out from under some burlap bags stacked in the back.

The offensive task didn't take long. Jean stood as they threw the last bit of dirt on the hastily dug group grave and wiped his forehead. "Monsieur L'Atrec, you and your family are welcome to ride with us to the Rhone, if that is the direction you need to travel."

David leaned on his shovel and shook his head. "We left our younger son with my wife's family in Grenoble. The dragoons happened upon us on our way home from visiting relatives in the countryside and decided to make sport of us." He threw a rock on the mound, and then picked up one of the dragoon's muskets. "We could use a weapon. May we take one of these with us?"

"Of course. Armond, help them with their team." Jean motioned to Philippe. "Go round up our horses. We need to get back to your mother."

David grabbed Jean and hugged him. "We owe you our lives. How can we ever thank you?"

"No need. I'm sure you would have done the same for us. Perhaps we shall meet again someday. God be with you."

A RIDERLESS HORSE TROTTED ALONGSIDE THE COACH. Madeleine and Elisabeth listened intently as Jean, sitting across from them inside the coach, related the grisly story of the ambush. Philippe sat beside his uncle, his bow resting in his lap, the quiver pulled from his back to the front of his chest. His eyes reflected his somber mood.

Charles sat on the edge of his seat next to his grandmother in the corner of the carriage, exuding naïve excitement. "Did you get a dragoon, Philippe? Did you kill one?"

"Hush, Charles." Madeleine reached across the crowded interior of the carriage and touched Philippe's knee. "My brave Philippe."

He looked at his mother, eyes filled with unshed tears.

"Son, you did what you needed to do to protect innocent lives from being taken." She pulled him across to her side and spoke softly into his ear as she cradled him. "I'm sorry yours was the eye that had to take aim and yours the arm that had to pull the string—but I am proud of you, so proud of your courage."

Except for the clatter of the carriage wheels on the bumpy road and the clopping of hooves, the inside of the carriage was silent for several minutes. Philippe buried his head in Madeleine's embrace and cried softly.

Charles looked at his brother with unspoken questions, sensing a change in him. "Philippe?"

"We'll talk later. I'm tired. I want to go to sleep." The newborn hero moved to the other side next to his uncle and made a pillow out of his quiver.

Madeleine patted Jean's knee. "Why don't both of you see if you can rest. Then you can relieve Henri and Armond after a couple of hours." She watched the two, uncle and nephew, bonded forever because of their devotion to protect family against an outside enemy, settle into a cramped position.

"Sleep, precious ones, sleep and bury the appalling events you've had to endure these past days. You need to renew your strength." Madeleine knew the next crisis could be around the coming bend in the road.

EIGHTEEN

The black water swirled around the two small boats carrying the remaining Clavell family and servants across Lake Geneva. Madeleine watched her beloved country slip away from her, wondering if she would ever return. She clutched her two sons tightly in her arms. Her mother was near her side, and Jean stood protectively behind them. Henri and the servants huddled together in the second boat. The only sound to be heard was the purling of the water.

Suppositions and questions plagued Madeleine's fatigued mind. When your homeland, the hills and trees and rivers where you have built a home and a life and raised a family, is snatched away, where do you go? When the tapestry of your life that you have woven together through the years with the threads of laughter and tears is rent, what patch is used to mend the tear?

She had no answers, only questions. Her maternal instinct proved to be more powerful than any other motivation, even at the point of her anguish over losing François and their home. Her heart broke at the thought of Vangie.

Mon Dieu, please take care of my baby girl. I cannot, but you can.

She pulled her boys closer to her side. All she knew now was that she had to protect her sons.

Madeleine had heard all her life about the martyrs who had given their lives for their faith, and now her family had been plunged into that role. She did not choose it, and she did not want it. What difference would it make in the long run, anyway? She was losing her husband, her daughter, and her country.

But even as doubts nipped at her thoughts, she knew she had no choice. The deep faith and heritage of her family held her as in a vise and forced her on. She could only pray that Louis would have mercy on François and that Vangie would fare well in a convent.

She swallowed a sob. *Oh, Dieu, let them know how much I love them and that my heart has been torn from me.*

Jean touched her shoulder gently. "Madeleine? Are you all right?"

She patted his hand. "Yes. No . . . ahhh. How do I answer that question when my heart is withering within me?" She swiveled around to face him and searched his eyes. He was so like François.

"My husband and my daughter are missing. Thanks to you, my sons are safe. Honestly, I don't know if I am all right or not. I don't know why our family has been caught up in these tumultuous times." Madeleine paused and wiped her tears with the hem of her cloak. "But I know our God is able to deliver us. We must trust him." She shivered and pulled her cloak tighter around her and her sons.

François, oh, François, please endure. I will wait for you. Please find us.

The mountains of Switzerland loomed on the horizon.

FRANÇOIS OPENED HIS EYES AND PEERED AROUND WITH-out lifting his head. The odor from his unwashed body made him want to retch. The blood around his wrists had dried and caked onto the coarse rope. He twisted his hands slightly. The pain was excruciat-ing, but he knew he must keep the rope from embedding into his skin. Infection was already setting in.

He realized he was chained in an open area surrounded by cells. Rats scurried in and out, drinking the filthy water from the cracks between the rocks.

A wiry old man in the cell next to him peered out through the bars, wheezing with every breath. "Aha. Awake now, are you?"

François peered up at the old man. "Where am I?"

"Why, son, you're in the king's private prison. *La Prise de la Bastille.*" The man went into a spasm of coughs that left him breathless and gasping for air.

François tried to shift his weight on the stones and realized his ankles were cuffed. He put his head on his knees and thought of Madeleine and Vangie and his sons. *Run, Madeleine, run. Take our boys and run.*

Every time he closed his eyes he could see Vangie's hair caught by the wind as Commander Boveé rode away with her. François couldn't even voice a prayer. *O Dieu, O Dieu, O Dieu* was all his muddled brain could offer. His eyes remained dry, though his heart was ripped apart.

A rumble from deep within the center of the prison began to grow until it reached the rim near the stairs where François was confined.

He looked up at the old man leaning against the bars. "What's going on? What's happening?"

The man nodded toward the door at the top of the stairs. "The guards'll be coming soon with our meal. The prisoners seem to know when it's time, and they start getting loud."

François knew that, in spite of the man's haggard appearance, his newfound companion was a man of culture. Only the upper classes were confined in the Bastille. "For what reason have you been shackled here?"

"Treason. I own a fleet of ships, and the king's policies were affecting my business in a negative manner. When I voiced my opinion, the king retaliated by conscripting my ships for the naval fleet." His stringy gray hair fell across his face. In a low, rattled whisper, he added, "And I am Huguenot."

"As am I."

"It'll go better for you if the guards don't know that. What crime have you committed, son?"

François laughed bitterly. "Aside from being Huguenot? The king and I are in love with the same woman—who happens to be my wife."

The old man began to laugh, ending in gulps for air. "You don't say! *Oui*, you don't mess with the king's women." He stared long and hard at François. "So you snatched away one of the king's beauties, eh? I must know your name."

François shook his head. "My name is François Clavell, and the story is long and tangled."

"François Clavell, François Clavell, stole the king's mademoiselle." The old gentleman laughed harder as he quoted his impromptu poem. He brought his crooked finger suddenly to his lips. "Shhh. Here come the guards."

The guards descended the stairs with large trays of food and barrels of drink. François had heard of the surprisingly humane conditions of the king's prison. He knew that it was a prison for the upper class—usually for people who had offended the king in some manner. Well, that was certainly true of him.

When they reached François, the guards began to goad him. "Ha! So this is the new prisoner. How do you like our quarters?"

François didn't answer.

"So? He's going to be a quiet one." The lead guard reached for his leg chains and unlocked them. "Just as well. The king wants to see him."

François stuttered, "Th-th-the king? King Louis?"

"Found your tongue, now, eh?" The guard jerked François to his feet and headed him toward the stairs. "Yes, King Louis. What other king were you expecting? You must be an important man. Nobody gets an audience with the king this quickly."

The guards released François' chains.

The old gentleman called after him, "May God be merciful to you, François Clavell."

The guards led him up the stairs and along a corridor to a small room. One of the guards, a stocky man with a thick black mustache, shoved him toward a washstand holding a pitcher of water, washbasin, and soap. A towel hung on the side of the washstand. "Wash your filthy body. The king will not tolerate the stench of unwashed flesh."

François groaned as they cut and pulled the rope from his wrists. The same guard opened an armoire on the back wall and removed clean clothes. "Here, put these on when you are finished washing." He placed a tin of salve on the washstand. His voice softened. "This might soothe those rope burns."

François looked into the unflinching eyes of the guard. *"Merci."*

When he had cleaned himself up the best he could with just a pitcher of water, they ushered him down a hall to a sparsely decorated but elegant chamber. They shoved him down on a bench alongside the wall. Two more guards stood on either side of a door at the far end of the room. A large, ornate chair stood toward the middle of the room.

François had lost all track of time, but he presumed it must be about midday, due to the rays of sun streaming in through the small window toward the top of the wall. How long he waited, he had no idea. He watched the shafts of sunlight move slowly across the stone wall until they no longer shone directly into the room.

Finally our destinies meet, Louis. Not only my king, but Madeleine's first love—the man who held my wife's heart for so long. What do you want of me? Was she successful in her plea to you? Did you even receive her? Was your love rekindled?

François shadowboxed with his adversary in his mind while he waited, ending with no solution.

At last the door burst open, and the fabled Sun King of France strode into the room. François struggled to his feet.

Louis stood in front of him, smirking. "So. This is the dashing François?"

François bowed slightly from the waist before his sovereign. He faltered and fell to his knees.

"Ah, yes. A very appropriate position. Just remain there." Louis turned to his entourage of guards and valets and ordered them out of the room. "Leave us."

"But, Your Majesty . . ."

Louis shook his cane at them and shouted, "I said leave us! Now!"

The king's personal guards hesitated.

"You too. I want the room empty."

The room cleared. François did as he was ordered and stayed on his knees. A long period of hushed quiet followed, interrupted only by the tapping of the king's cane.

François had heard about the king's short stature, but he was still shocked. He could tell he was probably a good head and shoulders taller than Louis.

"So, this is the man who stole my Madeleine from me." Louis pulled out his perfumed handkerchief, held it to his nose, and tapped François on the chest with his cane. He circled around him, looking him over from his matted, dirty hair to his worn shoes. "This fine country gentleman who has never bothered to pay homage to his king at court. Not such a handsome picture now, are we?"

Shame and embarrassment washed over François.

Louis stopped in the center of the room. "And a Huguenot. What is it about you people that you will go down and take your family with you just to stay Protestant?" He walked toward François. "We all believe in the same God, *oui?*"

"*Oui*, Your Majesty, but—"

"But what? If we believe in the same God, what peripheral issues could possibly matter? Don't you Huguenots understand that, because of your stubbornness, you are dividing our country? If we were one hundred percent Catholic, our nation would be strong, unbeatable."

"Begging Your Majesty's pardon, but we don't consider salvation by faith alone a peripheral matter."

"Aaach!" Louis sputtered and hit the chair with his cane. "Hang on to your precious doctrine of *Sola Fide* if you must, but convert. What harm could there be in that?" Louis' voice softened with a measure of empathy, and he bent down close to François' face.

François could feel the king's breath.

"If you convert now, I will spare your life, and I will call off the dragoons from your family."

Suddenly François realized that the king really didn't want to harm Madeleine, or anyone she loved. He truly did care for her. But he was trapped by his own decrees. In his weakened physical state, François battled with his conscience and his convictions. "Wh-what do I have to do?"

"Just say, 'I convert.'"

"And you will order the dragoons to leave my family alone?"

"By the king's order."

François felt himself crumbling. Surely the Lord would understand a compromise at this point. *It's not only my life at stake here—it's my family.* What harm would be done to the Huguenot cause for one man to convert to save his entire family? God is merciful and would forgive him.

"I-I . . ."

The king stared at him, waiting. And François felt as if all of heaven leaned forward as well, waiting with him.

At that moment, a wellspring of strength poured into François' broken body and disheartened spirit. From where it came he could not tell.

Fear not . . . When thou passest through the waters, I will be with thee; and through the rivers, they shall not overflow thee: when thou walkest through the fire, thou shalt not be burned . . .

An unbidden rod of courage shot up his back and through his soul like something alive within him. François struggled and stood and shook his head. "My King, I cannot. I could say the words, but would that change my heart? *Pas du tout!* You can kill my body, but my spirit will remain untouched."

François watched Louis' face redden with rage, but he continued, "Your Majesty, you say you still care for Madeleine. Do what you will to me, but spare her and our children. For her sake. Because of the love that you once shared."

"The love that we once shared." Louis turned and walked to the opposite end of the room. Minutes passed. Finally he spoke, his voice lowered to the point that François could hardly hear him. "Would you like to hear about that love? Has Madeleine ever told you the details of our passion for one another?"

The king walked back to François and stood directly in front of him and laughed, as if relishing some delectable memory. "Has she ever told you how we would meet early in the mornings and ride together; how she was my only true companion—the only one I could trust—the laughter and the good times that we shared; how I taught her to dance; how I was her first lover?"

Louis paced in front of François, taunting him. "Well, that is over, ended long ago. She had another chance to come to me. *That* would have rescued your family, but she refused. And now you refuse to convert. Unfathomable stupidity."

My Madeleine remained true to me! She refused the king's proposal. A slight smile flickered at the corners of François' lips.

The king turned quickly and walked toward the entrance. "There is no more to be said. Guards!"

The guards bounded into the room. "Your Majesty?"

"Take this man and execute him."

François inhaled sharply. The guards grabbed him by the shoulders and began to lead him away.

"No, wait." Louis walked back to François. He peered into François' eyes as if trying to detect any sign of weakness. "On second thought, take him to the docks. I commission him to the galleys. That way he will have plenty of time to think about his life and his family." Louis smiled grimly. "By the way, how old is your oldest son? About twelve?"

"*Oui.*"

"Hmm. Born soon after you married?"

"*Oui,* Your Majesty."

"As I said. Plenty of time to think in the galleys."

LOUIS WAS LATE. HE HAD TRIED TO SLIP AWAY AFTER *Mass, but an audience with one of his governmental officials had detained him. He galloped up to the gazebo, overrun with wisteria, dismounted, and tied his horse to a white oak tree. The dapple-gray nibbled on the grass beside the enclosure.*

He could see the lace on Madeleine's skirt peeking out from the lattice. She jumped up when she heard him approaching, and the sun highlighted the red in her mahogany hair as she ran out to greet him. She may have only been a young girl, but she aroused him like a mature woman.

"Forgive me for being late. I couldn't get away. There is always so much to take care of when we come to Versailles. Have you been waiting long?"

"It doesn't matter. You're here now. Let's ride, Louis." She lifted her face to him, and he kissed her. He tried to hold her, but she pulled away. "No, let's go."

"What's wrong, Madeleine? Have you been crying?" He held her face in his hands.

"Nothing's wrong. I just want to ride with you and forget that you are the king. I want us simply to be two people in love. Forget everything else." She pulled him toward their horses.

They spurred their mounts and galloped toward the countryside, away from the beginning construction of Versailles. Madeleine let her hair loose and tossed her head, laughing at the rare freedom they were enjoying.

Louis shouted to her and galloped in front. "Follow me!" He led the way to a mixed grove of oak and pine trees overlooking a meadow. Letting their horses graze, they sat, leaning against the trees. "Look, I have something for you." Louis reached in his tunic and pulled out a pouch. He handed it to Madeleine and sat up facing her. "Open it."

Madeleine fumbled with the strings and pulled out a small poesy ring. "Louis, I cannot accept this. It carries a promise of commitment, and you are . . . you can't . . ."

Louis stood and assumed the posture of his royal position—head up, shoulders thrown back, left foot forward. "I am the king. I can have whatever I want, and I want you." His voice softened. "I truly love you. Please wear it." He took the ring from her. "Look what is engraved on the inside."

Madeleine took it and read, "Toi seule pour toujours . . . Louis." She looked at this man, her first love, the king of France, and began to cry. "Do you really mean that, Louis? Will I forever be the only one for you?"

He did not answer her, but simply put the ring on her finger and kissed her.

Madeleine and her family left the court the next day. Louis sent messages, but she never answered. He dispatched messengers, but Madeleine was always out of the country when they arrived. When her father came to court periodically to attend to his duties, he avoided answering the king's questions about his daughter.

Then the affairs of France, his arranged marriage to Marie Thérèse of Spain, and his royal duties consumed Louis. He heard of Madeleine's marriage to a commoner who assumed the duties of her father's estate when he passed away. The years flew by. She invaded his thoughts often, but she had slipped through his fingers.

THE BIG LADY SHROUDED IN BLACK AND WHITE HELD OUT her arms to the screaming child.

"I want my maman—I want my papa!" Vangie's cries pierced the night as Commander Boveé handed her over. The little girl twisted and turned in his arms and beat her fists against his chest.

"This is a feisty one, Sister Marie-Aimée, but take good care of her. She is of special interest to the king."

The sister nodded and took the frightened child from his arms. Vangie kicked and screamed as the nun carried her to a tiny room and sat down with her on a small bed. Bread and cheese sat on a table beside the bed, but Vangie would have none of it.

The nun sang a quiet lullaby and spoke softly to the little girl, stroking her hair and rocking her back and forth. She prayed over the child. "Father in heaven, Blessed Mother, calm this panicked child and console her parents' hearts, wherever they are. Let them know their child is safe."

Vangie's cries subsided, and she fell asleep in the nun's arms, sniffling every now and then in her sleep.

"Poor child, she has no idea what is happening to her." Sister Marie laid her down on the bed, pulled a rough blanket over her, and kissed her on the cheek before blowing out the flickering flame in the candlestick on the bedside table.

THE BOAT CAPTAIN SIGNALED TO JEAN THAT THEY WERE approaching shore. They were now in Switzerland and out of danger.

Madeleine woke the boys. "We are safe, boys. Wake up and see a new world. No more hiding. No longer nightwalkers. We are free."

She stepped onto the dock and the wind caught her cape, whipping it in folds behind her. She breathed a deep breath of unrestricted, unfettered air. It felt good. In spite of the grief over François, Vangie, and the manor, she felt good.

"Maman, we are free. Come." She reached for Elisabeth and wrapped her arms around her mother's shoulders. "We made it. We are safe."

They stood shoulder to shoulder with Jean and the boys, Henri and the servants loyally by their side, weeping tears of relief, sorrow, and yes, even joy at what lay ahead.

NINETEEN

Elisabeth began to sing a familiar psalm—a privilege forbidden the Huguenots in recent years. "I will bless the Lord at all times: his praise shall continually be in my mouth . . . O magnify the Lord with me, and let us exalt his name together."

Madeleine, Jean, and Henri joined in immediately, singing heartily unto the Lord. Henri's robust bass voice rose above the rest as tears streamed down his cheeks.

Charles, timid and somewhat embarrassed that his family was singing in a public place, sidled up to Henri and slipped his hand into the old man's rough palm.

But in this bastion of Protestantism, passersby began to stop and sing with them: "The angel of the Lord encampeth round about them that fear him, and delivereth them . . . The Lord is nigh unto them that are of a broken heart; and saveth such as be of a contrite spirit. Many are the afflictions of the righteous: but the Lord delivereth him out of them all . . . The Lord redeemeth the soul of his servants; and none of them that trust in him shall be desolate."

The ending strains of the psalm rang out over the docks.

Jean removed his cap and voiced a simple prayer. "We thank you, O God, for our safe passage. Protect those loved ones we had to leave behind. We trust you now to guide us in this new place." He hesitated and looked around at the little band of brave souls and shrugged his shoulders. "What do we do now?"

Henri stepped up with his usual practical advice. "Well, first we need to secure coaches and unload our baggage from the boats."

Pulling a bag of coins from the knapsack that Madeleine had brought with her from the boat, she handed it to Henri. "Yes, Henri, would you see to that, please? We will wait for you in the marketplace, over there on the corner."

Madeleine gathered her brood around her and ushered them toward the street while Henri took Armond and disappeared in the crowd.

Philippe tugged on Elisabeth's sleeve. "Grand-mère, how do we know Geneva is a safe place for us? Why did we choose this city?"

Elisabeth began giving the boys a history lesson as they walked along the cobblestone streets. "Don't worry, Philippe. Geneva is the city to which John Calvin took his followers to develop a place where they could live out daily life according to the gospel. After that, Geneva became a refuge for persecuted Huguenots. The city government and families have rallied around others like us, fleeing persecution, offering shelter and even money. Here Protestants can lift up their voices to God without fear of persecution."

Philippe and Charles looked around them in wonder.

"Like us, huh?"

Philippe received the instruction stoically, but Charles seemed genuinely interested.

"Very much like us." Elisabeth paused for a moment. "Madeleine, on the journey here, I remembered a pastor and his family who sought shelter with us while your father was still alive. They had endured the same treatment that we've experienced in recent days and were on their way to Geneva." She sighed. "Little did I know at the time that we would walk a similar path. I thought—we all thought—we were protected by the Edict. And beyond that, of course, because of our connection with Louis."

She gave Madeleine a quick hug. "Not just *your* connection, dear, but because of your father's former position at court." She waved her hand. "That's all past. But I'm thinking that we might try to find the good pastor, and perhaps he could help us."

"I remember them." Madeleine's eyes brightened as she recalled the incident. "They had three little girls, and the two older ones slept in my room. I remember them because they were all so blonde, with beautiful blue eyes."

"Yes, those are the ones. Now if I can just recall their name." Elisabeth bit her lip. "Can you remember the daughters' names?"

"I believe the oldest daughter was Rachel. I don't remember the others . . . but their last name . . . was it Du Puy?"

"I think you're right. And the father was Gérard—Gérard du Puy. As soon as Henri returns with coaches, we shall set out to look for him."

Madeleine glanced around at the busy street. The marketplace where they found themselves was bustling with commerce. The Clavell party seemed to be right in the path of people coming and going, and they couldn't find a place to get out of the way or sit down.

"We can't just stand here until Henri and Armond find a coach. It may take them awhile." Madeleine spotted the imposing towers of a church. "That must be the Cathédrale de St. Pierre." She turned to Jean. "Take Daniel and go back to the boat to wait for Henri. When you get the baggage unloaded, pay the captain and guides with the money Henri has, and come to that church." She pointed to the towers. "We will wait for you there. Perhaps someone at the cathedral will know the Du Puys."

Philippe stuck out his chest and declared, "Maman, I can be of help to Uncle Jean as well. I will go with them."

"*Non!*" Madeleine dared not let her sons out of her sight again just yet. Composing herself, she said, "Why, son, don't you realize? I need a man to escort us through these crowds. I need you with *me*."

Philippe looked at the all-female party, save Charles—Madeleine, Elisabeth, Suzanne, Claudine, and Judith—and reluctantly agreed. "*Oui*, I suppose you are right."

Jean gave Madeleine some help. "Of course she's right, son. You take care of your mother and the rest of the women, and we will join you as soon as we get coaches."

Madeleine and the women, plus the boys, headed toward the church.

Trudging up a steep incline, Elisabeth called out to Madeleine, "I-I need to stop and catch my breath."

Madeleine came alongside her mother. "Are you all right?"

"Yes, I just need to rest." Elisabeth's breath came in gasps, and sweat broke out on her brow as she leaned against the wall of a building and fanned vigorously. "I'll be fine."

Elisabeth finally began to breathe easier and they continued, but Madeleine kept an eye on her mother.

The church was farther away than it appeared—and uphill all the way. The weary band of travelers finally arrived on the stone steps and went inside the huge, ornate double doors. Cool, dank darkness greeted them as they passed into the entrée.

"Just think," Elisabeth whispered, "John Calvin himself preached here."

A hush settled over the Clavell party as they paused to stare at the looming structure. A slight, rather grim-faced young man approached them from out of the shadows. "May I be of assistance?"

Madeleine gave a slight curtsy. "*Oui*, monsieur. We have just arrived from—" She hesitated, not knowing whether to divulge their plight. "Are you the pastor here? Are you in charge?"

"Madame, God is in charge here."

Philippe and Charles snickered. Elisabeth pulled the boys to her skirts. "Shhh."

"*Mais oui.* Of course." Madeleine turned on her charm. "We would not be here alive if our Father God were not in charge."

The young man's face softened. "You are refugees from France, I gather from your accent?"

"*Oui.* We have some old friends who we believe are pastoring a Protestant church here in Geneva, or nearby. Gérard du Puy. Do you perchance know of him?"

"One moment, *s'il vous plaît.*" The young man retreated into the shadows and down a columned hallway.

Madeleine looked at her mother and raised her eyebrows.

A moment later, out of the darkness bounded a slightly overweight, balding man with explosive energy and an open jolly face. "Welcome to Geneva and to Cathédrale de St. Pierre." His voice echoed through the cathedral as he opened his arms in a warm, welcoming gesture. "How can we help you? My assistant tells me you are searching for the Du Puys? Fine man. Fine pastor. Wonderful family. How do you know them? Are they expecting you?"

Madeleine waited for a pause to jump into the one-sided conversation, but found it impossible.

The pastor continued, "Oh, forgive my bad manners, I am Pastor Estienne Le Sueur, and this is my assistant, Jacob Veron." Pastor Le Sueur beckoned them to follow him. "Come, come. You must be weary if you have just arrived. Come to my quarters for some refreshment."

Madeleine hesitated. "I—the rest of our party went to secure coaches. They are to come here when they have accomplished that task. Perhaps we should wait outside for them."

"Oh, my child. Forgive my insensitivity. You are perfectly safe here." The pastor came to Madeleine's side, took her hand, and pressed it between both of his beefy palms. He patted the boys' heads and bowed to Elisabeth. "What you must have gone through these past days. Please, come. Do you need to rest? We have guest quarters."

All of a sudden, the euphoria of rescuing her sons, escaping from France, and arriving safely in Geneva left Madeleine like the wind leaving a full-blown sail. Tears sprang into her eyes. "I-I don't know. I don't want to presume upon your hospitality."

Then her firm resolve melted in light of the possibility of a safe harbor. Exhaling deeply, she nodded. "Oh, Pastor Le Sueur, *oui, merci,* that would be wonderful."

"Please, follow me. We will get you something to eat and a place to rest."

"The others—my brother-in-law and servants—will be here shortly."

"When they arrive, we will give them a meal and quarters as well. Rest as long as needed. Then we will help you get to the Du Puys."

The benevolent pastor gave his assistant instructions and then led them down a long corridor and up narrow stone stairs to guest quarters—Madeleine, her boys, and Suzanne in one room, and Elisabeth, Judith, and Claudine in an adjoining one. The rooms, although meagerly furnished, were comfortable, with a fireplace and beds, tables and chairs, and pallets for overflow guests.

Before Madeleine could even remove her gloves and hat, domestics entered with trays of bread and cheese and a pot of hot, steaming stew for both rooms. The attentive servants kindled a fire before they left, and the flames were soon crackling, bringing a warm glow to the plain room.

After indulging in the nourishing meal, Madeleine lay down on her bed, instructing her boys to spread out the pallets. Suzanne put the empty tray in the hallway, then timidly sat on the other bed.

Madeleine yawned. "Go ahead, Suzanne. Lie down and rest."

Within minutes all four were asleep.

WHEN MADELEINE AWOKE, DUSK HAD BEGUN TO SETTLE on the city. She looked out the window at the beautiful metropolis, the shoreline of the blue water of Lake Geneva. Across that water and the mountains lay her homeland. A wave of sadness swept over her as thoughts of François and Vangie invaded her mind. Would François ever hold her in his arms again? Would she ever embrace her daughter and kiss her sweet face?

Madeleine looked at her sleeping boys. She had to think about the children she had with her and do what was best for them. She went to the door and slowly pulled it open with a loud creak.

The boys stirred but did not wake up. Suzanne sat up in her bed. "I'm sorry, Suzanne. Go back to sleep."

"*Non*, madame. I feel rested now. Does Madame need anything?"

"Our small trunks are out here. Henri must have found coaches and brought us some of our things. Come, help me with them."

The two women brought the trunks into the room and got out clean clothing. Suzanne took a pitcher she found on a washstand and went in search of water.

Upon returning, Suzanne assisted Madeleine in her toilette. Madeleine sat on the plain chair, wishing for a vanity so she could check her hair, unsure what she needed to do next. She had been on alert for so long, she was finding it difficult to relax. She looked out in the hallway again. The servants were nowhere to be seen.

"I am going to find Jean and the others," she announced, "and then I will speak with Pastor Le Sueur. Stay here, please, and watch the children."

Suzanne curtsied. "*Oui*, madame."

Madeleine started down the dimly lit hallway. She passed several rooms, but heard nothing from behind the closed doors. She descended the narrow stairs and eventually found the pastor's office and quarters. Madeleine knocked quietly on the open door.

The portly gentleman was at his desk reading. "Come in. I was just wondering whether you would sleep through the night, or if we should awaken you for dinner." He rose from his chair. "Sit down, madame, please." His desk was filled to overflowing with books and Bibles. "Martha, come. They are awake. Come and meet Madame Clavell."

A large buxom woman, with a cheery smile that proclaimed welcome even before she spoke, bustled into the room. "Madame Clavell." She curtsied slightly, but left the curtsy quickly to envelop Madeleine in a smothering embrace.

"You are welcome here for as long as you need to stay. Estienne told me of your plight. Were you able to rest at all? Dinner will be ready soon. Do you need anything? Please make yourselves at home."

Madame Le Sueur's steady stream of conversation made Madeleine wonder to herself how either Pastor Le Sueur or his wife got a word in when the other was speaking. "No, we don't need a thing. Your hospitality has been overwhelming and welcome. Thank you."

She turned her attention to the pastor as Martha exited through a door behind his desk. Madeleine assumed their living quarters were behind the office. "Obviously my party has arrived. We found our trunks in the hall."

"*Oui*, madame. Your brother-in-law is on the same floor as you. Henri took the coaches and other servants to the stable and bedded down there." He smiled. "Quite a protective gentleman, the old one."

"*Oui*, he and his wife have been with our family since I was a child." Madeleine looked down at her hands resting in her lap. "Thérèse, his wife, was killed in our"—Madeleine stumbled over what to call their experiences of the past few weeks—"the persecutions we faced from the king's dragoons."

"Oh dear. I am so sorry."

"And my husband and daughter have been kidnapped." Madeleine looked at the pastor, and a lump arose in her throat. She swallowed hard. "My two boys were in hiding for over a month. We had to get them out of France." She began to cry softly. "I don't know what will happen to my husband and my daughter, but I had to protect my boys." She searched the pastor's eyes and found compassion in them.

"Did I do right by leaving France? Should I have stayed and tried to find them?"

"My child, you did the best you knew how to do at the time." He knelt before Madeleine and held her hand. "Do you know where they have taken your husband and daughter?"

"François was taken to Paris and Vangie to a convent, but we know no further details." Madeleine's heart began to race, as if it would burst from her chest. "Pardon, but I have no desire to revisit all this right now. My mind is far too muddled to think clearly. If you could just tell me, sir, where we can find the Du Puys, we will be on our way in the morning."

Pastor Le Sueur labored to rise to his feet. "Ah, these old knees aren't what they used to be. Comes from spending too much time on them, I suppose." He let out a soft laugh. "Of course, my dear. I understand completely. You need not share with me any more than you feel able to. But do go to our heavenly Father with your broken heart. It is he alone who truly understands."

Madeleine rose. "*Merci*, Pastor."

"As for the Du Puys, I sent a runner to their village shortly after you arrived. The last I knew, they were shepherding a church in a small village about an hour north of here by coach, but I'm not sure they are still at that location. I didn't want to send you there, only for you to arrive and find them gone."

"Thank you for your kindness. I don't know how to thank you properly." Madeleine curtsied and knelt before the man of God, and a tear escaped down her cheek. She grabbed his hand and pressed it to her cheek.

"Oh my, get up, my child. There's no need for that. We are on equal footing here. We are all God's children." He rubbed his hands together and chuckled. "Go prepare your family for the evening meal. Martha has planned a feast worthy of a celebration."

Indeed, the savory fragrance of onions and garlic and roasting meat had begun to permeate the study. Madeleine stood up, smiled, and wiped her cheek with her handkerchief. "*Oui*, something smells wonderful. We haven't had a decent meal for several days. *Merci*."

Madeleine started out the door. Pastor Le Sueur escorted her into the hallway. "I'll send a servant to let you know when we are ready for you."

Madeleine nodded. "Thank you. I'll go wake the others, and we will look forward to dining with you."

Alone in the darkened hallway, her thoughts turned again to François and Vangie. *What are they having for dinner tonight? Do they even have anything to eat? Are they warm? Is Vangie frightened? Is François even still alive?* She dismissed the unthinkable.

Madeleine reached the floor where they were quartered and saw Jean standing in front of the first doorway. Once again her emotions overwhelmed her. They rushed to the surface, like the deluge of a river after a thunderstorm, and she walked into the security of Jean's arms.

TWENTY

Days melted into weeks. Weeks rolled into months. And yet time dawdled, like a naughty child, testing his parent at every step along the way. The oppressive heat of summer reflected Madeleine's mood.

The Du Puys lavished hospitality on the Clavell family beyond what anyone could expect. The men fell into patterns of daily chores, helping Pastor Du Puy with his livestock and small crops. Philippe was learning the finer points of riding and helped in the responsibility of caring for the horses. Madeleine and Elisabeth's ball gowns lay crushed back into their trunks, and the two women assumed the life of the common folk rather than that of mistresses of a fine manor. Suzanne and Armond employed the clerical duties of Pastor Du Puy soon after arriving and now lived in a small cottage on the back of the property. They expected their first child in a few months. Life seemed almost normal.

Madeleine sat at the small desk in her bedroom writing yet another letter to Francina, inquiring if she had heard any court gossip that would lead to François' whereabouts. The domestic's reply to Madeleine's previous inquiries lay open on the hard wooden surface.

My dear friends,

I trust this correspondence finds you well. My good mistress's son has been willing to read your letters to me and is penning this reply for me. All is well here, but I am sorry to say that I have no information regarding your family. I will surely send word to you if I should overhear anything. Give Judith my love.

My regards to you and your family,

Francina

Madeleine crumpled her half-finished dispatch and threw it at the wall. She laid her head down on the desk and let the tears flow.

All investigations into François or Vangie's whereabouts had divulged nothing. Her trips to Geneva checking with Pastor Le Sueur at the Cathédrale, her wanderings on the docks hoping that she might stumble upon any kind of information, no matter how remote, produced no news.

She went to the window and opened it to let a breeze circulate in the escalating heat of the noon hour. Wiping her tears, she left the letter from Francina lying on the desk and went downstairs.

She walked into the kitchen, where Charles knelt on the floor polishing a wooden whistle Henri had carved for him. She sat down at the table, pulled the butter churn toward her, and absentmindedly jabbed the paddle up and down. She knew she couldn't simply keep helping with the garden, making an occasional stew, and hauling in a bucket of water every now and then. She needed to try again to find François and Vangie. She stared at Judith, who stood over a kettle of stew that hung over a low fire in the fireplace.

A biting whiff from a batch of onions that Claudine had just sliced stung Madeleine's eyes and pulled her thoughts back to the present and the chores at hand. "My goodness, those onions are strong. My eyes are watering just sitting next to the table."

Charles wiped his eyes with the back of his sleeve. "Mine too."

Madeleine ruffled his hair and chuckled.

Madame Du Puy came through the door and threw up her hands, clutching more onions from the garden in her arms, clumps of dirt filtering to the floor. "Ahhh, I bring you onions for the stew, and you've already pulled them." She emptied her arms of the dirty produce. "What am I going to do when you have to leave? You are spoiling me."

Madeleine managed a smile and got up from her chair. "You deserve to be spoiled. How can we ever repay your kindness and service to us?" She picked up a towel and wiped her hands on it. "Not to mention the unselfish way you serve your congregation." She lifted the top of the butter churn. "I think this is ready."

Madame Du Puy took the churn from Madeleine, clucking and protesting, and headed toward the sideboard.

Madeleine watched her spoon the creamy spread into a mold. "Vangie loved butter. Especially on hot bread. She would ask for more and more until it was dripping all over her hands."

Her mind raced back to the day the dragoons invaded their estate . . . Vangie begging Claudine for more butter . . . Commander Boveé watching. He was scheming where to take her even then.

As much as she tried to suppress them, Madeleine's thoughts continued to return to the devastating events of almost a year ago. "I cannot even entertain thoughts of my daughter without the threat of that contemptible Commander Boveé intruding." Looking around the room, panic crept into her voice. "Not only do we have to fight simply to exist, I have to struggle to think uncontaminated thoughts about Vangie. Evil wraps itself around my visions of her and strangles the life out of them." Madeleine ended her declaration stifling a sob.

The three older women stopped their chatter and stared at her. Elisabeth set her basket of vegetables on the table and hurried to put her arms around her daughter. "Dear, you must quit this, this torturing yourself with memories. I'm sure Vangie is fine."

Madeleine pulled away from her mother and spun around, knocking over a pitcher of milk on the table. "How can you say that?" She held both ends of the towel, snapping it in frustration in her clenched fists as she spoke. "How can you *say* that? None of us knows how she really is. Maybe she's not fine. Maybe she's sick or hungry or afraid. Maybe she's even . . ."

Madeleine could not bring herself to voice her darkest fear. The dripping of the milk off the edge of the dark wood table was the only sound for a few seconds.

She began to wipe up the mess. "I'm sorry. I'm sorry." She looked at her mother, and tears welled up in her eyes. "I can't stay here and do nothing. I have to go back and at least try to find her."

Elisabeth nodded and sat down at the table. "A mother's heart cannot rest while her child is in danger. But Madeleine, it's far too dangerous. And what will the rest of us do if something happens to you?" Elisabeth swiped absentmindedly at the milk with the tail of her apron. "However, if it were me, I must admit, I'd feel the same."

Elisabeth shook her head, rose, and walked out of the kitchen dabbing at her eyes. "Do what you have to do."

THE FAMILY ATE DINNER THAT NIGHT IN SILENCE EXCEPT for the bantering back and forth of the Du Puys' younger girls and Philippe and Charles. Rachel, the oldest, was now eighteen and helped her mother with serving the meal. Rebecca and Rosie, ten and thirteen, had proved to be comrades and good playmates for Philippe and Charles.

Jean jumped up from the table. "Horses—pulling up in the front." He sprinted to the front door with Pastor Du Puy, whose bushy blond beard glinted in the glow of the lantern he carried. Jean stepped to the side, into the shadows, as he allowed the head of the household to open the door.

"Ho there. Welcome to our home." Gérard's voice boomed out into the night.

As the light from his lantern illuminated the small lane with a hitching post, only one horse stood pawing the ground. A familiar figure alighted from the mount.

Gérard recognized him immediately. "Jacob, please come in."

The slender associate from Cathédrale St. Pierre stepped into the entry of the house and removed his gloves. Pastor Veron's eyes lit up when he saw Jean. "Monsieur Clavell. Praise God you are still here. I have news."

The Clavells and Du Puys hurriedly gathered in the great room of the house as Gérard ushered Pastor Veron into the center of the circle. The young man quickly declared the purpose of his nocturnal visit.

"Yesterday a rider came to the cathedral inquiring about your family. He seemed quite anxious to find you. He said he had information regarding your family."

Jean stepped forward. "Who was he? Did he give his name?"

"His name was Boveé."

A collective gasp filtered through the Clavell family.

"A dragoon commander—riding a white stallion?" Madeleine clenched her fists. "He has no authority to come into Switzerland looking for us."

"N-n-oo. This was a young man, very handsome. He said he was a courtier in King Louis' court and that he met you, Madame Clavell, at a ball last year."

"Pierre! How did he know to search for us in Geneva?"

Pastor Veron was searching in his pockets and pulled out a folded letter with his slender fingers. "He presented us with a méreau and asked if we knew you, and would we please see that you received his letter?" Pastor Veron shrugged his shoulders. "That's all I know."

"But he's not Protestant. Why would he have a méreau?" Madeleine took the envelope from their visitor. "You didn't tell him our whereabouts, did you?"

Pastor Veron vigorously shook his head. "*Pas du tout!*"

Gérard brought his lantern closer so Madeleine could read. The family crowded around.

"Who is Pierre, Maman?" Philippe questioned. His dark eyes were wide with fear. "Read it out loud."

Madeleine struggled in the dim light to read the message.

Madame Clavell,

I pray this note finds you safe. Our last meeting instigated this unexpected trip to Geneva, and I trust that you will agree to meet with me for further information. I plan to be at the Les Armures Hotel. I will stay until I hear from you.

Fondest regards, Pierre Boveé

"Why would our last meeting have 'instigated a trip to Geneva'? Our last meeting was when we were fleeing Versailles." She read over the short message again. "Further information? He must know something about François or Vangie."

She looked around at the bewildered faces of her family. "But why would he come all the way to Geneva to tell me? Why should he care?"

Jean spoke up. "Perhaps it's a trap, Madeleine. He is one of Louis' valets. What if Louis sent him here to bring you back?"

"Maybe." Madeleine sat down in a chair and tapped her fingers on the armrest. "But he had a méreau. Why would he have a méreau if he meant harm to us?"

Jean paced in front of her. "Don't be a fool, Madeleine. It wouldn't be hard to confiscate that off a dead Huguenot. Surely you are not that naïve."

Henri stepped forward and put a hand on Madeleine's shoulder. "Jean's right, madame. You mustn't trust anyone from King Louis' court. Least of all, the son of Commander Boveé."

"But Pierre helped us get out of Versailles safely." She looked at Elisabeth and pleaded with her eyes. "I don't think he would harm us."

Jean stopped his pacing. "You're right. This may be a trap, but I think we have to take the chance. If there is any possibility that the young Monsieur Boveé has information that might prove helpful in finding François and Vangie, I believe we have to investigate." He took Madeleine's hands. "I think I have a plan."

THREE MEN RODE AT A BRISK PACE SOUTH TOWARD GENEVA as the sun eased over the horizon. Pastor Veron took a slight lead. The small band pulled their cloaks around them in the chilly morning air.

They encountered farmers on the road to the city, plodding alongside their carts full of produce. Riders overtook and passed them. Some fell in behind them. The road grew more congested as the morning wore on. Jean and Armond, who'd hunkered down in their saddles in the slight chill of the early morning, began to sit taller and loosen their cloaks as the warm rays of the morning sun beamed down on them.

Approaching the city, Pastor Veron slowed his horse and then halted. "I need to turn east here." Pointing in the opposite direction, he explained to them the route they were to follow. "Take the main road into the market square down to Lake Geneva. The hotel is on the right bank. If you need directions, just stop and ask anybody. You can't miss it."

Jean nodded. "I think I remember seeing it."

Pastor Veron turned in his saddle. "If you encounter any difficulties, you know to come to the cathedral."

Jean and Armond acknowledged the instruction with a nod.

The austere young pastor continued, "I pray Godspeed for you—and discernment. Things are not always as they appear on the surface—nor are people."

In spite of the fact that Jacob's grim demeanor irritated him, Jean agreed. "*Merci*, Pastor Veron. Once again we are indebted to you."

A rare smile crossed Jacob's face, and he turned and rode away without another word.

Armond watched the young cleric depart. "Guess it takes all kinds, *non?*"

"I suppose so." Jean spurred his horse. "Let's get on with our mission. I want to find Monsieur Boveé as quickly as possible and get back to Madeleine with whatever message he has for us."

"What if we truly are riding into a trap?"

"That's a possibility, but we will be cautious." Jean pulled his hat down over his brow to deflect the brightening shafts of the sun climbing higher in the sky. "I think you'd best stay down the street a ways. Monsieur Boveé would recognize you, *oui?*"

Armond laughed. "Oh, *oui!* He will remember me. He rescued me from playing a part I did not want to play the night Madame Clavell met King Louis at the Trianon." His expression sobered. "Yes, he will recognize me."

"All right. I don't want to take that chance until we know what we are walking into. I will go into the inn first. I can check out whether there are dragoons or soldiers around—and try to locate Monsieur Boveé. Then I will send for you or come and get you."

The two young men found the hotel easily. Jean left Armond at a livery nearby with instructions to keep his eye out for anything suspicious, then made his way on foot to the inn. Merchants had already begun hawking their wares from wooden carts scattered helter-skelter throughout the cobbled streets, and the din began to rise, drowning out individual conversations.

Jean stopped at a vegetable cart not far from Les Armures and pretended to be interested in making a purchase. "Good crop so far this season?" He looked around for any sign of French dragoons.

"So far. We've had good rain. Care for a sample?"

Jean suddenly realized he was hungry. "What about strawberries? Do you have any strawberries yet?"

"I was just putting them out." The old man, his back stooped from years of labor and his hands dark from the sun, proudly showed Jean the prized red, sweet fruit.

"I'll take some."

"Yes. Certainly." The farmer tenderly placed them in a bag for Jean. "Frenchman, eh?"

Jean cocked his head. "Ah, *oui*." Jean paid the man and left quickly before he could ask any more questions.

Jean munched on his purchase as he entered the door of the hotel. It took a moment for his eyes to adjust to the dim interior. A dark, heavy wooden bar lined the wall in front of him. To his right, several round tables occupied a small room in front of the bar. A burly bearded man sat in the dining area at one of the tables. A middle-aged woman was serving the man from a kettle, which she hung back over the fire in a fireplace on the back wall. The scent of garlic mixed with the odor of old, oiled wood permeated the air.

Two gentlemen descended the stairs directly in front of Jean. He eyed them warily, but they paid him no mind and went directly outside.

The woman approached Jean. "May I help you?" What teeth she had were black and rotten, giving her a haglike appearance.

"Perhaps. I hope so." Jean looked around the room once more. "I am looking for an old friend and was told he is staying here—Monsieur Pierre Boveé?"

"Ahhh, yes. He has been expecting you. I'll fetch him."

Jean stepped toward her. "One moment, please. Is Monsieur Boveé alone?"

"Completely alone. He doesn't even ask for companionship in the evenings." She laughed raucously and started up the stairs.

"Would it be all right—could you just tell me which room he is in? I would like to surprise him."

The woman hesitated. "I guess he wouldn't mind." She pointed up the stairs. "Take a left at the head of the stairs. Last room on the right at the end of the hall."

Jean took cautious steps up the staircase. He winced as the last step creaked under his feet. He looked both ways at the top of the landing, turned left, and proceeded down the short hallway, stopping in front of the last room. He listened for any sound from behind the door.

It's still early. Maybe he's asleep. Jean hesitated. *Or perhaps he's gone out already.* He lowered his head and listened again. Suddenly the door swung open, and Jean found himself staring into the face of a man with a knife upraised in his left hand.

Jean leapt backward, knocking over a vase on an ornate table along the wall behind him. "Uh!" Jean doubled up his fist. "I was about to knock."

"And I was wondering who was listening at my door."

Jean kept up his guard. "Monsieur Boveé? Pierre Boveé?"

"Who is asking?"

Jean pulled the letter from his leather pouch and shoved it in front of Pierre's face. "Jean Clavell."

The barmaid from downstairs, breathing heavily, had made her way up the stairs with the burly man behind her. "What's going on here?" Beads of sweat broke out on her chubby face.

Pierre took charge. "Oh, we are so sorry. I simply startled my friend here, and we knocked the vase over." He clapped Jean on the back in feigned friendship and pulled him into the room, hiding the knife behind his back. "I will pay for any damages."

"Well, all right. But it's still early. People are sleeping."

"I'm very sorry, madame. Please forgive us."

The man turned around and went down the stairs as the maid picked up the pieces of the vase. "Mercy me. Roughhousing this time of morning. Don't men ever grow up?"

Pierre closed the door and turned to look at Jean. "And just who is Jean Clavell?"

Jean looked around the room and saw no evidence of any other party.

Jean gripped the letter in his fist and eyed the knife still in Pierre's hand. "I am the brother of François Clavell of Dauphiné, France, brother-in-law of Madeleine Clavell."

The two men faced each other, like two animals sizing each other up. Fight or flee? Comrade or enemy?

Pierre edged toward a table holding a washbasin and ewer. He put the knife down and held up his hands to placate Jean. "I am here as a friend and admirer of Madame Clavell."

"How can I trust that? Are you not a courtier in King Louis' court and the son of Commander Paul Boveé?" Jean looked at the young man's dress. He was attired as a commoner, not an elegant courtier.

"*Oui*, that is true." Pierre turned and opened a leather pouch that rested next to the now retired knife on the washstand. He pulled out a méreau. "This should convince you that I come as a comrade and not an enemy."

Jean took the méreau and examined it. "Where did you get this?

These are only given out during a Protestant service to those qualified to take Communion. You are not Protestant, are you?"

"Never mind how I got it. For now, I have news for Madame Clavell. Where is she?"

"You can give me any news you have for her."

Pierre and Jean again found themselves in a standoff.

This dashing, polished, handsome young courtier made Jean feel disheveled and untidy. What interest did he have in Madeleine? She was a married woman. *Perhaps he has news that François is dead, and he wants to win her hand.*

Jean reiterated his position. "You may tell me whatever you need to relay to Madeleine."

Pierre stood his ground as well and glowered at Jean. "I will speak only to Madame Clavell."

TWENTY-ONE

W atch, Maman. Look at me." Charles raced down the road in front of the house on a palomino mare that Armond had broken earlier that week.

Madeleine shielded her eyes from the sun and looked up from the flowers she was picking. "Good boy, stay with him."

"Watch." Charles flipped his head around to assure himself that his mother was indeed watching.

Madeleine knelt in the flower bed, surrounded by the new blossoms. *Watch me.* She wondered how many times she had heard her sons say that. Oh, that François were here to see what skilled equestrians his boys were becoming. Sadness flickered over her face. He would be so proud.

Cupping a handful of tiny blossoms, Madeleine bent over to sniff them. Tending to the flowers was her favorite chore. She loved the earthy smell, watching the buds swell and burst into brilliant colors, touching the delicate petals, and tracing the intricate design of each bloom.

She learned life lessons when she worked in the garden: how she needed to be diligent in pulling the weeds, or the beauty of the blossoms would be choked out. She tugged at a stubborn, thorny thistle that had twisted itself around the rhizome of an iris and refused to budge without destroying the flowering plant. Weeds in the garden reminded her of the weeds of evil. They were subtle. They first appeared as delicate leaves—no harm. And then they wrapped their life-sucking tentacles around the tender flowers.

Madeleine worked the soil with her small trowel to keep it soft so that moisture could soak the plants thoroughly. She cleared away the debris from around flowers so the sun could reach the plants. Cultivation, water, and light—if any one of these was missing, she knew the growth would be stunted. She wondered as she worked if she would be able to provide all the ingredients necessary for her boys to flourish without François. How was she going to keep evil away from them? She rocked back and held her dirty hands out in front of her.

"They don't look much like a genteel lady's hands," she said to herself. She turned them over. "But that doesn't actually matter anymore, does it?"

Madeleine struggled to her feet and looked up at the late afternoon sun. Jean and Armond could get home tonight if they found Pierre quickly and had no trouble. Gathering the flowers she had picked, she placed them carefully in a large, open-ended basket. She needed to get them into water.

"Maman!" Charles was coming back her way at a gallop. "Uncle Jean and Armond are coming, and some other man is with them."

Madeleine moved to the porch, still holding the basket of flowers in her hands. It must be Pierre. Her heart began to race. "Come here, Charles."

For once Charles did not question his mother. He dismounted, tied his horse to the hitching post, and came to Madeleine's side. He leaned into her and suddenly became shy. "Who is that man?"

Madeleine reached down and hugged Charles with her free hand. "He is a friend I met at Versailles. Don't be afraid. Perhaps he has news of Vangie and Papa." She wished she felt as confident as she sounded.

She watched the features of the men become more recognizable as they drew closer in a cloud of swirling dust. Jean waved. A sign that they have good news? Or simply to assure her that there was no danger from Pierre?

Jean jumped from his horse and bounded onto the porch. He gave Madeleine a crushing embrace. "Madeleine, we had no trouble finding Monsieur Boveé."

Charles looked up at his mother with wide eyes and began to tremble.

Jean swept the boy up in his arms. "It's okay, son. He comes as a friend."

Madeleine, still clutching the basket of flowers, watched Pierre dismount from his striking black steed and walk toward her, his appearance different without his court attire. But his elegant manners were the same.

He pulled off his hat with a flourish and bowed. "Madame Clavell, I am delighted to have found you." Looking at the basket of flowers still in Madeleine's arms, he continued, "The flowers you bear in your arms simply serve as a frame for your magnificent beauty."

He stepped onto the porch and reached for her hand, but Madeleine kept her dirty hands hidden beneath the flowers in the basket.

Madeleine curtsied. "We are not at court here, Monsieur Boveé. The flattering speech is not necessary."

"I speak but the truth."

Jean spoke up, "I must agree with Monsieur Boveé, Madeleine." He put Charles down. "This is Madame Clavell's younger son, Charles."

Pierre's charm extended to the child. "And a fine looking specimen of a young man he is."

Charles grinned and looked up at his mother.

Madeleine shooed Charles toward his horse. "Take your horse to the stable and tell Henri to come to the house immediately." As Charles untied the horse and started toward the stable, Madeleine called after him, "Don't put him up wet, *mon petit*."

"*Oui*, Maman." The young boy ran at a trot toward the stable, calling for Henri.

Elisabeth appeared at the door. "Oh!" The expression on her face reflected her surprise. "Oh my goodness. Monsieur Boveé, we meet again."

Pierre turned to Elisabeth and kissed her hand, which she extended in greeting.

Madeleine interrupted the formalities. "What news do you bring us, Monsieur Boveé?"

"Could we step inside, madame?"

Elisabeth took charge. "Of course. Forgive us." She led the way into the modest home. "Understandably, we are most anxious to hear why you have come to Geneva to find us."

Henri came in, his jaw set in a hard line, and joined the gathering.

The basket of flowers rested forgotten on a rough bench in the entryway.

Madeleine faced Pierre. "Please, monsieur, if you know something of our family, do not torture us any further with suspense. Whatever the news, tell us."

Pierre nervously twirled his hat. "I am privy to information regarding your daughter." A smile spread across his face. "She is alive and well."

Gasps of joy rippled around the circle of relatives.

Madeleine's eyes bore into Pierre's. "Where? Where is she? Is it possible to rescue her?" She reached out and touched the young man's sleeve. "How did you find her?"

Pierre continued to finger his hat nervously. "My father, during one of his infrequent visits, was boasting to me regarding his military prowess and told me of the kidnapping and the burning of your estate. He had no idea that I even knew who you were. I remembered the anguish I heard in your voice as I returned you to your apartment that night after your appeal to King Louis failed." He looked at Madeleine. "I kept thinking about your little girl and how alone and afraid she must be without her mother and the rest of her family."

He glanced around the room at the faces of the Clavell clan. "When the time was right, and my father had enough wine in him, I asked him to which convent he took her." Pierre squared his shoulders and stood straighter. "I visited the convent and spoke with the sister who looks after your daughter. She has agreed to help us. I am willing to take you to her."

"How did you know to look for us in Geneva?" Madeleine asked.

"Would you believe me if I said it was a lucky guess? Or perhaps one of the king's servants knew of your whereabouts?"

"Francina!" Madeleine exclaimed. "But why would you risk your position in King Louis' court to come and tell us?"

Pierre looked steadily into Madeleine's eyes. "I have my reasons. Perhaps someday I will reveal them to you."

Madeleine hesitated. "And what of my husband? Do you have any knowledge of what has happened to him?"

Pierre shuffled his feet. "I know nothing about your husband."

Henri voiced his concern. "It is much too dangerous, madame. What guarantee do we have that Monsieur Boveé is telling us the truth?"

"I assure you," Pierre said, his distress evident. "I have brought you nothing but the truth." He stepped back. "You will simply have to trust me."

THIS TIME FOUR HORSEMEN RODE OUT FROM THE DU Puy farm. The determined little *coterie* headed straight west out of Geneva, then south toward Lyon. Jean and Pierre rode in the lead, with Armond and a smaller figure in the rear.

Jean dropped back. "Armond, go up front, please, with Pierre."

Armond spurred his horse and rode ahead.

Jean spoke to the fourth rider. "Remember to keep your muffler up and your hat pulled down around your face. And don't talk!"

Madeleine grinned and peered out from under her broad-brimmed hat. "The hat I can pull down and the muffler I can keep wrapped around my face, but not talking?" She laughed. "I'm not so sure about that."

"Well, if you want a successful mission, that would be best."

Her tone turned somber. "Yes, I am well aware of that. I will be cautious."

They rode along side by side, not conversing for a few moments.

"Let's catch up with Pierre and Armond. I want to ask Pierre something." She took off, leaving Jean to wonder what she was up to.

She drew alongside Pierre. "I've been thinking about something."

"What is that, madame?"

"You need to stop calling me *madame*."

"*Oui*, you are right, but I don't care how we disguise you, you are much too beautiful ever to pass for a man." Pierre's eyes betrayed a growing affection for Madeleine.

"Your courtly demeanor is lingering much beyond its benefit."

Pierre protested. "But, madame—or whatever we agreed to call you—"

"Matty, for Matthieu, in case we slip into *Madeleine*. Remember?"

"I remember." Pierre let the reins rest on his saddle as he turned his attention to Madeleine. "Is this what you rode up here to discuss with me?"

Jean joined them, and the horsemen rode four abreast now.

Madeleine continued, "I was wondering why your father didn't take Vangie farther away from Grenoble than he did. Lyon is so close to our home, and to Geneva, as well."

"I thought about that myself, ma—er, Matty. Probably several reasons—his insufferable arrogance being foremost. He didn't suppose you would be bold enough to attempt a rescue. Or even find out where he had taken her at all. Second"—Pierre chuckled—"I imagine he soon wearied of dealing with a kicking, screaming three-year-old and was more than ready to pass her off to somebody else. My father is not exactly patient with children."

Madeleine grew serious. "You don't think he would have been cruel to her, do you?"

"My father is not cruel or abusive, simply very loyal to duty and attentive to his orders and the task at hand." Pierre looked at Madeleine. "Did you find him cruel during his stay at your estate?"

Madeleine shook her head. "No, not cruel, but very cold and insensitive." She shuddered to think of Vangie in the commander's care.

Pierre changed the subject. "We should be at the Filles de Sainte-Marie, Visitandines, by tomorrow evening. Soon, if all works as planned, your baby will be back in your arms."

Madeleine smiled at the thought of holding her daughter once again. "She's not a baby anymore. She's four years old." Suddenly an inconceivable notion struck her. "What if she doesn't want to come with us? What if she doesn't remember me?"

Jean entered the conversation. "Don't torment yourself. Of course she will remember her mother, and surely she will want to come with us."

Armond abandoned his usual quiet mode and echoed the same sentiments. "Of course she will."

Pierre goaded his horse. "We had best pick up the pace if we intend to be in Lyon by tomorrow."

THE SOFT, EARLY EVENING RAIN COURSED DOWN THE THICK outer walls of the convent, forming rivulets along the stone walkway in front of the black wrought-iron gate. A small but heavy wooden door lay embedded in the rock beside the gate.

Pierre approached the door and pulled on the bell cord hanging over the door. He had changed into his court apparel and exuded a confidence that Jean found difficult to share. The blue-and-silver musketeer uniform Pierre had ordered Jean to don reeked of body odor from the former owner and was too tight for Jean's muscular girth. Raindrops dribbled off both their plumed hats.

A round face surrounded by a black-and-white habit peered through iron bars over the small window in the door.

Pierre took charge. "We are here in the service of King Louis."

The nun opened the door. "*Oui*, monsieur." The door creaked on its hinges, and the nun ushered the two men inside. "How may we be of assistance to the king's messengers?"

Pierre pulled a letter from inside his embellished jacket, quickly flashing in the dim light what appeared to be the king's seal. "I have a message for Sister Marie-Aimée."

The nun bowed slightly at the waist. "I will take you to her. Please come this way."

The sister moved down a walkway and through arched columns surrounding a courtyard. The halls began to fill with the songs of the nuns attending evening vespers. A bell atop the chapel commenced to toll.

"I apologize. We seem to be interrupting your evening recitations."

The nun turned toward him, acknowledging his remark, and continued down the archway without making a reply. She turned right at the end and then stopped in front of a bench against the stone wall. "Please wait here. I will get Sister Marie-Aimée for you." She left quickly in a whorl of black and white.

Minutes passed. The singing and the bell ceased. A low, almost indistinguishable hum hung in the courtyard. Jean realized it was the nuns reciting their prayers.

Pierre stood and began to pace back and forth in front of Jean.

Perturbed, Jean stood as well. "What's taking her so long?"

"She's at evening prayer. We will probably have to wait until they are finished."

Just as Pierre was completing his sentence, Sister Marie-Aimée

came into view. "Monsieur Boveé. I thought it must be you." She neither sat down, nor did she invite the men to do so.

"Thank you for seeing us, Sister Marie."

"I surmise you have come for the child?"

"Yes. Will there be any trouble getting her out of the convent?"

"We must act quickly. Come with me." She did not question the
presence of a musketeer.

They returned the way they had come in, but stopped and walked
through a door leading to the kitchen where bread, cheese, and wine
lay on the long table in preparation for the evening meal. One lone lay
sister, wearing a white veil, stood at the far end of the room removing
another fragrant loaf from the large stone oven.

Pierre eyed the fresh bread. They passed into another hallway and
then entered a room with several beds lining the walls.

"This is where the younger girls sleep, along with some of the novi-
tiates as their companions." Sister Marie-Aimée pointed to the first
bed. "That is Evangeline's bed. Her belongings are in the chest at the
foot. Gather them up while I fetch her."

The two men quickly stuffed Vangie's clothing into a bag Sister
Marie-Aimée had handed them before she hastened out the door at
the opposite end of the room. Jean pulled the soft musketeer hat down
around his face and stepped behind Pierre, just in case Vangie recognized him and blurted out his name.

The door opened, and Sister Marie-Aimée came back in carrying
the child, who had her head buried in the nun's shoulder. "It's all right,
my child. This nice man is going to take you on a little trip."

With her head still buried in the nun's habit, Vangie's muffled voice
protested. "I don't want to go on a trip."

Pierre reached for the little girl and with a soft, gentle voice coaxed her. "Come, Vangie. Everything will be fine. We will take good care of you."

Vangie continued to resist and cling to Sister Marie.

"Vangie." Jean stepped out from behind Pierre and put his finger to his mouth to signal her to remain quiet. Upon seeing her uncle, the child scrambled from the nun's arms and ran to him, almost knocking him down. She began to whimper.

Jean heaved a sigh of relief. He stroked her long silky hair and shushed her. "Shhh, child. Don't cry. We will indeed take good care of you. Don't you worry." He rocked her in his arms and hugged her tight.

"Well, Monsieur Boveé, it seems the 'musketeer' has won the affections of the child away from you rather quickly." Sister Marie looked at Jean, smiled, and patted Vangie's head. "What a precious child she is. It's not right these children should be ripped from their parents' arms."

Pierre bowed. "Sister, I know your assistance in this matter is putting you at great risk." He took her hand. "*Merci*. May God bless you."

"I must endeavor to do in every action only the Divine Will, my son—and with the greatest possible love. We must hurry now. Leave by the back gate. If anyone stops you, show them your letter and keep walking."

Pierre nodded, slung the child's sack over his shoulders, and motioned to Jean to leave.

Sister Marie stepped toward Jean and Vangie and spoke to the child. "Vangie, dear, I will miss you." She cupped Vangie's face in her hands. "God be with you. God make his face to shine upon you and give you peace." A tear rolled down the nun's cheek as she kissed the little girl. "Now quickly—leave before the sisters finish their evening prayers."

"*Merci*, Sister." Jean hesitated.

"Go!" Sister Marie-Aimée shooed them toward the door. She turned and exited the opposite direction.

The back door led to another, smaller courtyard. Jean spied the gate. "There it is."

They hurried toward it, only to find it bolted and locked.

Jean looked about in terror. "What now?"

"Over the top." Pierre threw the sack over the wall and easily scaled to the ledge around the crown of the wall. "Hand the child to me."

Jean hoisted her up on his shoulders. "Stand on my shoulders and reach for Pierre, so he can grab your wrists."

Vangie was shaking. "I'm scared." She clung to Jean's tunic and would not let go to stand on his shoulders.

Jean pried her fingers loose. "Vangie, you must let go. I'll hold you. You won't fall."

"No! No!" Vangie shrieked above the hum of the sister's prayers.

Pierre caught hold of her wrists and pulled her small form up as if she weighed nothing. "Good girl. Come, Jean. Quickly."

Jean joined them and then leapt to the opposite side. "Hand her to me—carefully now."

Pierre jumped to the ground, and they began to run toward the edge of town where they had left their horses tied in a grove of trees—and where Madeleine and Armond anxiously waited.

Just as the trees came into sight, the bell in the convent began to peal.

TWENTY-TWO

Jean handed Vangie over to Madeleine's outstretched arms. In one fluid motion, the three men leapt into their saddles, and amidst the stamping and neighing of horses, took off. Vangie glued herself to Madeleine as they galloped into the night. Madeleine longed to stop and gaze at her child, but dared not. The bell from the convent continued to ring, but no horsemen followed them, and eventually the tolling of the bell faded away.

Deep into the dark hours of the night, Pierre called the party to a halt and dismounted. Vangie had fallen asleep. Jean got down from his horse and took the child from Madeleine as she descended from her mount.

She claimed her daughter back from Jean and sat on a fallen tree trunk. "It's too dark. I can't see her." The mother stroked the child's face and kissed her over and over. "In just these few months, how she has grown."

Pierre surveyed the area and listened carefully for signs of anyone following. "We've gone as far as the horses can go without rest. I don't think we are being followed. We will camp here for the night."

Jean took over now that they were on their way. "Armond, see if you can find some wood dry enough to start a fire. I'll take care of the horses." He tugged at the tight breeches. "Then I'm getting out of this costume and into my own clothes."

Pierre laughed. "I don't know, Jean. I perceive you may have missed your calling. You cut a fine figure as a musketeer."

Jean grumbled as he tore off the tunic and tossed it at Pierre.

The courtier stuffed it in his knapsack. "Say, I'm hungry. How about the rest of you?"

Madeleine rocked her sleeping daughter back and forth on the tree trunk. "I'd forgotten all about food, but yes, I could eat something. Do we have anything left?"

Pierre grinned and pulled out from his cloak a loaf of bread and a circle of cheese he had pilfered from the convent kitchen.

Jean was horrified. "Pierre! We are not thieves."

Pierre held the bread and cheese in his hands as he pleaded his case. "Now, a moment, *s'il vous plâit*, to plead my case." He assumed a mock proud stance. "Madame, in the Old Testament, did not David and his men eat the consecrated bread because they were on a holy mission? I say we are on a holy mission, and we are justified. I just wish I could have absconded with some of the wine as well."

Armond, picking up wood to start a fire, joined in the laughter. "I agree."

Vangie sat up in her mother's lap, rubbing her eyes. She blinked and looked around the circle of men, then back at Madeleine. "Maman!" She threw her arms around her mother's neck and snuggled close. She looked at Jean and then Pierre. "Who is that?" she asked, pointing at the young courtier.

"This is a friend I met at Versailles, who arranged your rescue." She smiled reassuringly at Vangie. "His name is Pierre."

Pierre knelt beside the two. "I am pleased to finally meet the princess that we have all been trying to rescue."

Looking at his formal appearance, Vangie asked, "Are you a prince?"

Pierre threw back his head and laughed. "Why no, I'm not. But for you, beautiful princess, I could try to become one—and then wait for you to grow up, so we could get married and live happily ever after."

Vangie giggled.

Pierre reached inside his tunic and took out a méreau. "Here you go, *ma princesse*—for you to remember me by." He pressed it into her hand and kissed her cheek.

Madeleine shook her head. "Pierre, do you ever stop?"

"Not when it comes to beautiful women."

Madeleine smiled. She would be eternally grateful to this dashing young man. Still, she could not fathom why he would take the risk to quiz his father, go to the convent and set up an alliance with the nun, then lead a rescue party to reclaim her child. She watched him as he strode away and poked at the fire. How could he be Commander Boveé's son and harbor such charity within his heart at the same time?

THE RESCUE PARTY WAS UP BY DAWN AND READYING FOR departure.

Pierre led his horse around and faced the group. "This, I am afraid, is where I leave you, my friends."

"What?" Madeleine jumped to her feet. "Why? Where will you go?"

"To Paris, Versailles. Back to court."

"How can you return to court after last night? Surely word will reach Louis that you were involved in Vangie's escape."

"Only Sister Marie-Aimée knew my identity, and she was a co-conspirator. I suppose it's possible that I will be found out, but there are so many at court, I seriously doubt it." Pierre picked Vangie up, tossed her in the air, and spun her around. "Remember, *ma petite princesse*, I'll be waiting for you to grow up."

Vangie squealed and begged, "Do that again, Pierre!"

Pierre swung her around again and then held her in his arms. "Since you are our little princess, why don't you just call me Prince?"

"Okay, Prince."

Pierre chucked her underneath her chin and smiled. "I like that much better."

He set Vangie down and gave Jean and Armond perfunctory hugs.

Jean's voice sounded hoarse and choked up. "How can we ever thank you?"

"No need." Pierre executed his most elegant court bow and reached for Madeleine's hand. This time she extended it willingly. He lingered over the kiss. Maintaining his hold he softly murmured, "I pray that we will meet again someday."

"May God be with you, Monsieur Pierre." She could not bear to connect this kind young man with the name Boveé.

"And with you. *Au revoir.*" Pierre mounted, turned his horse sharply, and left without another word. The sticky mud, left from the night rain, muffled the horse's hooves as he rode into the thin ribbon of pink on the horizon.

Madeleine picked Vangie up and rested the child on her hip. Her voice, soft with wonder at how God had arranged circumstances, nevertheless was firm and strong. "*Père Dieu*, thank you for bringing that young man into our lives. Protect him from the deceit of Louis' court. Make a way for him. We pray the same protection for ourselves as we journey back into safe territory. And for François, Lord, wherever he is—let him know you are with him. Amen."

Jean and Armond echoed their amens and finished their preparations to depart.

Madeleine watched Pierre as he disappeared from sight. *And, yes, may you and I meet again someday.*

A HIGH-PITCHED SCREAM PIERCED THE NIGHT. MADELEINE bolted awake, reached down, and picked Vangie up from her pallet. Sweat beaded on the child's forehead, and her hair was damp and warm. Madeleine rocked her daughter in her arms and could feel the child's heart pounding through her nightgown.

"Don't be afraid, Vangie. Maman is here with you." She wiped a strand of Vangie's hair from her eyes. "You are safe." The little girl began to calm down as her mother soothed and assured her. "Was it the same dream, *ma petite?*"

Vangie nodded her head. "It scares me. Something black and white is holding me on a horse, and I can't get away." She put her arms around her mother's neck and pulled herself closer. "I keep calling for you, but you never answer me. I can't find you."

"I know it's scary, my sweet Vangie. But it's only a dream. It's not real." *Not anymore*, Madeleine added to herself.

At least the dreams did not come every night as they had in the beginning. Madeleine continued to rock her daughter until she fell asleep again. She did not return Vangie to her pallet, but put the frightened child in bed with her.

Madeleine closed her eyes, but sleep escaped her. *François, where are you? What am I to do—remain here waiting for you? Try to find a place of our own somewhere else? Do you need rescuing as Vangie did? How do I find you?*

Her attempts at sleep were punctuated with tortured thoughts of François alone, cold, and hungry. His face, gaunt and dirty, haunted her dreams. Finally she dozed off in a fitful facsimile of sleep.

THE NEXT MORNING ELISABETH OPENED THE DOOR TO Madeleine's bedroom and stuck her head in just far enough to call to her daughter. "Wake up, sleepyhead. Time to get up." Upon seeing Vangie once again in Madeleine's bed, Elisabeth began to back out quietly.

Madeleine stretched and yawned. "It's all right. I was just waking up."

Elisabeth slipped in. "Dreams again?"

"Yes." Madeleine covered Vangie with the quilt she had kicked off during the night. "Though it's almost been a whole week this time." She kissed the sleeping child and eased out of bed. She pulled a robe from the bedpost and wrapped it around her shoulders as she stared at Vangie. "My eyes never get their fill of looking at her."

Elisabeth, too, watched the child as she slept. "There is nothing as serene and beautiful as a sleeping child."

Madeleine shivered and began to get dressed. "And our little princess is the most beautiful of all." The nickname Pierre coined during the rescue had stuck. "Well, you can tell summer is about gone. The mornings are getting cool again." She glanced toward the boys' pallet in the corner of the room. "I see the boys are up."

Elisabeth nodded. "Long ago. They are already in the barn with Henri and Armond, tending to the livestock. Are you coming?"

Madeleine slipped into her shoes and hurried after her mother. "Right behind you."

The Du Puy household was already bustling with the daily morning routine. Madeleine spooned some porridge out of the kettle hanging in the fireplace into a bowl.

Madame Du Puy was kneading bread at the worktable. "Another bad night?"

Madeleine got a spoon and sat down at the table with a pitcher of milk. "Not too bad. She's getting better all the time."

Charles bounded into the kitchen brandishing a wooden bucket filled with eggs. "Look what I found! The chickens made a new nest in the loft." He shoved the pail excitedly in Madeleine's face. "Where's Princess?" Charles had hardly let Vangie get out of his sight since she had returned to their family.

"She's still asleep—and don't go wake her up. Let her sleep."

"Did she have another dream? The same one? Why won't it go away?"

Madeleine grinned at her son. "Yes—yes—and I don't know." She finished her porridge and stood up to clean her bowl. "Have you eaten anything?"

Charles set the bucket on the table and was already running out the door. "*Oui*, Maman."

A moment later he reappeared. "Maman! Come out! It's Pastor Le Sueur."

A small black coach had pulled up in front of the house, and the two families gathered to greet the portly pastor and his wife. Madame Le Sueur, carrying a basket laden with pastries, alighted with some help from Pastor Du Puy.

Pastor Le Sueur bubbled over with his usual good-natured greetings. "We received word that the little girl had been rescued, and we wanted to come and meet her." He embraced each warmly, including the children. "Well? Where is she?"

Madeleine enthusiastically returned their hugs. "I'll go get her. She's still asleep."

But as Madeleine turned to go inside, the subject of their conversation appeared in the doorway, shielding her sleepy eyes against the morning sun. Her mother caught hold of Vangie's hand and walked toward the pastor and his wife.

"This is Vangie, our little princess."

Madame Le Sueur bent forward to speak to the child. "My, what a beautiful princess you are."

Vangie began to tremble and scream. "Get away from me! Maman! Maman! Don't let them take me! Get away! Get away!"

Madeleine could hardly control the hysterical child. She looked at Madame Le Sueur's black hat and black dress with its white collar, and retreated into the house. "I'm terribly sorry. Please excuse me. I'll get her calmed down and will be back in a moment."

Madeleine carried the child upstairs and tried to reassure her. "Vangie, did you think Madame Le Sueur was a nun?"

Vangie nodded and sniffled.

"She is not a nun, *ma petite*. That is Pastor Le Sueur and his wife from Geneva. They helped us when we escaped from France. They love us."

The child continued to whimper and cry, but Madeleine managed to calm her down and dress her. When they returned downstairs, the little girl cut a wide swath around the pastor and his wife, keeping her eyes on them as she circled the room, then darted out the door to play with the other children.

After sampling some of his wife's tasty pastries, Pastor Le Sueur summoned Madeleine aside. "A messenger came to the Cathédrale earlier in the week. I do not know where he was from, nor do I know the contents of the message." He handed her a simple parchment envelope with her name penned in familiar handwriting.

My dear Madeleine,
I have learned that François has been sentenced to the galleys.
I am so sorry.
   It is best that you consider him dead and move ahead with your life.
   My love to all. Give my little princess special regards from her prince.
                                        As ever, Pierre

FRANÇOIS TRUDGED ALONGSIDE AND BEHIND HIS FELLOW prisoners, stepping only as far as the chains would allow. The collar around his neck hung heavy and chafed his skin with each step. Other lines of unfortunates, many of them Huguenots, some criminals, had walked for many miles to reach the coast. Emaciated, weak, and filthy, they filed alongside and were assigned to the various ships.

François received his orders to be put on board a *galère* named *La Fidelle*, commanded by a Commodore de La Bourbonnais. The ship looked to him to be about a hundred and fifty feet long and fifty feet broad, with one deck, which covered the hold. The deck rose in the middle and sloped toward the edges to allow for the water to run off.

A rough-looking sailor approached François upon boarding. "You look like one of substance. Suppose you share some of your wealth with me, and I'll see that it goes well with you here."

François tried to ignore him, but the sailor would not let him alone. Finally the exhausted former seigneur answered the persistent sailor. "Leave me be, sir. I have nothing. It has been stripped from me already."

"You will not trifle with me, Infidéle! You are Huguenot, are you not?" The sailor jibed at him with a stick. "You could have enjoyed my protection, but your refusal will cost you. You've not heard the last of me."

François watched the ruffian stride up to the *sous-comite*, converse with him for a moment, then point in François' direction. The galley master, a silver whistle around his neck and a whip of cords in his hand, approached François. "My colleague informs me that you uttered horrid blasphemies against the Holy Virgin and all the saints in paradise."

François gasped. "No, sir. I did no such thing. He demanded money from me, and I have none."

"You are Huguenot, *non?*"

"Yes, but . . ."

The *sous-comite* blew his whistle and ordered François to remove his shoes. "We'll teach these new Huguenot recruits not to trifle with the authority of the king. Prepare to receive the *bastinado.*"

"But, sir, I have done nothing to deserve this."

"Silence! Or it will go harder with you."

A sandy-haired sailor approached with a grim smirk on his face, swinging a cane. "We haven't even set sail yet, and we are having a bit of rebellion here?"

"Take care of it and get back to your duties straightaway."

"Aye, sir. As you say, sir." The bully forced François down on the bench.

At that moment, as the sailor prepared to swing the cane at François' bare feet, a large man with graying hair and the rank of an officer came on board. He stopped in front of François. "What is the nature of this man's offense? How has he had time to cause any trouble?"

The sailor shrugged his shoulders. "I'm just following orders, sir. Ask the *sous-comite*."

"Hold your cane—and for that matter, your tongue—while I investigate."

"Aye, sir."

François began to shiver, not from the cold, but from the anticipation of the cruelty to be imposed upon him. Guilt or innocence seemed to have no meaning. He braced himself for the inevitable.

The officer returned, bent down, and asked him, "How came you to be guilty of such folly, as well as insolence, as to blaspheme the Catholic faith?"

"That is a false accusation, sir. I said none of those things. My religion forbids my insulting the faith of others. I simply had no money to give one of your sailors who was demanding it of me."

"I see. You seem to be a man of integrity, although one in chains. Many of our 'workers' these days seem to have arrived at their duties through no reason, except that they are Huguenot." The commander walked back and forth in front of François, scrutinizing him through eyes hooded with wrinkled, leathery eyelids. "Release this man, and put the cane away. No man is to be issued punishment of the basti-nado, except by my direct orders."

"Aye, Commodore."

It was a lesson François never forgot. Even in the hellish pit of the galleys, God did not leave his child without a rescuer that arose from a most unsuspecting place.

François was shoved toward a bench, covered with sackcloth and a cowhide, and chained to the apparatus along with six other men. Fifty benches lined the galley, twenty-five on each side. He bumped some-thing at his feet and found a board raised from the deck that he sur-mised must serve as a footstool to keep their feet out of the water.

He soon learned how to row, sitting naked with one foot on the footstool and the other resting on the bench before him, holding in his hands an enormous oar. He learned how to lengthen his body, stretch out his arms to push the oar over the backs of those in front of him, and then plunge the oar into the sea in rhythm. Labor that exhausted one in half an hour was sustained for hours. Many around him fainted from the fatigue and misery, only to be brought back by the whip. Sometimes they would be given a bit of bread dipped in wine if they fainted. Sometimes the weak ones would simply be unchained and thrown into the sea.

François vowed to stay strong. His faith grew stronger as his body grew weaker. He prayed to the rhythm of the rowing. He sang the Huguenot psalms to the rhythm of the rowing. He thought of Madeleine and his children to the rhythm of the rowing. And he waited.

TWENTY-THREE

Madeleine trudged through the motions of each day's chores. She had watched her life shatter before her eyes, but she had become numb. Caring for the children was her only incentive to rise each morning. She removed Pierre's letter from her apron pocket and reread it. Each time she read the message, her heart churned within her, and tears stood ready to spill over onto her cheeks. Why she read it over and over again, she did not know. It said the same thing every time. *François is suffering at the oars of a galley ship, and may already be dead.* She battled back and forth in her mind. They didn't know for sure that François was dead. He might survive. He might be able to escape.

But she knew she had to face reality. Hardly anyone survived the galleys—and if they did, they were so sick and diseased that they barely existed. Even if their bodies were alive, their minds were ravaged. But she so loved François that she could not relinquish her hope. She was willing to spend the rest of her life nursing him back to health. That she knew with certainty.

But was hope a luxury she could afford? What if he never returned? Their children needed a father to provide for them. How long should she wait? The constant introspection tore at her mind, ripping it into ribbons of doubt.

Madeleine heard Vangie and the boys laughing as they chased each other outside, throwing snowballs.

Vangie ran up on the porch screaming, "Maman! Make them stop!" Her unruly mahogany-colored curls, exactly the color of Madeleine's, escaped from under her cap and dripped wet from the hurled snowballs.

Madeleine yelled at her aggressive sons. "Boys! Stop that! She's too little—besides, she's a girl." She watched as Vangie ran back to taunt her brothers.

Madeleine held the door open for a moment and looked at the dreary winter reminders of death—dead trees, dead flowers, gray skies. She was unable to enjoy the pristine beauty of the fresh snowfall. She pulled her shawl around her shoulders. "Br-r-r-r. Winter lingers much too long here." Madeleine found it hard to believe that it had been nearly two springs ago that the dragoons invaded their manor.

Elisabeth's coughing pulled Madeleine inside. The older woman reclined on a *canapé* in front of the fireplace.

Madeleine crossed in front of her mother and went to the fireplace to stoke the fire. "I don't care how much wood we put in this fireplace, it doesn't seem to get any warmer in here." She sat down in front of her mother on a footstool. "May I get you anything? Would you like another blanket?"

Elisabeth shook her head. "Not right now." She spoke with difficulty. Her comment ended in a coughing spasm, and she gasped for breath.

"That potion the doctor had us make for you is doing no good. I'm sending Daniel to fetch him again."

"In a moment, Madeleine. Just sit here with me for a while." Elisabeth took her daughter's hand. "*Ma petite*, I am concerned about you. You must get on with your life. That's what François would want you to do." She paused and struggled for air. "Do you understand what I'm saying?"

Madeleine shook her head vigorously. "No, Maman, what are you saying? That I should try to find another husband? I can't even think about that right now. François might . . ."

Elisabeth stared into the fire. Madeleine could hear her mother's chest rattling as she labored to breathe.

"You must face the facts." Elisabeth leaned up on one elbow. "I know François was young and strong. Even at that, it's been over a year. Very few survive even for that length of time. And we've not heard from him. If there had been any way to get word to you, he would have done that. You must think—" A fit of coughing interrupted her sentence. "Think about the best situation for the children." She ended in another coughing convulsion and collapsed into the pillows.

Madeleine rearranged the pillows for her mother and tucked the quilt around her legs. "As long as there is a chance that François is alive, I cannot entertain thoughts of finding another mate." She took a handkerchief out of her apron and dabbed at her nose. "I am furious that Louis would be so cruel to our family as to subject someone I love to the galleys. That is not the Louis that I knew."

Elisabeth put her hand over her eyes and sighed. "Madeleine, that is probably the most sensible comment you have made concerning Louis. He is *not* the Louis you knew. We all tried to tell you that before you set off to Versailles to try to collect on old declarations of undying love."

Madeleine corrected her mother. "No, Maman. It was Louis who tried to collect on old declarations of undying love. I simply appealed to him for mercy."

A long, awkward silence dampened their conversation—each woman lost in her own thoughts. The fire sizzled and popped. Madeleine could hear the laughter of the children still playing in the snow outside. Elisabeth closed her eyes. Thinking her mother had dozed off, Madeleine started to leave.

"Madeleine, sit back down, please."

Madeleine complied and came back to the footstool.

Elisabeth reached for her daughter's hand, but stared blankly into space. Then, her eyes filling with tears, she looked directly at Madeleine. "What I'm trying to say is—I-I really don't think I am going to be around much longer to help you."

"Nonsense, Maman. You will be better soon. You can't leave me too. I won't let you!" Madeleine pulled her mother's frail frame into her arms, and tears rolled down her cheeks. "You're going to be just fine. You simply need to rest and stay warm." She eased Elisabeth down into the pillows. "I'm going to get you some tea."

"Yes, dear. That would be nice. *Merci.*" Elisabeth's voice was only a whisper.

MADELEINE SAT WITH HER MOTHER THROUGH THE NIGHT. Jean joined her and kept a watch on the fire. Pastor Du Puy checked on them periodically. Elisabeth's breathing became more labored, and Madeleine cooled her fever with a damp cloth and encouraged her mother to drink sips of tea.

At one point Elisabeth looked at Madeleine and said, "What are you doing here so late? François will be concerned."

Then suddenly, toward morning, she lifted her right hand toward the ceiling. "Do you see them?"

Madeleine looked around the room and saw nothing. "No, Mère. Lie back down. There's no one here but you and me."

"Yes, there in the corner. Don't you see them? They have come for me."

"Maman, what do you see?" Madeleine's eyes widened, searching the corner of the room. "Are you seeing angels?"

Elisabeth looked at her daughter and nodded and smiled. "And there's *Père* and Dina and a young man with her. Oh, don't you see them? Look at the colors. I've never seen such colors. And the light. It's brilliant. Oh, how beautiful!" She lay back on her pillow with a smile on her face and lapsed into a deep sleep.

Madeleine stifled a sob and looked at Jean, who had come to the bedside and heard all Elisabeth had said. "It's her time, Madeleine. Let her go."

Elisabeth's breathing grew shallow, and by morning she was gone.

Madeleine rocked back and forth on the stool, moaning and praying. "*Mon Dieu, mon Dieu.* Why have you taken her from me? I need her. What do I do now?"

She would not leave her mother's side so that Madame Du Puy and her husband could prepare the body for burial, and she flung Pastor Du Puy's hand off her shoulder. "Don't tell me she's in a better place. I need her here with me. Doesn't God care what *I* need? My husband is probably dead. I have no home. My mother didn't have the privilege of dying in her own bed—she died on a borrowed couch, for God's sake!" Sobs racked her body. "I can't even bury her next to my father."

She raised a tearstained face to Pastor Du Puy. "Don't you give me any religious platitudes. If God loves me so much, why has he abandoned me? Do you have an answer for that, good pastor? Tell me, do you?" Madeleine started toward the stairs. "It's because of God that we are in this mess in the first place. We should have agreed to convert and play King Louis' game. At least we would all still be alive, and my husband and children would be enjoying their own home. Or perhaps I should have agreed to become Louis' mistress. Even that would be better than this." She flew up the stairs, leaving an astonished audience of family and servants behind.

Jean started after her, but Henri stopped him. "No, Jean. Give her time to grieve. She will be all right after a bit."

HENRI DROVE THE TEAM BEARING HIS LONGTIME MISTRESS'S coffin to the Cathédrale de St. Pierre in Geneva. Madeleine, a sleeping Vangie on her lap, spoke in low tones to Jean as they swayed back and forth in the coach. "I know she would have wanted to be buried next to Father, but that was impossible." She looked at Jean, her dark eyelashes wet with tears. "Do you think she would understand?"

Jean's arm rested loosely around her shoulders. "*Absolument.* Under normal circumstances we would have done that, but we are not living in normal circumstances."

Madeleine nodded. "I know." She laid her gloved hand on Jean's knee. "What would I do without you? You have been the true hero."

Jean blushed, even through his olive skin. He untangled his arm from Madeleine's cloak and pulled on his gloves. "I'm here for you and the boys as long as you need me. I love Philippe and Charles as my own . . . and with Dina gone, I don't have any . . . any other responsibilities." He paused, and unshed tears filled his eyes. "I have no place else I can go, or want to go."

"Your place is with us, Jean, and I need you."

Jean nodded and turned away from Madeleine to look out the window at the wintry scene.

The coach turned and came to a stop in front of the cathedral. Madeleine tied the black taffeta bow on her bonnet tighter under her chin and shook Vangie awake. "We're here, *mon petite.*"

The rest of the family, servants, and friends in three coaches following the lead carriage descended in a cloud of mourning black into a white veil of snow. Pastor Le Sueur and Jacob came out in the threatening snowstorm to help the party inside.

Pastor Du Puy came alongside Madeleine and Jean on the steps to the Cathédrale. The snow blew in their eyes and stuck in the pastor's beard.

Madeleine took his arm. "Gérard, the night that my mother died— I didn't mean—I am so sorry for what I said. I—well, I apologize for my outburst. Forgive me."

"Think nothing of it, my child. You had just cause to feel the way you did. And besides that . . ." He smiled. "God can handle our outbursts, and I imagine Elisabeth was amused as well."

The funeral service consisted of some of Elisabeth's favorite psalms, a few words from the pastors, and a quick interment at the cathedral, as the snowstorm was building in intensity. The actual burial would wait until spring.

Pastor Le Sueur addressed the family after the service. "I would venture to say that you are not going to make it back home tonight. We will put you up for the night."

MADELEINE LAY IN HER BED AFTER ANOTHER OF MADAME Le Sueur's hearty meals. She knew she had to make some decisions. Where would they go? What would they do? She wished she had her mother here now to lend her wisdom.

Mon Dieu, can I still pray to you? Do you hear my prayers? Are you even concerned about our plight? You did see us safely back into France, and for that I thank you. And you did make a way for us to find Vangie.

Madeleine wiped at the tears that trickled down onto her pillow.

I suppose I have been ungrateful, haven't I, when everything didn't go exactly as I wished? I am beginning to realize that even when trials and death and suffering descend upon us, it doesn't mean you have abandoned us. I ask your forgiveness. If there is not hope with you, then we are devoid of hope. Would you give me direction as to what I am to do next?

She quoted aloud the verse that had been her anchor through the unimaginably difficult days of the past two years. She needed to hear the sound of her own voice citing the Scripture. "And thine ears shall hear a word behind thee, saying, This is the way, walk ye in it, when ye turn to the right hand, and when ye turn to the left."

I'm listening, Dieu, I truly am. And I am going to continue to pray for François until I know for sure he is gone. Would you please send ministering angels to help him?

THE FEEBLE ELDERLY MAN SAT AT HIS DESK GOING OVER the books from his fleet of ships. His time in the Bastille had taken its toll on his body. Although treated reasonably well in the king's high-class prison, the dampness of the air and the dank conditions disagreed with his creaky joints. By the time he was pardoned and released, his business was in chaos.

He slammed a heavy ledger shut with a bang. "Bah! What does one hire an associate for, if not to keep accurate records? I cannot even balance the assets and debits columns."

Dust billowed from the books as he took them down from the shelves one by one. His thinning gray hair crept out of the band that he had tied at the nape of his neck and fell into his face over his eyes.

His crooked, arthritic finger skated down the lists of employees, including the galley slaves—the expendable human commodity that propelled his ships. He stopped at a familiar name. "What's this?" He scratched his chin through the sparse stubble of a beard. "Could it be?" He muttered the catchy little singsong phrase, "François Clavell, François Clavell, stole the king's mademoiselle."

He rose from his desk, picked up his gold embossed walking stick, put on his hat, tucked the book under his arm, and walked out of his office door directly onto the dock. The smell of the sea always served to rejuvenate the old gentleman.

Farther down the landing pier, his crews were unloading a large shipment of goods from Spain. The captain of the fleet barked orders to the men. "Can't you go any faster? Lift hearty there, mate!"

The owner of the fleet approached the crusty sea captain. "*Bonjour!* How goes it?"

The captain, chewing on a stained pipe, switched the nasty device to the side of his mouth and spoke around it. "*Bonjour*, monsieur. Well, if these sisters would move faster, we could be on our way yet today, but it looks like it will be tomorrow before we can set sail." He took the pipe out of his mouth and spat on the wooden platform.

Opening the book, the older gentleman stabbed his finger at the name. "I want to see this man."

The captain looked at the log. "A galley slave? You want to see a galley slave?"

"Those are my orders. Bring him to me immediately." He pointed in the direction of *La Fidelle* tied to huge wooden posts where the cargo lay stacked. "He should be on *that* ship."

TWENTY-FOUR

Cold. Icy, bone-penetrating cold. Madeleine struggled against the silence. Her mouth twisted in soundless efforts to scream. Whispers shouted into the stillness of the night. *Dead, Madeleine. François is dead. Give up. Nobody survives the galleys. You will never see François again.*

Macabre images of bloody backs straining against the oars of the galleys mocked her. Her breathing quickened, and she huddled under the heavy quilt. Ghoulish eyes teetered on the edge of her consciousness. She fought against the darkness, yet the sense of evil persisted, invading her mind and tearing at her soul. This was no dream. She was fully awake. Sweat trickled down her neck and dampened her gown.

Madeleine reached across the bed and touched Vangie. Her daughter stirred and turned over as Madeleine rearranged the quilt the tiny legs had kicked off during the night. Shivering, she lay back down. Within the darkness, the clammy atmosphere persisted, wrapping around her like a wet blanket. She could see nothing. She put her hand in front of her face—only black, inky gloom. *Is this what it's like to die? Completely alone in suffocating darkness? Is this what it's like for François?*

She felt along the floor with her feet and slid them into her slippers, grabbed her robe, and checked for the candle on the bedside table. Finding it, she moved quickly to the fireplace. Groping for the poker, she touched the cold metal handle, hoisted the tool, and began to stir the embers. Placing a piece of kindling next to the candlewick, she coaxed a flickering flame from the sparks.

She checked on her two sons, asleep on their pallets. Madeleine exhaled a small stream of vapor into the frigid early morning air. Odd—it felt as if there were no warmth left on earth—as if she'd been abandoned to the pitch-black dampness of the grave.

She returned to the fireplace, and even though the fire began to take hold, no warmth issued into the room. Charles moaned in his sleep. "Papa. Don't . . . don't . . . !" His voice trailed off into his dreams.

Vangie whimpered.

The curtains, closed against the windows, started moving. Ah! That was it—she must have left a window open when retiring for the night. Madeleine threw aside the fabric to shut the window, but the pane was firmly closed. Dumbfounded, she watched the curtains continue to sway. She stepped back, her heart pounding.

A breathy voice hissed from the windows, *Madeleine.*

A shudder ran down her spine.

You may as well give up. He's dead—François is dead. He died a torturous cruel death, all because he wouldn't deny your so-called God. Odious laughter filled the air. *That's what is going to happen to you if you don't give up. And what horrible things will happen to your children when you are gone?*

Madeleine's skin crawled with fear, and she lurched backward, covering her ears with her hands. "Stop it! Stop it! I know who you are—you are the Father of Lies, and I will not listen to you." She began to tremble, but her voice resonated with power. "Be gone from us in the name of Jesus!"

She rushed to the door and wrenched it open, calling into the hallway, "Pastor Du Puy! Pastor Du Puy! Come quickly—something's happening in here!"

Vangie sat up amidst the rumpled bedclothes and began to cry. Philippe, ever the protective older brother, leapt from his pallet and raced to the fireplace for his musket. Charles sat on his knees rubbing his eyes and blinking at the confusion. The curtains ceased to sway as the fire licked cheerily into action, and the icy atmosphere diminished. The roosters in the barnyard began their early morning serenade.

Hair askew and skinny bowlegs emerging from beneath his nightshirt, Gérard, with his rotund wife behind him, stumbled into Madeleine's room. "In the name of Jesus, what's all this commotion?"

Jean bounded up the stairs. "Madeleine!"

Madeleine clutched her robe around her. "All this commotion has nothing to do with Jesus—it's the devil himself, that's what it is." She quickly related the events of the past few moments.

"Ooh, *oui*, that would be old Beelzebub himself harassing you."

Nobody spoke for several seconds. Jean leaned against the banister. The children stared at their mother, and Charles climbed into the bed beside Vangie.

Madame Du Puy turned and started out the door. "Everything seems to be in order now. Shall I go start breakfast?"

The kindly pastor scratched his beard. "Of course, of course. You must do that." He watched his wife leave the room, and when she was gone, he asked, "Are you all right?"

Madeleine wrapped her arms around herself and sighed. "I suppose so. Yes, I'm fine."

"Very well, then. Get dressed and come downstairs." He put his hand on the door latch and surveyed the room. "We need to discuss this. And do not allow fear to overwhelm you. God does not abandon his children."

Madeleine hustled Charles and Vangie, still in their bedclothes, down the stairs with Philippe, who had pulled on his trousers. She dressed herself hurriedly and followed.

The household began to spring to life with its usual early morning bustle, unaware of the supernatural events that had occurred in the room over their heads. Jean went outside to tend to the livestock. Henri entered through the back door with a pail of fresh milk, followed by Suzanne with her apron full of brown eggs gathered from the chicken pens.

Pastor Du Puy sat at the end of the large trestle table with his Bible open. "Sit down, Madeleine. Let's talk about your encounter this morning."

Madeleine sat down across from the pastor. Turning pages in his Bible, Pastor Du Puy stopped in the New Testament book of Ephesians. "I'm thinking the devil is putting thoughts into your mind to give up in your attempts to find François, because he knows François is still alive."

She leaned toward the pastor. "My thoughts exactly."

"Of course. Otherwise, why would he bother?" Gérard turned a few more pages and read, "For we wrestle not against flesh and blood, but against principalities, against powers, against the rulers of the darkness of this world, against spiritual wickedness in high places."

"That's what we witnessed upstairs." Madeleine settled her children at the table with bowls of hot boiled meal. "But why would the devil think us a threat? All I want is our family back together."

"Exactly. A strong family, united, who believes in and follows God is a threat of major proportions to the devil. You come from a courageous heritage, Madeleine. You are raising your children to reverence God. You have personally opposed a profession of faith that speaks out of one side of the mouth, but lives according to fleshly desires."

"You speak of Louis?"

"I speak of all who make a mockery of what the Scriptures teach. Those who profess a belief in God but continue to live in wickedness and debauchery. All who kneel in piety as they discharge their duty, but care not for the poor, nor have compassion for the hungry." Pastor Du Puy put his hand over Madeleine's. "My dear, only eternity will reveal what is at stake in these days. Your true enemy is not Louis. The enemy of our souls, Satan himself, is your true enemy and the one who stands ready to battle for your defeat at every turn."

Madeleine looked at the kind countenance of this man of God seated across from her. He had come to her rescue many times in the past two years. Her eyes filled with tears. "I don't want to battle with the enemy. I'm just a woman—a wife and mother. I want my husband back, and I want to go home."

"So was Deborah in the Old Testament, just a woman—and Abigail and Esther. Mary, the mother of our Lord, was just a woman, and Priscilla and Phoebe—and Joan of Arc."

Madeleine shook her head. "Surely you cannot be comparing me to those women—and certainly not to Joan of Arc. I have no battle to fight with the king, except to have my family back and to live in peace."

"No, my dear. I am not saying that you are to don the armor of a knight, take up a sword, and gallop in front of an army. But I am saying that as St. Joan fought a battle for what she believed was God's cause, you are also fighting a battle for the furtherance of his kingdom. But it is a spiritual battle." Pastor Du Puy closed his Bible and clasped his hands in front of him. "That is why you are being harassed by Satan."

Madeleine stood and clenched her fists at her side. "I'm tired of fighting, and I'm tired of running." The tone of her voice escalated and perched on the edge of hysteria. "I don't want to hide any longer in a foreign country in somebody else's house. I want to go home—to my own home—and raise my children with my husband on our estate. And I want..."

Her words hung in the air as Madame Du Puy paused with her spoon in hand, dripping porridge into the kettle. Henri and Suzanne stared at their mistress's outburst. Her children watched wide-eyed as their mother railed.

I want . . . I want. She sounded like a spoiled child. Madeleine lowered herself wearily back to her place at a table that did not belong to her, in a kitchen that had been offered to her family as a welcome refuge, and buried her face in her hands.

"But I can't, can I?" She looked at Pastor Du Puy, tears trickling down her cheeks. "It's impossible, isn't it? It will never be the same."

Vangie crawled onto her mother's lap and began to wipe the tears away with her sleeve. Philippe's lanky form unfolded to stand behind his mother, and Charles scooted over beside Madeleine and laid his head on her other shoulder.

"Gérard . . ." Madeleine's defenses crumbled in the face of the unsettling events of the morning. "What am I to do? My mother is gone. François is lost to us, at least for now, and nearly all of our money is gone. I know not where to turn."

Pastor Du Puy shook his head. "I'm not sure either. We will pray, and God will show you. He will speak to you, but you must trust what you hear from him and follow his direction."

Find François.

Madeleine cocked her head and paused. The command was as strong as if God had shouted it from heaven. After a moment she spoke, and her voice had grown calm, her words measured. "Even as you were speaking, I believe God revealed to me what I am to do."

"Go on."

"I must try once more to find François."

"And if your search turns up nothing?"

"If my search is in vain, I will consider going to the New World to start over." Madeleine drew her children close and looked at the Du Puys. "You two have gone the second mile with us—much beyond what anyone could need or expect—but it is too painful for me to be this close to France and not be able to return. Perhaps in a completely different environment—one where we are free to worship and seek God according to our own beliefs—we can begin anew." She shifted Vangie on her lap. "You do understand, don't you?"

"Completely. But let's not be hasty. We can talk about a trip to the New World later." The pastor shuffled his feet as he shifted his weight on the bench. "I hate to think of you tackling a feat such as that—a woman alone, with children. Of course, you have Jean, but he's young. Surely he will eventually have a family of his own." He shook his head. "No, let's exhaust every possibility we can think of here first."

Gérard stood and began to pace. "We need to formulate a plan to find François. However, I'm not sure I have any ideas. We can't go to every seaport in France and look for him."

"No, of course not." Madeleine hesitated. "Perhaps . . . perhaps I shall contact Pierre again to see if he has any more news."

Gérard shook his head. "Don't you think he would have communicated with you if he knew anything else?"

"Possibly. But I have to try something. Pierre is still our best source." Madeleine stood and walked to the window. "I feel . . ." She stopped and continued to stare to the south, toward her homeland. She touched her chest. "The heart that truly loves senses what is alive in the spirit—and my spirit perceives that François is alive."

The reluctant warrior turned toward the early morning gathering with new resolve in her voice. "That's what we will do. I shall send word to Pierre to meet me at the Cathédrale in Geneva and see exactly what he knows."

The striking figure of the handsome courtier riding away after Vangie's rescue remained in her mind. They could not have made it this far without him. Vangie would have remained lost to them. Would he be willing to risk his position, and conceivably even his life, once again, to help them? The idea of seeing him excited her, but she quickly put the thought away.

Pastor Du Puy joined Madeleine at the window. "Consider this, *ma chérie*. He may have lost his good standing in Louis' court after helping you rescue Vangie from the convent."

"Well then, I suppose we shall soon find out."

TWENTY-FIVE

François heard scuffling, but dared not open his eyes. He could not bear to watch the rats scurrying among the putrid conditions of the galleys, scavenging for any crumb of bread dropped on the slimy boards or for a bite of unprotected human flesh. He drew his hands up to his chest to protect them from the vermin—and then realized he was in a bed—not on a hard wooden bench.

He inhaled—not the stench of urine and human waste, but the welcome aroma of a bubbling stew. Had this all been a horrible nightmare? Was he back home?

François licked his parched lips and squinted through half-open eyelids. The indistinct shape of a bespeckled elderly gentleman talking to a servant appeared. The servant held a kettle by its handle, covered with a protective cloth. François watched as the servant pulled some glowing coals to the side from the flames and nestled the kettle into them, then left the room.

The old man shuffled to a rocker and dragged it close to the fire. Pulling a shawl around his shoulders, he began a rhythmic movement back and forth in the rocker and picked up a Bible. The boards creaked as the old man tipped forward and backward.

François pushed up on one elbow and groaned. Pain raged through the tender lesions on his back as bandages slipped away from his wounds.

"Ah, finally, you are awake." The man stood and moved to François' bedside. "Take it easy, son. Your wounds are still festering." He pulled his spectacles down on his nose and examined the sores.

François struggled to sit upright. "Who—who are you? And where am I?"

"You don't remember me?"

"I'm sorry, sir, but I don't." François winced as his rescuer explored the lacerations.

"My name is Isaac Fourié, but you wouldn't know who I am by name. I own the fleet of ships to which you were sentenced as a galley slave."

"But . . . why am I . . . ?"

"Shhh. Be patient, my boy. I'll answer all your questions, at least the ones I can—in due time. First things first. Let's take care of this before we talk." Monsieur Fourié turned to a bench at the foot of the bed on which servants had left clean white cloths and hot water. He tore the cloths into strips and with gentle hands applied ointment and a clean dressing to François' back. "There, that should feel a little better."

"Are you a physician?"

"I am not, but I will gladly tend to your wounds. As I told you, I run a fleet of ships. Are you hungry?"

"Thirsty—I'm so thirsty."

"That's to be expected. You've lost a lot of blood."

Monsieur Fourié uncorked a bottle of wine and assisted François in sitting up. "This will help with the pain as well as your thirst."

François gulped the tangy liquid and sank back into the pillows. "Thank you."

"You are very weak and in need of more than just wine." The kind gentleman ladled some hot broth into a bowl from the kettle in the fireplace and set it down on an ornate table next to the bed. He plumped the pillows behind François to support him and began spooning the brew to François as if he were a child.

The hot mixture of vegetables and broth warmed his throat and belly, and he took the spoon and bowl from his benefactor and began to feed himself.

"Easy now. Not too much too fast." The old gentleman chuckled and took the nearly empty bowl away. "Your stomach will rebel if we put too much in too quickly."

François sighed and laid back down in what he now realized was a luxurious canopy bed, piled with soft quilts and pillows. A tiny ray of sunlight poked through a slit in the heavy draperies. He couldn't tell if it was morning or afternoon. He closed his eyes and sank into the smooth coverings, grateful for the sanctuary. He turned his head and watched the old man as he gathered the bloody dressings and rang for a servant. Wispy gray hair fell across his benefactor's face out of his queue.

Suddenly François' mind raced back to the old man he had met in prison—the stringy gray hair falling across his weathered face. "*O mon Dieu,* you are the one from the Bastille!"

Monsieur Fourié smiled at François as the servant entered and picked up the medical supplies. "Yes, you are right. *C'est moi.*"

"This is your house? How did you get out of . . . how did I get here? Why am I here?"

Monsieur Fourié sat on the bed beside François and began to weave his tale of his release from prison soon after meeting François. "I was in the Bastille upon a whim of our illustrious king. I defied him, and he merely wanted to exert his authority. Upon returning to my shipping business—which I must say had declined to a tawdry state of disarray during my absence—I ran across your name in the list of galley slaves and wondered if it could possibly be the same young man I had met in the king's prison."

He chuckled. "François Clavell, François Clavell, stole the king's mademoiselle. If it hadn't been for that little jingle in my head, I never would have recognized your name among the others. God does indeed work in mysterious ways, does he not?"

François stared at the obviously wealthy gentleman. "You are very kind, sir. I am indebted to you." He turned his hands over and rubbed his sensitive wrists that iron cuffs had encircled only the day before. "But what do you intend to do with me?"

"*Do* with you?" Monsieur Fourié gave a hearty laugh, jarring the bed.

François winced.

"Oh, how thoughtless of me. I am sorry." Isaac eased himself off the edge of the bed. He pulled his rocking chair across the floor and resumed the creaking rhythm. "Do you recall that I am Huguenot as well?"

François nodded.

"My sentence to the Bastille came about because the king was angry with me for challenging his orders to turn my fleet of ships into war vessels. When I recanted and agreed to allow a percentage of them to be confiscated for that purpose, he released me from prison. Of course, he could have taken them himself with a sweep of his hand, but Louis has his good side—at times."

François scoffed. "That I have failed to observe firsthand. However, my wife assures me it is the case."

Isaac smiled. "In addition to any kindly leanings the king might have had toward me personally, we are somewhat related—or shall we say, connected." He rubbed his thin goatee as his smile warmed to a chuckle. "His mistress is my cousin, and I suspect she appealed to him on my behalf."

"Madame de Montespan?"

"*Oui.* And quite a woman she is." Isaac leaned forward. "I am passing on my good fortune to you. As soon as you are well and able to travel, you are free to go."

He pushed his feeble frame up from his chair and paced in front of the fireplace. "I am afraid that my time in our king's 'special facility' has taken its toll on me as well. My arthritis pains me. I am weak, and I am old. It's to be expected. You-you have a chance to recover and resume your life. Our paths didn't cross by accident. God directs human events, and I am simply his instrument of healing toward another of his flock."

François' eyes filled with tears. "I am indebted to you, my friend. May God repay your kindness. But I have nothing to offer you at this time." He swung his legs over the edge of the bed and hesitated before putting his feet on the cold floor. "If I could just get to my estate and my family . . ."

Isaac stood and held François' elbow as the younger man attempted to stand.

"Let me walk a bit. I need to try to get my strength back."

The frail pair, the arthritic old man and the young man weak from dehydration and malnutrition, slowly placed one foot in front of the other as they moved across the room.

Beneath the tall, heavily draped window, François collapsed onto an elegant couch. "Where are we? I mean, how far am I from Grenoble?" He pulled the drapery aside to view the countryside. What he saw were not the rolling hills, rivers, and trees he was accustomed to, but the teeming docks of the waterfront, billowing sails of fleets of ships, and seagulls and fish merchants. "What seaport is this?"

"Brest. You are in Brest."

François groaned. "I couldn't be any farther from Grenoble and still be in France." He lay back on the small couch. "I must get back to my wife and children. They need me."

"Yes, of course they do. But of what benefit will you be to them if you die on the way? You need to heal first, then we will get you home." Isaac pulled a quilt from the back of the couch and covered François' legs. "Try to sleep, son."

François closed his eyes. He would doze, and then his consciousness would rise to a dream world of undulating waves, creaking oars, and the cruel cracking of a whip ending in unbidden moans wrenched from François' throat. Then he would sink once again into the welcomed relief of sleep.

THE FIRE HAD DWINDLED; A CHILL CAME OVER THE ROOM. François awakened and realized he was still on the couch. Struggling to sit up, he reached toward the window and pulled the draperies aside. Clouds, like brilliant orange torches lit by the setting sun, poked their fingers into a darkening night sky and hovered over the watery horizon. Monsieur Fourié was nowhere in sight.

François forced himself to stand on wobbly legs and watched the approaching nightfall. He pushed on the leaded windowpane, and the putrid whiff of rotting fish from the nearby dock assaulted his nostrils. The memory of lashes and iron cuffs and beatings rushed over him.

Daylight struggled against the encroaching nightfall as if it begrudged giving up its light to the darkness. Seagulls screeched, and the docks began to empty. Vendors pushed their carts under cover for the night. *Le Fidelle* floated lazily atop the calm water of the port, tugging on the huge ropes that lashed it to the dock.

Strange. From this vantage point, it was a beautiful ship. Most of the passersby had no idea of the horror encased within the vessel that enabled it to make its journeys. How many men struggled against the oars, like the waning sunlight, and had given up their lives to the impinging darkness?

Why has God in his mercy declared that I am to live? Why has he so graciously rescued me? François had no answers.

Weary and emaciated, he returned to his bed. He picked up the flask of wine. With a trembling hand he poured himself a glass as the rim clanked against a fine crystal goblet. He gulped down every last drop before surrendering himself to the welcome indulgence of the soft mattress.

Images of his daughter caught in the arms of the dragoon commander as he carried her away atop his stallion tortured his mind. Commander Boveé—that name would be forever etched in his memory. Was Vangie in a safe place? Or was she cold and hungry?

François' physical pain tormented his thinking so much that he could not seem to formulate a clear strategy to reunite with his family. But he knew he must join them as soon as he could. More cruel questions jabbed at his memory. *Did the boys escape from the cave? Did Madeleine rescue them from their hiding place and take them to Geneva? Is Jean with them? Does Madeleine even know I'm alive? Does she know I was sentenced to the galleys? How could she possibly know? What if she has given up on finding me? How long has it been?* He had tried to mark the passing of time even while on the ship, but eventually lost track. Could it possibly be that two years had passed?

François' dark eyes blinked open and his heart raced. He tried to sleep, but memories of Madeleine punctured any attempt to escape into the blessed world of non-thought. He poured himself another goblet of wine—and then another. The room began to spin. At last he fell into a troubled slumber.

TWENTY-SIX

Pierre pulled on his gloves and made his way through the maze of halls and out into the teeming outer courtyard of Versailles. Diplomats from around the world rushed from the stables and gathered in clumps, debating over one political issue or another. It was easy to spot the new arrivals.

The splendor of Versailles never failed to overwhelm Pierre, no matter how long he was there or how many times he returned. The palace seemed to have a blossoming soul of its own. Constant construction challenged the imagination with what would appear next. Water gushed from fountains, urns, and statues amidst the lavish botanical display, renowned as one of the most abundant and magnificent gardens in the world. Louis' penchant for exotic plants confronted the beholder at every turn and overflowed with lush color. The king's appetite for bigger and better seemed to be insatiable.

Entering the huge stables, Pierre beckoned a servant to fetch his horse, then removed from his tunic the letter Francina had delivered to him the night before.

The domestic's merry countenance never failed to lift his spirits. She had curtsied and handed him an envelope with familiar handwriting. "Monsieur, I have news from my relatives in Geneva."

The wide Boveé smile raced across his face. "Ah! Does the family fare well?"

"*Oui*, monsieur. If you please, the note is for you. I do believe you have an admirer." She smiled and curtsied again and left.

Pierre had looked at his name on the envelope. In spite of his determination to insulate his heart, his hands trembled as he broke open the seal.

My dear Pierre,
I trust this finds you well in your position at court.

Pierre chuckled at Madeleine's cleverness. He knew she was wondering if he had been discovered for his participation in rescuing Vangie from the convent.

Will be in Geneva on the first Sabbath of next month. I would like very much to see you. Would it be possible to meet me at our regular place?

Regards, M

Our regular place. The overtones were those of a lover's note. Pierre's heart quickened and his hopes rose at the possible implications. He knew she meant the cathedral where she and her family had found refuge as they had fled France. Pastor Le Sueur had been a compassionate and reliable contact point.

Pierre had watched Francina's plump figure disappear into the darkness of the massive hallway. He folded the letter, tucked it safely away inside his tunic, and returned to his evening duties.

Now a young stable boy brought Pierre's horse to him. Pierre slung his gear behind the saddle and tied it securely.

Pierre looked at the innocence and eagerness etched on the boy's face. "Would you like to be a courtier in the court?"

"*Oui*, monsieur. I would like that very much."

"I wish it were mine to grant to you, my boy. But, beware. The outward grandeur of the court hides a tangled web of intrigue and pitfalls."

"*Oui*, but is it not the most exciting life to lead?"

"The familiar soon becomes boredom."

Pierre had whatever, and whomever, he desired with merely a nod of his head or the whisper of an intention. He danced with the most beautiful and elegant women in the country, but it was Madeleine's face he saw in each partner, and it was her voice he heard in the music.

"I do not think I would ever become bored with King Louis' court." The boy held the bridle of the prancing stallion. "Are you going on a long journey, sir?"

"I'm not sure." Pierre mounted his Percheron. "But if God is kind, it may turn out to be the journey of a lifetime." He tipped his hat and waved to the lad as he galloped toward the gates of Versailles.

MADELEINE STEPPED OUT OF THE CARRIAGE AND LET HER hand linger on the door handle. She looked skyward. The square towers of John Calvin's cathedral echoed the faith to which the Vaudois and Clavell families had given their lives.

"Jean, would you find Pastor Le Sueur and let him know we are here? Judith and I will wait for you."

Judith descended from the carriage complaining of the rough ride. "I'm not as young as I used to be."

"I know, and I am indebted to you for agreeing to come with me."

Judith removed Madeleine's case from the coach and set it on the cobblestone walk.

Before Jean could reach the top of the cathedral steps, the heavy door creaked open and the dour face of Pastor Le Sueur's assistant poked through.

"Ah, Monsieur Clavell. What a pleasant surprise. Come in, come in." Pastor Veron pulled the door back, and a slight smile creased his usually sober appearance.

Madeleine reached the top step and offered her hand. "Pastor Veron. How nice to see you again."

Pastor Veron held her hand in his limp, delicate one, too soft for a man's hand. "I will let Pastor Le Sueur know you are here. What brings you to Geneva?"

"I suppose you could say business. Once again we require a meeting place and, of necessity, are appealing to your gracious hospitality."

"Of course, madame." He nodded and ushered them into the impressive foyer.

Jean cradled Madeleine's elbow as she started into the dimly lit hallway.

"I'll be fine. You can tend to the horses. Judith will stay with me."

Jean hesitated. "But . . ."

"Go on, Jean, I'll be fine. See that our carriage is taken care of. Then come inside and join me."

Jean reluctantly left her side.

Pastor Veron indicated the way with a wave of his hand. "Please follow me. I know Pastor Le Sueur will be eager for an update. He is studying for his sermon on the morrow."

Madeleine and Judith's footsteps echoed through the corridor as they hurried to keep up with Pastor Veron.

"Any word on your husband?"

"I'm afraid not."

"Oh. I'm truly sorry."

For the first time, Madeleine detected a note of genuine compassion in the wiry assistant's voice. "Thank you."

They continued in silence down the darkened hallway and entered the musty office that once before had been a welcome refuge for the Clavell family. Hunched over his books, the man of God in this historic place of worship did not look up immediately.

Madeleine hesitated to venture farther into the office, although Jacob strode straight to the front of the desk and cleared his throat. "Ahem, monsieur—we have visitors—the Clavells."

"Oh!" Pastor Le Sueur stood and rushed to greet Madeleine, knocking a book off the stack.

Madeleine curtsied as the portly gentleman approached her.

"Madame Clavell, how wonderful to see you again." Laughing, he took her hand. "We think of you often and wonder how you have fared. Your children—are they with you? And the Du Puys, are they well? Any word on your husband?"

Madeleine giggled. She had forgotten Pastor Le Sueur's propensity for verbosity. "We are all well. The Du Puys send their best wishes. The children stayed behind with them. Jean and I have come to make one more attempt to locate François." She looked around for a chair.

"Forgive me, madame. Please, sit here." Pastor Le Sueur pulled a heavy chair to the front of his desk for her as he perched on the edge of the dark piece of furniture.

Madeleine eased herself onto the cushion. "Ah, this feels good after that carriage ride." She evaded the pastor's eyes and looked down at her hands as she spoke. "I have sent for Pierre Boveé. He is the most reliable resource we have at court. God's hand is directing us to continue our search for François, but we need information, and Pierre is our best option." She sat forward in her chair. "I pray you can support our effort by offering us a rendezvous point."

Pastor Le Sueur stroked his beard. "I know of no reason why we cannot assist you in your quest to find your husband." He searched Madeleine's eyes and reached for her hand. Several seconds passed.

"My child, may I speak frankly?" The pastor did not wait for an answer. "You must guard your heart. Much more is at stake in these uncertain days than the satisfying of one's emotional longings. As long as François lives, you are bound to him."

"Of course, monsieur. I would not—"

"I know. I am confident of that." The paternal pastor patted Madeleine's hand as he talked. "But whichever you feed the most— one's heart or one's convictions—will become the stronger, and in the final analysis will claim victory. Be cautious. Do not allow your heart to dictate your actions."

Madeleine lowered her head and nodded.

The pastor continued, "God knows the end from the beginning. He has predestined your mission. Look at the strategic areas in which he has placed you to speak up for his glory. You had the king's ear—and from what I can discern, a piece of his heart."

"Yes, but he didn't listen."

"Never mind what appears to be. All God requires of you is that you be faithful. Only God knows what goes on in a man's spirit. It's possible, in fact very probable, that the Holy Spirit will use your determination to hold your convictions firm to prick the king's heart. Perhaps even as we are speaking."

Barely above a whisper, Madeleine answered, "Thank you, Pastor. I will heed your warning."

THE NEXT MORNING PASTOR VERON ushered the CLAVELL party to a pew close to the front and seated them for the service. An elder stood at the entrance giving méreaux to those who were faithful and qualified to take Communion.

As always, a sense of awe prevailed when Madeleine entered the legendary house of God founded by John Calvin. And memories of her mother's funeral in the cathedral only a few months before wafted in and out of her mind. Hidden emotions sprang to the surface, bringing unbidden tears. She dabbed at her eyes with her handkerchief.

Jean reached over and touched her hand without looking at her.

Pastor Le Sueur opened the service with the traditional reading from the Psalms: "My help cometh from the Lord, which made heaven and earth."

Then he continued with the confession and absolution and the singing of the *Kyrie Eleison*. Madeleine experienced great comfort in the rituals of the church, and to be able to take Communion in Calvin's church lent an almost mystical presence. Another elder stood at the

Communion table and collected a méreau from each parishioner before they received the bread and wine.

The good pastor preached with fervor and conviction on God's peace. As he concluded his sermon, the peace of which he spoke suddenly transformed into reality and encircled Madeleine's heart. She leaned over and whispered to Jean, "We are on the right path. I perceive it in my spirit."

Jean looked at her and smiled, whispering, "I sense it as well."

Jean stood as the service concluded and assisted Madeleine and Judith out of the pew. Halfway down the aisle, Madeleine stopped short. There, seated in the shadows in the back, a familiar figure bowed, appearing to be deep in prayer.

"Pierre?" Madeleine's soft voice nevertheless carried over the pews and through the cathedral.

The courtier, more handsome than she remembered, stood and moved quickly toward Madeleine and her party. He took her hand, kissed it, and bowed elegantly.

"Madeleine, uh . . . Madame Clavell . . . I am delighted to have been summoned here to meet with you. How can I be of service?" He held her hand beyond the social expectations.

Madeleine's heart raced, but she calmed herself. "Thank you for coming. I didn't expect you until later today. I've never . . . that is, I didn't know you . . . I didn't know you had a leaning toward God."

"Don't all men have a need to know their Creator?"

"Yes, but . . ."

"Is that why you have summoned me to the famous cathedral—to question me regarding my faith?" He cocked his head and grinned at her, and she realized he was teasing her. "Why have you requested my services once again?"

The small group moved toward the entrance, and Pastor Le Sueur broke away from chatting with congregates to greet Pierre. "Welcome, Monsieur Boveé." He pounded Pierre on the back in greeting. "Come, Madame Le Sueur has prepared a sumptuous meal for us. Decisions can be made more easily on a full stomach." His hearty laugh rolled through the sanctuary as he escorted them to his quarters.

Pierre gave his arm to Madeleine as they followed Pastor Le Sueur. Jean hurried to her opposite side, not willing to give up his responsibility as temporary head of the Clavell household. Judith scowled at the jousting of the two men.

King Louis listened to Father Bourdaloue drone on about the poor and the mistreatment they suffered. Outwardly the king listened attentively and nodded, but inwardly he wondered what this had to do with him. He attended Mass daily, and he took Communion and prayed at the proper times. There were moments he felt guilty for his lust and adultery, but the government's lack of concern for the poor and prisoners did not concern him. Let the Church take care of them.

For the briefest of moments, a flicker of faces from his past flashed through his mind—the so-called "man in the iron mask," François Clavell—but the rationalized conscience of the regent did not light on them for long. More concerned about his personal absolution over last night's tryst, he bowed his head and muttered a brief prayer of memorized confession.

Louis did not understand the consecration and humility of the devout. Religious duty, he understood. But the attributes of sacrifice, dedication, piety, and religious fervor escaped his mind-set. Especially that of the Huguenots. Why not simply convert and avoid losing one's family, business, and home? Believe what you must, but do it in the context of a united church of France.

Then Madeleine's face loomed in his imagination. And Louis began to be aware of annoying qualms concerning his treatment of her, her faith, and her family. He shook his head. The queen frowned at him. He ignored her.

He returned to the privacy of his thoughts as the priest continued. He tried to picture Madeleine's son. What did he look like? How old was he, exactly? He had to be about the same age as his Louis, the Dauphine, maybe a bit older. If Madeleine's son were . . . if he were . . . if he and Madeleine had had . . . if they had had a son, he would be older than his Louis. And that would give him claim to the throne.

The king's heart began to pound, and sweat beaded up on his brow. He took his lace handkerchief out of his sleeve and dabbed at his forehead. The queen looked over at him again, questioning him with her eyes. He gave her a tiny, imperceptible nod, letting her know he was fine.

No, he wouldn't allow himself to think about that. Madeleine would have told him. Or would she?

"I WAS PLEASANTLY SURPRISED BY YOUR SUMMONS." PIERRE leaned in close to Madeleine and spoke so only she could hear.

Jean turned his head and inclined his ear toward them.

"Yes. I . . . I need you . . ."

Pierre's eyes betrayed his heart. "Whatever you need, Madeleine. I am at your service." He brushed her hand, hidden by the tablecloth. "I am so happy to see you again."

"I-I am glad to see you as well." Madeleine moved her hand. She blushed. "We need to talk." She placed her napkin on the table and rose. "Where can we go for private conversation, Pastor Le Sueur?"

The pastor glanced at the trio, Jean, Madeleine, and Pierre, as he helped himself to another serving of potatoes. "You may use my study. No one will disturb you there."

Jean and Pierre both leapt into action to assist Madeleine. Pierre deferred to Jean and followed the lead of the brother and sister-in-law. Jean glared at the debonair courtier.

Entering the gloomy study, Madeleine turned and faced the two men. She studied their faces—the tanned, swarthy face of her brother-in-law and the handsome features of the suave courtier. "Pierre, we are indebted to you once again, for having made the long journey here at our summons."

Pierre raised his eyebrows at the use of the plural *we*.

"We need your assistance in making a final attempt to locate François."

"I see." Pierre turned his back to Madeleine. He composed himself and put on a façade of platonic concern. "Madame, surely you don't think he is still alive after having been sentenced to the galleys. Surviving the torture of that injunction is practically impossible."

"I feel . . ." Madeleine placed her hand over her heart. "I sense in my heart that François is alive, and unless I do everything I know to find him"—she chose her words carefully—"I cannot go on with my life."

Pierre shook his head in disbelief. He walked toward the bulging bookcases and tapped his fingers on a dusty shelf. "I know this is painful, but if François died on board a ship as a galley slave, they would simply—"

Pierre halted in midsentence as Madeleine's eyes darkened.

"Simply what?"

"The slaves are offered no sense of dignity whatsoever. The bodies are simply tossed overboard. We would never be able to find out exactly what happened."

Madeleine set her jaw in an effort to control her emotions. "Don't you understand? We must try. Whatever we find, at least we will have some sort of answer."

Jean remained by Madeleine's side. "If there is even the slightest possibility that my brother is alive, we must try to find him."

Madeleine stepped toward Pierre. "You are our only hope. We know of no one else who could possibly gain access to the galley records and get word back to us." Her voice broke as she pleaded with him. "Won't you please help us?"

Pierre looked at the one woman who had captured his heart, as she stood, broken and vulnerable before him, begging him to save her husband's life. "Very well. I will do as you ask. But I must warn you again, there is almost no chance that he has survived."

He faced the two Clavells, then moved to Madeleine and took both her hands in his. "You must be prepared for whatever we might find—or not find."

"*Oui*, I understand. I am prepared."

"And if . . ."

"Pierre, we must not waste our time speculating on what only God knows."

"Yes." Pierre sighed. "I shall leave in the morning and return by way of Paris. I will make inquiries as discreetly as possible." He addressed Jean. "Take good care of her."

Jean's mouth tightened. "Rest assured, I intend to do exactly that."

Pierre took Madeleine's hands in both of his and kissed them. "*Au revoir.*" He moved toward the door of the study and paused as he put his hand on the doorknob. "I will not send a message. I will come to you personally and bring whatever results I find—good or bad. May God have mercy on us all."

TWENTY-SEVEN

Madeleine sat at the vanity in the plain guest room in the cathedral brushing the tangles out of her hair. "Judith, help me with this, please. I cannot reach the back."

The servant placed her mistress's robe on the bed and took the hairbrush from her. "What are you going to do with this in the morning? You are brushing out all the stiffening."

"Dear Judith. Always concerned with appearances. We're just traveling back to the Du Puys'. I'll wear my bonnet. Don't worry yourself."

"What was that?" Judith halted with the hairbrush in midair.

"I heard nothing."

Judith cocked her head. "There it is again. Someone is knocking on the door."

"Hand me my robe."

The servant helped Madeleine into her robe and scurried to answer the barely discernible knock. "Monsieur Boveé! Madame is preparing to retire." Judith's lips pursed into a disapproving downward turn.

"Please, I must speak with Madame Clavell."

"I'm sorry. I'm afraid that is impossible."

Madeleine pulled the door open all the way. "It's all right, Judith."

"But, madame . . ."

"I said it's all right." Madeleine motioned to the young man. "Come in, Pierre."

Pierre looked around, but remained in the doorway. "I need to speak to you . . . alone."

"Very well. Judith, you may be excused."

"Madame . . ."

"I will see you in the morning. See to it that our things are ready to go immediately after breakfast."

Judith curtsied and started for the door, grumbling under her breath.

"Judith."

"Madame?"

"I appreciate your concern, but everything is fine. No need to worry."

"But this does not look—"

"I am past worrying about appearances. Our life has degenerated around us, and we are in a struggle for our lives. Pierre is here to help us. There is no danger or impropriety here. You can rest easy, and I will see you in the morning."

Madeleine held the door open, and the servant departed. Pierre moved into the room, and Madeleine shut the door and leaned against it. "What is it, Pierre? Are you having second thoughts about helping us find François?"

"No, I'm willing to help. I'm not optimistic about being able to find him or even any news about him. But I will do all I can."

"Then why—why are you here?"

"Because there are things I want to say to you—matters you need to know about."

"Do you know something about François you're not telling me? What is it? Do you know he's already dead?" Madeleine's voice rose in panic.

"No, no. Calm down." Pierre moved toward Madeleine and took hold of her hands. "I know nothing about François beyond what I have already said."

"Then what is it?" Madeleine paused, and an uneasy silence blanketed the room. "I am waiting to hear what you have to say."

Pierre dropped Madeleine's hands while at the same time gathering her in his arms. "I must express my heart."

Madeleine gasped and tried to pull away from the handsome courtier. "No, Pierre, we must not. Please, please don't."

Pierre held her fast. "Hear me out. I don't intend to pursue anything you don't want." Pierre relaxed his grip, but did not let her go. He gazed directly into her eyes in the soft glow of the light from the bedside candle stand and stroked her hair. "But you must know—surely you have suspected—that I have fallen in love with you."

Madeleine pulled away from him, shaking her head, but he grasped her shoulders and made her look at him.

"I can have any woman I want at court, but you are the only woman who has ever captured my heart. From the first time I saw you flirting with me from behind your mask at the ball in Versailles I was smitten. At that point I simply considered you another conquest, another prize to add to my collection. But as our paths continued to cross, and I was drawn into the drama of your family's struggles, the challenge turned into admiration for your courage—and then to love."

Madeleine relaxed, resting her head against his chest. He wrapped his muscular arms around her, and she began to cry. "This cannot happen. I will not allow it."

"Is there a possibility for us? Is there any chance that you have similar feelings? I must know." His breathing quickened. "How—how can the one woman I have ever loved not return those emotions? How can fate be so cruel as to dictate that the only one I have ever loved be forbidden to me?"

"I cannot lie." Madeleine pulled back and looked into the dusky gray eyes of the man who had been her rescuer more than once. Who wouldn't be tempted by this dashing, handsome courtier with the wide smile that he could turn on at a moment's notice?

"Yes, I must admit that I have feelings for you. When I watched you ride away after rescuing Vangie from the convent, my heart welled up with emotion for you. The passion I had begun to feel for you frightened me. And each time we meet again, the emotions return and sweep over me. B-but I cannot permit this to develop any further." Tears were pooling in her eyes and dripping over the edge of her eyelids. "I love François, and I am committed to our marriage."

Pierre fell to his knees and groaned. He grasped Madeleine around her legs and wept softly. "I love you. *Mon Dieu*, help me, but I am hopelessly in love with you."

Madeleine ran her hands through his hair and knelt in front of him. "Not here, and not now. My commitment is to my husband, and I love him. I love my family, and I am committed to them. I cannot . . . I simply cannot."

The two stood, holding each other's hands. Moments passed as they searched each other's eyes—the silence broken only by their breathing.

Pierre finally whispered, "This is the response I suppose I expected. I would never try to persuade you to go against what you believe and who you are. You would not be able to live with yourself if you went against your convictions."

"You must promise me that you will never again express your love to me—not while there is any hope that François is alive." Madeleine's faint voice faltered. "P-promise me."

Pierre drew Madeleine's hands to his lips and smothered them with kisses. He raised his head, still holding on to her. "I want you to know that you will always have my heart—only you. You may see me with other women or hear of me with other women, but my heart will always belong to you."

Pierre embraced Madeleine gently and buried his face in her hair. A barely audible choked whisper passed over his lips. "You have my word. I will never speak of loving you again." He backed away and bowed. Lingering for a moment at the door, he gazed at her as if he were committing to memory every detail of her face. "My solemn word."

Then he was gone.

FROM THE WINDOW OF HER ROOM, MADELEINE WATCHED Pierre saddle his horse in the early morning dawn. Heavy dew dripped from the edges of the steep roof. She saw no stable boy in view to assist him. The courtier went about the task with efficiency and mounted. Without warning, he looked up at Madeleine's window. Their eyes met.

Pierre touched the edge of his hat, and then tapped his chest over his heart. Madeleine nodded and raised her hand to wave good-bye, but Pierre gouged his spurs into the flanks of his horse, turned his back, and rode away.

FRANÇOIS AWOKE WITH A THROBBING HEADACHE. HE rolled over and groaned as he eyed the wine bottle on the bedside table. The wounds on his back continued to remind him of the *sous-comite's* whip, but the stabbing pain had subsided to a dull ache. Monsieur Fourie's ointment was doing its job.

The clear brightness of the early morning sun streamed through the draperies where François had pulled them aside the night before. He sat up and shoved the covers away. Someone had left a loaf of bread and a quarter round of cheese on the table. He tore the bread apart and downed it eagerly. He tipped the wine flask over, finding only a few drops left to drip into his glass.

François' mind began to race. Even through the wine-induced headache, he was thinking more clearly than yesterday. He had to get word to Madeleine as quickly as possible. Where should he start? If she and the children were safe, and the danger had passed, she would return to the estate. Perhaps Louis had relented and granted her his protection once again. Or if she had to flee to Geneva as they had discussed, she might have left some kind of message at the manor. Perhaps she left Henri or Armond behind to keep the estate running.

He pushed himself up from the bed and limped to the window. He peered through the slit, then pushed aside the folds of the drapery and watched the pier come alive. *Le Fidelle* still floated at the dock. Sailors lugged cargo up the gangplank.

François shuddered and released the window hanging. It swung against a servant bell cord. François reached for the weighty rope and pulled on it—then again and again.

Two servants rushed into the room, followed by a breathless Monsieur Fourié. "Monsieur Clavell! What is wrong? How may we help you?"

François turned from the window. "I must get word to my wife. Please get me a messenger—now."

"Yes, yes, indeed." Monsieur Fourié turned to his servants. "Get some breakfast for our guest. And call for Joost. Tell him to prepare for a journey."

The servants scuttled out of the room. Monsieur Fourié put his arthritic hand on François' shoulder. "We'll have a messenger on his way to Grenoble immediately, my son. Trust God."

François' shoulders sagged as he sat on the couch beside the window. "I must get word to her as quickly as possible. What if it's too late? I don't even know if . . . I don't know where . . ." Frantic, he looked at his benefactor, then buried his head in his hands. "Don't give up on me, Madeleine. I'm alive, and I will find you. Don't give up."

TWENTY-EIGHT

François' face was fading from her memory. As the carriage jostled over the bumpy road, carrying the small party back from Geneva to the countryside, Madeleine closed her eyes and willed herself to recount details of her husband's appearance—his dark eyes, the scar across his forehead, his thick, dark hair. Images of their bygone lives on their estate back in France flashed across her mind: François teaching the children to bridle and saddle their own horses; evenings together by the fireplace after dinner; the look in his eyes when he teased her; the security she felt in his arms; and then the terror on his face as he shouted the warning that the dragoons were invading.

His face danced around the rim of her memory and then vanished the moment she attempted to capture it with her mind's eye. She wondered if his already slender frame was now emaciated from his sentence in the galleys. Was the brightness gone from his eyes? Even worse were her thoughts of the torture she was certain François faced. She shook her head and refused to allow the morbid picture to be painted in her mind.

Another face pervaded her thoughts, crowding out the fading image of her husband: that of Pierre Boveé. He had risked his career and his very life to help Madeleine rescue her daughter from the convent and continued to offer himself to her service. Now he had exposed his deepest emotions and declared his love for her.

Early that morning when he left her in Geneva and rode toward France, she had watched his figure disappear from view and sent a whispered prayer heavenward. *God be with you, Pierre. God. Mon Dieu. Do you really know my God, Pierre? Heavenly Father, I cannot return his love, but I do care deeply about him.*

Her emotions were a labyrinth of contradictions. She remembered how Pierre had bowed in prayer in the cathedral in Geneva. Strange. Was he a follower of Jehovah God? A true believer? Or did he simply put on a semblance of godliness when convenient? She didn't know. In reality, she didn't know this man at all who had become a major part of her life—didn't know anything about him—except that their lives had become profoundly entangled.

Madeleine knew that her family members were not the only victims of persecution. Vangie was only one child among thousands who had been kidnapped and whisked away from their families, François only one of countless men and women who had been imprisoned, tortured, sentenced to labor, even killed for their faith.

She wondered if Pierre even knew of the Vaudois family's renown for their courageous stand against the persecution of the Huguenots. Critical as those struggles for their personal religious freedom were, they served only as a small piece of a larger mosaic. Madeleine well knew that her personal longings paled in comparison to God's encompassing plan for the church in history.

But at this point she really didn't care if her family was pivotal in the drama. She only knew that she was tired of the hiding and running and that she wanted her family back together—and that the longer François remained missing, the more her heart turned toward Pierre Boveé, this familiar stranger.

The carriage jolted to a stop. Judith's head snapped upright. Madeleine heard her brother-in-law shout for the horses to halt, and then he opened the door of the coach and poked his head inside.

"The inn is just ahead. We'll stop to eat something there. But I wanted to water the horses first here at the river. We won't have any problem getting home by dark."

Madeleine nodded, and she and Judith escaped the confines of the coach. "That's fine, Jean. How much farther to the inn?"

"Probably not fifteen minutes."

Jean unhitched the horses and led them to the gurgling stream. Madeleine trailed behind them. Only the sloshing of the horses on the river's edge interrupted the tranquil scene. Madeleine gathered her skirt around her, sat on a stump, and stared downstream. "Jean, what if no records exist of François in the galley archives? Have you thought about what we shall do if Pierre is unable to find François?"

Jean hung on to the reins of the thirsty horses, but turned toward Madeleine and shook his head. "Truthfully, up until now, I have not allowed myself to entertain that thought. My older brother—he's—he's always been my hero." He gazed across the river. "However, as much as I detest the thought of going on without him, I suppose, if we must—plans need to be made—just in case." He struggled to express his thoughts. "I know we can't continue to presume upon Pastor Du

Puy's hospitality forever, but talking about proceeding with our lives without François is difficult for me."

"I understand." Madeleine stood. "Through no fault or decision of your own, you have been thrust into the position of head of this household." She touched his arm and looked into his eyes—eyes so similar to François'. "I don't know how I would have managed without you. But we need to face the fact that we may have to make some hard decisions on our own if-if we can't find François."

Jean shifted the reins to one hand and took Madeleine's hand with the other. "We'd best be on our way if we are going to get home by nightfall."

They walked back to the coach together, each deep in thought. Madeleine sensed they were embarking upon a new chapter of their lives. Jean was a man of character and integrity. He had saved the lives of her sons. He was shouldering the responsibilities of their family during François' absence, not seeking a life of his own. She would be indebted to him forever, but how long could she expect him to sacrifice his life for theirs?

These two held the uncertain destiny of the Vaudois and Clavell heritage in their hands.

FRANÇOIS STARED OUT THE WINDOW AT THE HARBOR. He tapped absentmindedly at the writing materials Isaac had left for him on the desk in the upstairs bedroom.

Seagulls screeched and dove through the air catching insects, then alit on the wooden posts of the docks. *Le Fidelle* still rode alongside the wharf, but the activity on board signaled preparations for a voyage.

He squinted his eyes as if doing so would allow him to see more clearly the details of the ship where he had labored at the oars, his body wasting away from hunger, torture, and despair. The memory of the chant of the *comite* roared in his ears. His eyes filled with tears, and emotions too strong to hold back any longer began to well up from a place deep in his gut that had been cruelly hewn by a vicious taskmaster. The toxin of his confinement and hopelessness had festered in that dark place for almost two years. Now the putrid boil demanded to be lanced. There was no stopping it. He buried his face in his hands and wept as he never had before.

François heard a noise at his door and looked up to see Monsieur Fourié.

Isaac stepped through the doorway toward François and put his hand on the younger man's shoulder. "My friend, are you in pain?"

François struggled to gain his composure. "Ahh-hh-h, no—no, my body is not in any more pain than is to be expected." He looked at the kind gentleman. "Thanks to your compassionate care, I-I am healing." François sighed. "But my heart is in agony."

Unsteady on his feet, François stood and leaned on the desk. "I must get to my wife as soon as possible."

"I have sent for a courier," Monsieur Fourié said. "You are much too weak to travel."

"Please, sir. Don't stand in my way." François stopped in front of Isaac and searched the wrinkled eyes of his angel of mercy. "I feel my strength returning every day. Will you help me? Please?"

Isaac shook his head, his wispy gray hair floating around his face. "Ach! It's against my better judgment, but I know better than to try to dissuade a man who has been so cruelly separated from his loved ones. I will help you." He sat in the chair at the desk and leaned across the table. "If I were able, I would go with you myself."

"Thank you, my gracious friend. I am once again in your debt."

"Nonsense. No more than you would have done in my place."

"I will repay you as soon as I reclaim my holdings. Madeleine has . . ." François' voice trailed away. He realized he had been assuming that Madeleine had returned to the estate and picked up their previous lives. But what if she had not? What if she too were destitute? "Isaac, I don't even know if I have means to repay you."

"That is the least of our worries. Who knows if I will even be around long enough to be repaid?" He rocked back and forth with his hands on his knees and chortled.

A tall, muscular man with curly red hair knocked on the open door.

"Ah, Joost. Come in." Isaac motioned for the young man to enter.

Joost strode into the room, twirling his hat between his hands. He exuded an air of confidence, though he couldn't have been more than twenty years of age.

Isaac affectionately pounded the young man on the back. "François, this is Joost, my grandson."

"Monsieur Fourié, this journey will be long and arduous for sure— and quite possibly dangerous," François protested. "I couldn't risk the life of your grandson on my behalf."

"You will find no braver man in my household—and none any more skilled with the sword. He is an expert horseman and knows the country roads between northern and southern France better than you know your own estate. He is young, but has served in the king's army for almost four years already as a courier."

"The king's military?"

"Oui, monsieur." Joost stepped forward. "But I now serve a higher Master. I came home to study for the ministry."

Isaac cleared his throat. "A bit of a fanatic, I fear, but a good man."

Joost grinned at his grandfather. "And no more reliable courier in all of France."

"I have been separated from my family for two years at the whim of King Louis. I must get word to my wife and children that I am alive. My wife was a childhood friend of Louis' and recently declined his invitation to return to court." François wavered. "Do you understand the danger that might present itself?"

Joost glanced at his grandfather. "*Oui*, monsieur, I understand."

"Can you be ready to go by tomorrow?"

"*Oui*, monsieur. I have only myself to prepare. I am not married—at the moment anyway." He grinned, showing a deep dimple in one cheek.

"Oh? A sweetheart, perhaps?"

"Perhaps, but no serious commitment. I am still unencumbered by family responsibilities."

Isaac stepped up beside his grandson. "Joost just returned a few weeks ago from his duties in the king's service and seems to be unable to settle into his studies yet." The boy's grandfather winked at him. "He has been restless for a new adventure. This mission for God will fill the bill just fine. He has 'escorted' Huguenots across the border before. He seemed to have an uncanny ability to mesh his official duties for the king, while providing safe passage for those of our faith."

"I see. Well, Joost!" François grabbed the young man's shoulders. "I shall look forward to being in the company of such an auspicious courier of King Louis—and one who seems to enjoy the protection of Almighty God!"

TWENTY-NINE

"Send for Pierre Boveé."

King Louis' ceremonial morning *lever* having been completed, the attending courtiers eyed each other. Only the *whish* of the linens being stripped from the king's bed could be heard in the room. The king's hunting wig rested on a pedestal, ready to be used later that afternoon.

Louis dismissed the royal wigmaker and strode toward the door leading to his office, still holding his morning cup of scented, distilled white wine, seasoned with sugar and spices. The fragrance of amber trailed after him.

"What is it?" He glared at his attendants. "Where is Monsieur Boveé?"

One of the courtiers stepped forward. "If it please Your Majesty, Monsieur Boveé left on a trip last week."

"Trip? No, it does not please me." The king's voice echoed through the now-silent room. "He did not have permission to leave. Did he ask permission to leave?" The king's eyes surveyed the room, and his ministers and attendants averted his gaze.

A tense silence fell on the room. Eyes downcast, all shook their heads. Several muttered, "No, Your Majesty."

"Well, does no one know where Monsieur Boveé has gone—without permission?" The monarch's voice quivered with mounting rage. He pounded the floor with his cane. "No one?" He spun around as he approached the door, and his voice lowered to a sinister growl. "Has he gone to Paris?"

The same courtier who dared to answer previously, bowed, "*Non*, Your Majesty. I recall hearing someone remark that Monsieur Boveé had to leave suddenly to deal with a personal problem."

The Sun King's countenance softened. "Very well." He chuckled. "A personal problem, eh? A beautiful mademoiselle, no doubt?"

The king's attendants followed suit and laughed under their breath.

"See to it he is summoned the moment he returns." The magnificent King Louis went into his office and motioned to his ministers for the door to be closed behind him.

King Louis' secretary of state, Colbert, followed the monarch into the office. His usual dour, reserved manner descended on the room. "Why should the whereabouts of a mere courtier concern Your Majesty this morning? We have more important matters to which we need to turn our attention."

"Ah! Of course, you are right, Monsieur Colbert. Always the diligent one. What have you for me today?" Louis paused at his desk and thumbed through a manual. "What does the treasury report say? We are doing well, are we not? The French revenue has doubled in the last ten years."

The keeper of the king's affairs shook his head. "Once more, Your Majesty, I plead with you. The expense of building Versailles has gotten out of hand. Mansard's grand apartments, dance halls, galleries, and offices will bankrupt the treasury if we don't do something." He walked to the window. "And the gardens—bowers, trellises, grottoes, fountains, waterspouts—and, *mon Dieu*—the orange trees. Where do we stop? You already have the grandest gardens in all of Europe."

Louis held up his hand. "We will not discuss this again, Colbert. You are a genius at finding and managing the treasury. Take care of it." He handed the report to the secretary. "Anything else?"

Colbert turned his back and sighed. "Yes, Your Majesty. I have become aware of increased, shall we say, pressure upon the Huguenots. As long as they remain politically loyal and obedient, the Protestants are a valuable asset to the economy and commerce of France. We do ourselves no favor by forcing them to flee because they fear persecution or pressure to convert."

"Of what do you speak? Be more specific."

Colbert confronted his king. "Sire, we have closed their hospitals and colleges, forbidden them to serve as public officials, kidnapped their children to reeducate them in convents—and now the latest assembly has decreed that mixed marriages be declared null and void and the children illegitimate. This is not to our advantage." He paused. "It is my observation that the public opinion against these people is because—" Colbert hesitated.

"Because what, Colbert? Go on, say it."

"Because they are more astute businessmen than their Catholic

303

counterparts. The economy is flourishing in the villages where the Huguenots dominate."

"Enough. Our people remember stories from their Catholic fore-fathers of the burning of farmsteads and the desecration of the Host in village churches when the Huguenots had the upper hand. Does not the stability of our government rest on the social order? And the social order rests on morality, and that will collapse without the sup-port of a state religion. No, Colbert, you are wrong. We must unify the nation. *Un roi, une loi, une foi*—one king, one law, one faith."

"France cannot 'unify' when Huguenot villages and homes are being ravaged by dragoons, and Protestant funerals, weddings, and church services are being attacked by Catholic uprisings. The dra-goons are ignoring the protection offered the Huguenots by the Edict of Nantes, which you have upheld. Your Majesty, I implore you, this must stop."

Louis' face turned red, and he stood, pounding the table with his fist. "I will not discuss the Huguenots any further! It is your job to find the revenue we need to run this government, not to discuss the state religion. Leave religion to Cardinal de Bérulle and the priests." The king waved his hand. "You are dismissed."

"But, Your Majesty . . ."

"I said you are dismissed. Leave me now."

Colbert backed out of the office, bowing as he left.

"Wait."

Colbert stopped and faced the monarch.

"Fetch my correspondence and bring it to me."

"Yes, Your Majesty. I shall return shortly."

Louis sat motionless in his chair. He picked up his cane and, mov-ing to the window, pulled the heavy drapery aside and watched the gardeners below. He knew Colbert was right about the expensive gardens. Versailles' formal grounds were becoming known as some of the most beautiful and elegant of their kind. But he wasn't satisfied. He still wanted more.

He gripped the edge of the weighty fabric and squeezed it in his fist. But the Huguenots—Colbert was not right about this thorn in the flesh of France. They must be dealt with.

And Louis couldn't think about the Huguenots without thinking of Madeleine. He was certain that her determination to cling to her Protestant faith had prevented her from coming to him. In spite of his vendetta against the Huguenot religion, Louis felt within himself a surprising compassion toward those individual families caught in the rising public tide of vengeance against them. For one generation Catholics were persecuted, then for the next forty years, the axe fell on the necks of the Huguenots. Why couldn't they simply offer outward obeisance to the Catholic Church? Let them believe what they pleased, but pledge allegiance to the Church to unite the nation.

Louis was resolute in his conviction toward the unity of the state, but his heart went out to those individuals in his kingdom who suffered—especially to one.

PIERRE BOVÉE INSERTED HIS KEY INTO THE LOCK OF THE door to his apartment at Versailles. It was late, and all he wanted to do was collapse on his bed. The door swung open without his having to turn the key. He remembered distinctly locking the door when he left.

The handsome courtier placed his hand on his sword. The room was pitch-black.

The door creaked, announcing to anyone waiting within that Monsieur Boveé had returned. He stepped inside, and a dark figure sprang from the bed, ready to attack.

Pierre recognized the form. "Father! What are you doing here?"

"Ah, Pierre." The figure relaxed. "I didn't know when you would be back." Commander Paul Boveé moved to the table and lit a candle. "Good to see you, son." He gave Pierre a perfunctory slap on the back.

"Yes, well, good to see you too." Pierre tossed his hat and gloves onto a chair and sat on the edge of the bed to remove his boots. "However, I've been riding for days and have been looking forward to sleeping in my own bed." The boots clunked to the floor. "So, I am shoving you out."

"But of course. I will go back to the quarters with my men." The older, but still dashing, commander of the dragoons flashed the broad Boveé smile. "I just thought I would take advantage of a soft mattress if the opportunity afforded itself. And since you had graciously left a key to your apartment with me . . ."

"The door was unlocked."

"I guess I forgot to lock it when I went to bed. I do apologize."

Pierre looked at his father, who had been distant and indifferent toward him most of his life. What precipitated the sudden interest in their relationship now?

"No harm done. It startled me, that's all." Pierre indicated the couch with a nod of his head. "You are welcome to the couch. But I must warn you, it is not very comfortable."

Pierre watched his father gather up his clothes. Perhaps the commander was becoming sentimental as he grew older, or regretted that he hadn't married Pierre's mother and had left them struggling. Or did he want to claim his son for bragging rights now that Pierre was climbing in court society? Or possibly something more sinister—maybe he was attempting to pry into Pierre's acquaintance with Madeleine Clavell.

"*Merci*, but I will go on down with my men."

Pierre was relieved. He would prefer to avoid being questioned about his whereabouts.

"By the way, where have you been? On a mission on behalf of the king?"

"You could say that."

"And you've been riding for several days?"

"Yes."

"Hmm, I see. Don't want to talk about it, eh?"

"I am exhausted. I've been in the saddle for days."

"Believe me, I understand that." Commander Boveé pulled on his boots, put on his floppy dragoon cap, and stuffed his other belongings into his pack. He slung his gear over his shoulder. "I have become aware of an interesting development and wondered if you might have heard any gossip among your fellow courtiers."

"And what might that be?" Pierre pulled off his tunic and emptied what little water was left in the pitcher into the basin.

"Sorry, son. I didn't know you were coming in tonight."

Pierre sighed, dipped the towel into the water, and wiped his face. "If you hadn't been here, there probably would have been no water at all in the pitcher."

"I made a stop at the Filles de Sainte-Marie, Visitandines a few weeks ago. It seems a little Huguenot girl I rescued and took there for safekeeping has been kidnapped." Commander Boveé eyed his son intently. "I don't suppose you've heard anything about that."

Pierre threw the towel on the washstand. He could feel panic tugging at him. He lay on his bed and breathed in a long sigh. "Ahhh—this feels heavenly." He crossed his legs and pulled his arms up behind his head. "Now, why would I be privy to that kind of information? Why should I even concern myself with the escapades of a Huguenot family? Besides that, I am in no mood for speculative conversations tonight."

"Of course. I don't have orders to ride out for a week or so. I will see you in the morning."

"Not too early—I plan on sleeping as long as I can." Pierre closed his eyes and hoped his father could not detect the pounding of his chest.

"Sleep well. Good night, son."

"Good night." Pierre got up and went to the door and locked it behind the departing figure of his father.

Son. Pierre didn't trust the man. But he was too tired to think on it for very long. He pulled off his breeches, fell into the formerly occupied bed, and was snoring almost immediately.

THUNDEROUS BANGS ON THE DOOR INVADED PIERRE'S dreams. He swam his way through the fog of the early morning vision and groaned as he realized someone was at his apartment door. He stumbled out of bed, muttering to himself, "I told him I wanted to sleep late this morning."

Pierre threw open the door, slamming it against the wall. "I told you . . ."

Instead of his father, an adolescent page stood in the darkness of the hallway gaping at the bleary-eyed courtier. "The king wishes to see you immediately."

Pierre ran his hand through his long, disheveled hair, and held it out of his eyes. "Wha . . . what is this? I'm not on duty."

"The king has been calling for you every morning. He is not happy that you left without permission and wishes to see you at once." The boy shifted from one foot to another. "What shall I report to His Majesty?"

"I need some time to freshen up." Pierre knew he dared not enter the fastidious king's presence without completing his toilette. "Bring me fresh water and help me. Hurry." Pierre turned to the washstand and handed the empty pitcher to the page.

"*Oui*, monsieur. I shall return quickly." The page took the pitcher and hastened down the hallway, his shoes clattering on the hard black-and-white tile.

Pierre grumbled, opened his armoire, and pulled out suitable clothing to attend the king's morning rituals. He sat on the edge of his bed and leaned forward, his elbows on his knees, holding his head in his hands. "I feel like I have been drinking all night."

"Sir?" The page stood at the doorway with the pitcher sloshing water on the floor.

"Come ahead, come in. Pour the water into the basin." Pierre handed the boy his coat. "Unbutton my tunic."

The page went about his duties, and Pierre quickly washed up. He dressed in his court clothes and dismissed the page, taking care to lock his apartment door behind him. Adjusting his wig, he hurried toward the king's quarters.

Pierre knew he must calm himself. He stopped and took a deep breath before he entered the anteroom with the other courtiers.

His fellow courtiers jostled Pierre good-naturedly as he passed through the group: "Look who is here!" "The king's been asking for you." "Better have your story ready."

He grinned and greeted them as he walked toward the king's office door.

He nodded to the guards as they let him in. Pierre saw the king and Colbert huddled over Louis' desk at the far end of the room. Colbert straightened up to greet Pierre. He held a large, leather-bound book in his hands.

Louis motioned to Pierre to come closer. "Ah, Pierre. You have returned at last." He lowered his voice. "I understand you had 'personal business' to attend to?"

"*Oui*, Your Majesty. Please forgive my haste in leaving without your permission. The lady's message was urgent, and I—"

"What did I tell you, Colbert? I knew it had to do with a woman. All is forgiven." Louis dismissed the apology with a wave of his hand. "I was angry at first, because I thought you had gone to Paris without my leave." He smiled. "However, if the summons was urgent— well—you had to go, didn't you?" The king looked at Pierre with a lascivious grin.

Was the king aware that he had gone to meet Madeleine? How could he know that? Scattered thoughts raced through Pierre's head. *Calm down. As far as the king is concerned, there's no connection between Madeleine and me.*

Pierre played along with the king. "What is one to do when a beautiful lady calls you to her side—and her husband is gone?"

"An absent husband? Ah, that was the distress then? Sounds like a worthy mission to me." The king guffawed. "Enough of your amorous escapades. I have a question to ask you."

"I am ever at your service."

"Do you remember the beautiful Madeleine Clavell whom I assigned you to escort to the Porcelain Trianon a couple of years ago?"

Pierre knew he was walking a tightrope, but in a split second decided that to be evasive would arouse suspicion. "*Oui*, Your Majesty. Who could forget such a woman? And as I remember, you had a special interest in that one. I don't blame you—"

Again the king interrupted him. "Simply a childhood first love. However, her family has been a source of irritation to me. She's Huguenot."

"I gathered as much that night." Pierre cleared his throat. "But why is she of concern to you, sire? I've not seen her in court since."

"No, that is precisely my point. She has disappeared, along with her daughter. I sentenced her husband to the galleys, and if he is still alive, he is a man most miserable." Louis continued to rearrange the papers on his desk. "Your father reports to me that someone kidnapped her daughter from Filles de Sainte-Marie, Visitandines, where I had assigned her for reeducation and safekeeping. And now Madeleine is nowhere to be found." The king looked up suddenly at Pierre. "You wouldn't happen to know anything about any of this, would you?"

His father was at the bottom of this.

Pierre scoffed. "Why would I trouble myself with a married Huguenot—despite her startling beauty? I can have any woman I might desire in your celebrated court." Pierre bowed. "With your permission, of course."

"Um—yes. Precisely." King Louis stood. "Since you know what she looks like and were with her for an evening, I have a mission for you."

"Sire?"

"I want you to find out what has happened to her. I ordered her family estate south of Grenoble destroyed, and, as I said, her husband sentenced to the galleys."

"Perhaps that would be the place to start. If I could question her husband, he might know where she is."

"Maybe—if he is still alive." Louis turned to Colbert. "Find the galley records for Pierre."

"But, Your Majesty, there are hundreds of names in the galley archives. That could take weeks."

"How many ships have we currently in the royal navy that employ galley slaves?"

"Forty, Your Majesty."

"Surely those could be reviewed in a timely manner."

"But there are also the merchant ships that employ galley slaves. And we keep no record of those slaves. Those galleys are in every port in France."

"What about the prisoners who have been sentenced to the galleys from the Bastille? Are those records kept separately from the general ledgers?"

"*Oui*, those are kept in the records of the Bastille."

"Then we are in luck. I sentenced François Clavell to the galleys directly from the Bastille. His 'assignment' should be among those documents, *non?*"

Colbert sighed, knowing better than to argue any further with the king. "I shall see to it immediately." Then he gave Boveé a sly smile. "Perhaps Monsieur Boveé now has Your Majesty's permission go to Paris after all, but on business this time?"

Louis laughed. "To be sure."

Pierre listened to the conversation in disbelief. Was this more cunning court innuendo? Or was it a trap? If not a trap, it was too good to be true—to receive an assignment from the king to pursue the very undercover mission he had agreed to undertake for Madeleine. Pierre walked from the presence of the king stunned at his good fortune.

THIRTY

François hurried down the stairs in the early morning darkness. His legs trembled beneath him, but he felt stronger today than he had in two years. His nagging cough had succumbed to Isaac's nightly soothing syrup of warm honey and wine. The lesions on his back had healed and were no longer painful, only tender. He could hear the chatter of the cooks in the kitchen as he made his way toward the back of the house. His mouth began to water as he entered the kitchen and smelled the porridge already bubbling in the kettle hanging in the fireplace.

"Monsieur Clavell." Startled by the sudden appearance of their houseguest, the head domestic, Sara, paused in her meal preparation. "You are up early, sir, and looking as if you feel much better."

"My strength returns daily, thanks to your good care—and good food." François touched the scar on his forehead and grinned at the servant.

She ducked her head and murmured a quiet *merci*. A dark-haired toddler peered up at François from behind her skirt.

"Hello, there, *chérie*." François knelt down and chucked the tot underneath her chin. "You're a pretty one. You remind me of my Vangie."

"Vangie—short for Evangeline?"

"Yes, she would be five years old by now. I hope she remembers me."

"Oh, she will. This is my granddaughter. She gets up at the crack of dawn with me every morning. Don't know why she won't sleep. Guess she's afraid she will miss something." Sara laughed and wiped her rough, red hands on her apron and pulled a bowl down from the cupboard. "Be seated in the dining room, and I'll get you some breakfast." She fussed over François as if he were an honored guest.

"Thank you, but I'd rather eat here in the kitchen." He pulled on the heavy bench and sat at the servants' long trestle table.

The domestic protested, but spooned up a generous portion of steaming meal and cut a thick slice of bread to go with it.

François dug into the porridge with gusto. "My appetite is returning."

"Are you leaving us? Is that why you are up so early this morning?"

"Yes, I am off to try to find my family. We have been separated for two years, and I am desperate to discover their whereabouts."

Joost burst into the kitchen, bellowing greetings to the staff. He slapped François on the back and sat down beside him. "*Bonjour!* It is a beautiful morning, *non?* A perfect day for an adventure."

François liked this young man—capable, confident, and positive. Although nearly twenty years younger, Joost would be an ideal traveling mate; he possessed the added dimension of trust in God, as well as being savvy in the ways of the French military. François felt he had found the perfect companion—in faith and purpose.

The two men downed their breakfast quickly and proceeded to the stables, where saddled and bridled horses stood ready.

Joost indicated a chestnut mare for François. "This is Madame. We named her that because she has been the queen of the stables ever since she was a filly. She's a solid steed. Not too skittish anymore, but you'll get speed out of her if we need it. Best tempered horse we ever had."

François patted her head, and the mare nickered at him.

Joost laughed. "Looks like you've already made friends."

"*Bonjour*, my lads. You weren't going to leave without telling me good-bye, were you?" Isaac emerged from the back door.

"No, Grand-père. I was just introducing François to Madame."

Isaac came alongside François and handed him a leather pouch. "You may find this helpful along the way."

François took the pouch and fingered the coins through the leather. "My friend, you have showered me with more than I deserve. How can I ever repay you?"

"No need. I am going soon to meet the Lord. I feel it in my spirit. Do not concern yourself with repayment, but focus on reuniting with your family and furthering God's kingdom. Most of us never fully understand how our lives matter in the bigger picture. We feel small and insignificant and unworthy. But his plans are written for us in his Book, and we must seek them out to the best of our ability."

Isaac turned to Joost and held on to his arm. "I am proud of you. I leave to you the legacy of our heritage. Carry it on well."

"Grand-père, what are you talking about? Are you ill? I cannot leave if you are not well."

"I'm rattling on like an old fool—just the musings of an old man. I will see you when you return." Isaac gave Joost a hug, then pulled François to him as well. "Now, off with you. Don't try to ride too far each day, Joost. He's still mending."

"We will be cautious. And I will return as soon as I can."

Joost and François mounted and waved good-bye. They rode onto the cobblestone street in front of the dock, past *Le Fidelle*, and headed southeast. François shuddered and turned his back on the floating prison.

PIERRE GUIDED HIS HORSE OUT OF THE GATES OF THE Bastille, through the eastern main entrance, and headed southwest to the coastal port of Brest. In his hand he clutched a piece of parchment on which was scrawled the name *François Clavell, Le Fidelle, Brest*. He figured he could make the trip in a week or so, riding south to avoid the mountains. The early spring would still be producing snow showers, but heading south he should enjoy pleasant weather.

Pierre's emotions fluctuated between satisfaction in locating François and despondency over what would mean the certain loss of Madeleine; then sadness if he would have to report to Madeleine that her husband was dead. The turns of life were at times indeed cruel beyond bearing. *Does God even care about the plight of humans? Does he not see? Is he deaf that he cannot hear the groans and the cries for mercy of his people?*

Pierre's thoughts of a search for a God who reaches down to man and involves himself in the affairs of earth consumed him as he rode along. Madeleine's God was a tangible force in her life. He envied her faith in such a God. He was tired of court life, deceit, women at his every whim. The life he lived was a façade, and he wanted reality. He truly wanted to know God. But he knew not how to find him.

After riding for a couple of hours, he pulled his horse over to a grove of trees, sat on a log, and let the reins drop loose so his horse could graze. He pulled out a flask of wine and the piece of parchment with François' name circled. He could just return to Switzerland and tell Madeleine he had found nothing.

But he knew he couldn't do that to her. If François were still alive, she could have her family back again. But if he did find François, how would he get the man out of the galleys? He would have to devise a plan at that point.

Pierre's thoughts returned to his relationship with God—or his lack thereof. He pulled off his hat and put it on the log beside him. He looked up at the sky through the leaves of the overhanging oak trees and watched the clouds for a few seconds.

Oh, God, I don't know about all this. I'm confused, but somewhere deep within me, I am feeling a tugging of my spirit toward you. If you are real, if you care anything about a lowly human subject, I-I need you.

Pierre found himself kneeling in the soft moss beside the log. Wildflowers waved their multicolored heads at him as a brisk breeze blew his hat off the log. Butterflies flitted about, darting from flower to flower. The breeze tousled his hair and cooled his face, and a distinct impression settled in his heart. *All is well, Pierre. You don't have to wonder anymore. I am with you. Peace, be still.*

The breeze ceased. Pierre sat back on the log and watched the gentle rhythm of nature around him. He was aware of a compelling sense of peace, of well-being—as if a load had been lifted from his shoulders. Was this real, or was he imagining this shift in his heart?

How long he remained on the log, he didn't know. He turned to retrieve his hat and stopped as he observed a butterfly teetering on the brim. The butterfly remained, then flew to his hand and alit for a moment. Pierre carefully brought his hand closer to observe the intricate patterns and brilliant colors in the wings of the delicate creature before it flew away. He was seeing God's creation with new eyes.

Pierre mounted his horse and left the sacred spot reluctantly. He still didn't have answers to all his questions, but he had a perception that he now possessed a relationship with a heavenly Father who did know the answers. Now all he had to do was seek and follow God. How to do that, he hadn't a clue.

"God . . ."

His horse turned his head and looked at Pierre.

"I'm not talking to you." He patted the stallion's neck. "I'm talking to God." Pierre started to laugh. He laughed as he had never laughed before—loud and unrestrained. "Pierre Boveé, talking to God." He let the reins rest on the saddle horn and threw open wide his arms. *God, thank you. Thank you!*

Pierre searched for the words to express himself. In amazement, he suddenly realized what it was that he was experiencing. "I feel clean. That's what I'm feeling—clean."

Mon Dieu, thank you for whatever this is that has happened to me. I don't know if I'm crazy or what—but it feels wonderful.

He picked the reins up and spurred his horse. *Now show me what to do and where to go.* Merci, merci, merci!

JOOST TURNED IN HIS SADDLE AND CALLED TO FRANÇOIS. "How are you doing, my friend?"

François nodded and waved. "I'm well. Keep going."

They had been traveling for five days, and in spite of the long hours on horseback, François continued to gain strength.

"If you think you can make it a little farther, I'd like to go on into Nantes. I know an inn where we can lodge for the night. We might even take a couple of days for you to recoup."

"That's fine. We'll see how I feel after we get there. A good night's sleep in a bed will probably do me well."

François continued to be amazed at the knowledge beyond the years of this young man. Joost knew the roads and towns like a map. They had lost no time taking wrong turns.

As twilight settled over Nantes, Joost led them to a roadside inn. Several horsemen and king's emissaries moved in and out of the main entrance. The two travelers hitched their horses to a post on the side and went in to see if they could find a room. The interior of the tavern bustled with shouts of greetings and the roar of loud conversation. The smell of roasting meat welcomed them, and they grinned at each other.

Joost indicated a table. "Sit down, François, at that table by the window. I'll get us a room."

"I'll go get the table, but I believe I'll stand for a moment. It feels good." François claimed the table, tugged his gloves off, and twisted the kinks out of his back.

Joost walked to the desk, where he was greeted by the innkeeper, a small, well-built man with a bushy moustache. "Good to see you again, Monsieur Fourié. Where have you been lately?"

"I've returned home, Albert—no longer in the king's service."

"No wonder we haven't seen you around. Is your family doing well?" The innkeeper retrieved a key out of a compartment on the wall behind him.

"Yes, thank you. I need a room with two beds this time." Joost nodded toward François.

Albert replaced the first key and withdrew another one, which he handed to Joost. "This one's right next to your usual room." He shoved the registration book across the desk. "Who is your friend?"

"An acquaintance of my grandfather's. His name is Clavell, a seigneur from the Grenoble area. He's been ill, and I'm escorting him back to his estate." Joost laughed. "I guess Grand-père thought I needed something to do." Joost paid the innkeeper and went to the table François was holding for them.

"Busy place," François said.

"It's always crowded. This is a favorite stop of the king's couriers, soldiers, and courtiers. Food's good. Beds are comfortable. And it's on a main thoroughfare."

Joost and François pulled out the heavy wooden chairs and sat down.

"Besides that," Joost continued, "it's a good place to keep your ears and eyes open for information away from the formality of the court."

A sturdy barmaid hurried to their table. "Well, hello, stranger. Where have you been? What will you have—your usual?"

Joost smiled. "Yes, and plenty of it. We are starving."

"Be right back."

True to her word, the barmaid returned promptly and plunked a hearty serving of roast, cabbage and potatoes, a loaf of bread, cheese, and steins of ale on the table. The two men devoured their meal and then lingered a bit, joining in the good-natured bantering with the men at the surrounding tables.

Before long, François yawned.

Joost handed François the key. "Why don't you go upstairs? I'll be up shortly, but don't wait up for me."

"Don't worry."

PIERRE PULLED UP TO THE CROWDED INN SLIGHTLY AFTER dark, hoping he could still get a room. As he opened the door, he saw the innkeeper deep in conversation with a group of the king's couriers. Pierre walked over to the group. "*Bonsoir*, Albert."

"Ahh-hh, Monsieur Boveé," said the innkeeper. "How are you? This must be the evening for old customers."

"Oh? Who else is here?"

"Joost Fourié. He's over there at his usual table."

"Good, I shall join him. Do you have any more rooms—for an old customer?" Pierre reached for his money.

"For you, I always have room. In fact, I have one next to Joost's. He needed a room with two beds this time. He has a friend with him."

Pierre looked over at Joost's table. "I don't see anyone."

"His friend has already retired. I think they've been traveling for several days."

"*Merci*." Pierre took the key, then moved through the jostling crowd to Joost's table. He shouted over the heads of the men. "Joost Fourié—hello!"

"Pierre!" Joost jumped up and embraced his former colleague. "I have missed you."

"And I have missed you as well. I thought you were in Brest."

"I am, but my grandfather has sent me on a mission. And yourself? What are you doing in this part of the country?"

"Oh, a mission for the king. In fact, I am on my way to Brest to check on a galley."

"Which one?"

"*Le Fidelle.* Know anything about it? Is it in port?"

"That's one of my grandfather's ships, and you are in luck. It is in port. Anything amiss?"

"No, no, not at all. Simply following up on some routine matters." Pierre changed the subject. "Albert said you had a friend with you. Will I be intruding if I join you for a bite to eat?"

"I would be honored to have you join me." Joost slapped the table and sat down. "Have a seat. My friend has already retired."

The two men exchanged court gossip. As the evening wore on, the din lowered.

Pierre leaned toward Joost. "May I ask you something?"

Joost finished his ale. "Of course. This sounds serious."

"It is, I suppose." Pierre searched for words. "As I recall, you went home to begin to study for the priesthood? Is that right?"

"Partially correct. In my faith we do not have priests, but I do plan to study to be a clergyman, a pastor."

"You are Huguenot?"

"Correct."

The fact that they were that night in the very locale where the Edict of Nantes went forth to protect the religion of the Protestants kept creeping into Pierre's thoughts. He glanced around the room. Who was Catholic and who was Protestant?

Joost's demeanor grew guarded. "Why is that any concern of yours?"

Pierre put up his hands to alleviate his friend's uneasiness. "I am one who is seeking God. I mean you no harm." He looked down for a moment, then searched Joost's face. "Can you help me?"

Joost hesitated. "I thought Catholics were seeking conversions to your side, not the other way around." The awful truth of Joost's statement pierced Pierre to the bone. "I don't care whether God is Catholic or Protestant. I just want to know him."

Joost relaxed. He put his hand over Pierre's. "My friend, God is neither Catholic nor Protestant. He is more than and above all religions. He wants to have a personal relationship with his children through Jesus Christ." Joost paused.

Pierre was still leaning forward, so he continued, "That's what the crucifixion and the resurrection were all about—Jesus becoming the mediator between God and man."

Pierre nodded. "This is all beginning to make sense to me. I never understood it until—well, until the other day. I was riding in the woods on my way here and . . ." Pierre told Joost about his plea to God and the breeze—and even about the butterfly.

Joost burst out in laughter. "You don't even know what happened to you, do you? Do you realize what you did?"

Pierre was confused. He didn't know whether to be insulted or laugh with Joost.

Joost lowered his voice. "The Spirit of God has quickened your heart, my friend. You have moved into new life in the Lord. It's what the Scriptures call salvation, the new birth. You are a new creature in Christ."

"Does that mean I'm Huguenot now?"

"Not at all. It simply means you are a true believer."

"What do I do?"

"At some point you need to be baptized. You need to find someone to walk alongside you and teach you the Scriptures. But for the moment—nothing. Just thank the Lord and rejoice in him."

Pierre sat back in his chair and remained silent for a time. He looked at Joost and smiled, tears forming in his eyes. "Why am I crying?"

"Those are tears of joy—tears of tenderness toward the movement of the Spirit of God. Pierre, my new brother, you will never be the same."

Joost and Pierre talked deep into the night at the table by the window. All the other guests had departed or gone to their rooms when they finally retired, long after midnight.

Pierre paused before opening his door. "Will I see you again in the morning?"

"Perhaps. But if not, *au revoir*, until we meet again. I will be praying for you."

"Thank you. Surely God directed our steps to meet at this inn tonight. Does that sound foolish?"

"Not at all. There's no doubt God brought us together. Sleep well."

"Good night." Pierre unlocked his door and went into his room.

He sat on the bed, then he knelt beside it. "God, I don't really know how to pray or what to say. All I know to do is to thank you for touching me. Thank you for arranging the encounter with Joost tonight. Now what am I to do next? Keep on traveling to Brest?"

Pierre sensed nothing, so he shrugged his shoulders, got up, and prepared for bed. *I suppose I'll continue on my way until he tells me something different. Who knows what I shall face in the morning?*

THIRTY-ONE

Pierre heard movement downstairs, the clank of pots and pans, and knew that breakfast must be underway. Doors slammed down the hall, and he heard the thud of footsteps on the wooden stairway. He threw the covers back, jumped out of bed, and dashed some water on his face. He really wanted to see Joost again this morning.

"God, I'm asking you to guide my way today." He stuffed his gear into his pack and opened his door. "Uh . . . Amen."

Joost's door stood ajar. Pierre walked to the open doorway and looked in. The room was cleared out.

He went downstairs and glanced around. No Joost. Pierre was disappointed, but he would try to find his friend again in a few months. He picked up some bread and cheese from the buffet and had the servant fill his wine flask. As he was paying her, he heard a familiar laugh from outside. Joost!

Through the diamond-shaped windowpanes he could see his friend saddling his horse. A slender man, probably in his late thirties or early forties, sat on a chestnut mare beside him. Pierre grabbed his pack and ran outside, still holding the bread in his hand.

"Joost! I thought you'd already left."

"*Bonjour!* And I thought you were going to sleep all day." Joost held the reins to his horse. "I'm glad you caught us. I want you to meet my companion."

Joost introduced Pierre, who tipped his hat. "My pleasure."

"Pierre, this is François Clavell, from Grenoble."

Pierre took a step backward and dropped the bread he was holding. "Wha . . . what did you say your name was?"

"François Clavell."

Pierre stared at the man.

François dismounted. "Are you ill? You look as if you've seen a ghost."

Pierre leaned against the hitching post. He looked toward the sky. Then he looked at Joost. "I-I don't know what to say."

Joost stared at his friend. "What are you talking about?"

"Monsieur Clavell, I was on my way to Brest to find you—sent by the king."

François stepped back, and Joost moved in between the two men, his hand on his sword.

Pierre threw up his hands. "No need for alarm. I was also commissioned by your wife, Madeleine." He shook his head. "This is very complicated."

"Madeleine! Where . . . is she . . . ?"

"She is well, and anxiously awaits word of you." Pierre nodded toward the door of the inn. "May we go back inside? Believe me. What I have to tell you is going to make your journey much faster."

The trio moved inside and sat once again at the table by the window. As Pierre unfolded his story, both men had many questions. The news of the demolished estate saddened François, but knowing his beloved family had escaped soothed his sorrow. François told Pierre of his confrontation with Louis and his time in the galleys, and Pierre told François of their daring rescue of Vangie from the convent. Joost listened and rejoiced with them and wept with them.

After nearly two hours of talking, the men decided to spend another night at the inn and depart for Switzerland in the morning. Joost left his two friends, whom God had brought together in the way only God can, and went to look for Albert to reserve rooms for another night.

He returned to the table. "We are all set. I'm going to go unhitch the horses and put them back in the livery."

François pulled Joost's chair out. "Sit down first."

"What is it?"

"I would like to go by the estate first, before we travel to Switzerland."

Joost tossed a room key to Pierre. "But, François, the manor is in shambles, and Madeleine is not there. That will be a painful visit."

"True, but I need to see it for myself. I need to walk through the grounds and see if anything is salvageable. I want to check on our people—if there are any left."

"I understand." Joost rose from the chair and started toward the door. "On second thought, François, I'll put your horse away, but I think I'll ride into town and pick up some food for our trip. You two have much more to talk about. I'll be back this evening." He looked heavenward. "Thank you, Lord, for this divine encounter."

He waved to the two new comrades. "We'll get an early start in the morning."

AFTER THE INITIAL SHOCK AND EXCITEMENT OF FIND-ing François, Pierre sank into a quiet depression. Finding François sounded the death knell to any hope of continuing his connection with Madeleine. She would no longer require his services, would no longer have any reason to summon him. Perhaps someday he would see her in court. No, on second thought, he realized that she would never again set foot in Versailles. It had become too danger-ous for her.

The three men rode in silence for miles, Joost leading the way. The sun had reached its zenith when Pierre leaned over his saddle and called out, "How long do you think it will take us to ride to Grenoble?"

"It depends on François' stamina. Riding hard, we could make it in ten days. But I think we ought to count on about two weeks."

Pierre smiled. "That's fine with me. I'm in no hurry to get back to court." He reined his horse closer to Joost's. "That life seems far distant now. The world of politics and balls and high society feels artificial. One is constantly on edge trying to guess the true meaning of anoth-er's words. I thought I liked the intrigue of the cat-and-mouse games, but not anymore. I'm weary of it."

Joost nodded. "Why do you think I left? I found a higher cause to serve."

Pierre felt as if he had not only traveled from one side of France to the other, but as if he had entered another country. His perspective of his life, his country, his father, his religion, all had shifted—altered forever.

Joost kicked his horse to a faster gait. "We'd better pick it up, or we'll be three weeks getting to Grenoble." He turned toward François. "If you are up to it, let's put some miles behind us."

François took off his hat and swung it in the air. "I'm right behind you. Let's go, Madame, let's make tracks to *my* madame. Madeleine, here we come!"

"Pierre, I do believe he's feeling better." Joost gave a whoop, and the trio galloped toward the east.

DUSK WAS DESCENDING ON THE LUSH COUNTRYSIDE OF southern France. François had taken the lead the closer they got to Grenoble. He turned in his saddle. "This is it. This is the road to the estate."

No one spoke as they started through the archway of trees leading to the manor. François sat taller in the saddle, preparing himself for what he knew awaited them.

The stone walls of the house loomed against the increasing color of the evening sky as if attempting to retain the dignity of former days. The roof had caved in, and the wooden doors bore scorch marks of the flames that had licked around them from the inside. François reined in at the well beside the driveway where Madeleine had heard his first shouts of warning when the dragoons descended on them, forever changing their lives. One lone hitching post remained beside the front door.

François dismounted and tied his horse to the well, motioning for Joost and Pierre to tie theirs to the hitching post. The roof was gone, but the two chimneys on either end of the house remained, standing like silent sentinels over the wounded chateau. The turret on the back seemed to be intact.

He leaned against the massive front door with his shoulder and pushed. It resisted him but slowly gave way, scraping against the rubble on the floor. François groaned as he surveyed the interior of the once elegant home. Vandals had ransacked anything that might have remained, and droppings indicated that animals had bedded down in the living room.

François sifted through the debris with his foot, stooping to examine an object here and there. Joost and Pierre trailed behind, staring at the devastation.

Pierre shook his head. "To think this was my father's doing. And only because you stood strong in your faith." With tears gathering in his eyes, he looked at François. "I am so sorry. I am embarrassed that I bear the Boveé name. Can you forgive me?"

François spoke barely above a whisper. "This was not your doing. This was the act of soldiers obeying orders from a misguided king."

"Yes, but look at the destruction. There is no good reason for this kind of ruin among civilized men. We all serve the same God, do we not?"

"We do," Joost said, "but this is the result of *religion*, state-ordered religion—not genuine faith in God."

François spotted a shiny object in the charred ashes. He picked up the metal box and blew the soot away. Opening it, he found the set of toy soldiers Charles had been playing with the day the dragoons came. He remembered Madeleine picking one up that the boy had dropped as he rode away to hide in the cave with Jean.

François stuffed the small box in his tunic and climbed over the heavy beams, making his way to the kitchen. The huge stone mantel overhanging the fireplace remained. "It could be rebuilt." François nodded his head, talking to no one in particular as he inspected the ruins. "But it will not be the Clavells who will have that privilege. Not in my lifetime, anyway."

He stepped over the rubble in front of the fireplace. "Come here, Joost, and lift me up on your shoulders."

The young man hoisted François easily. François began to tug on a large, smooth stone above the mantle. He worked it loose and pulled it out, scraping his knuckles as he did.

"Ouch! I do that every time."

Joost, his footing not steady amidst the debris, warned François, "Hurry. I don't think I can hold you much longer. What are you doing?"

François smiled as he pulled a metal chest from the recesses of the wall. "Let me down. I found what I was looking for. I was hoping that Commander Boveé's troops were in such a hurry to burn the house that they didn't take time to search for any valuables."

Joost shrugged François off his shoulders and stepped back.

François opened the chest. "We always kept a stash of coins and some of Madeleine's jewels hidden here for safekeeping."

Pierre laughed, the nervous tension released by the retrieval of the treasure. Joost and François joined in, ending in breathless chuckles.

Pierre finally spoke. "My father would be livid to know that he was outsmarted by a mere country Protestant."

The men continued their laughter and walked out the back door, hanging askew by its hinges, and down the path to the barn. The gardens were overgrown with weeds, but some of the perennials had returned and were attempting to paint a colorful palette on the landscape.

The barn stood unscathed, except for the disrepair of time. François pulled on the door. It creaked, but it opened.

"We can sleep in here tonight." He indicated the stalls. "I've spent many a night in this barn helping a colt into the world." He passed the stall gate where only faint brown spots remained of the bloodstains from the dragoon Jean had killed. He ran his hand along the rough wood.

François inspected the tack room, but vandals, or soldiers, had long ago helped themselves to the fine saddles and bridles that the Clavells once stored there. The hay in the stalls was old and rancid.

The forge and the anvil were still in the center of the barn—too heavy for vandals to tackle. François waved toward the blacksmith tools, remembering repairing the wheel of Madeleine's carriage the night before she left for Versailles.

"We can build a fire and heat water here." He found a bucket in the corner of one of the stalls. "I'll go coax some water from the well. You two get a fire going."

The evening passed in hushed tones as if the spirits of those who once lived on the estate were listening. Joost asked François questions about his responsibilities as a seigneur, how he met Madeleine, about their children. The shadows from the fire in the forge danced on François' face, and he told about the night Jean killed the dragoon in the barn. Joost and Pierre now sat near the spot where the life of a young dragoon left this earth.

François stoked the fire with a stick. "Pierre, you have been quiet tonight."

"I am stunned at the havoc that has been heaped upon your family in the name of God. Even though my father is an officer in the dragoons, he was never around in my childhood. He left us when I was only a little boy. I didn't know . . ." Pierre's eyes welled up and red-dened. "I suppose up until now I have walked through life consumed with selfish ambition, heedless of what was happening to others. I cannot find words to express the sadness in my heart."

François put his hand on Pierre's shoulder. No words needed to be said. These two men's souls had been hammered and melded together on an anvil of persecution. One had been in the fire and the other had been part of wielding the hammer that fashioned the tool, but both were a part of the process.

That night Pierre put aside the yearnings in his heart for Madeleine. In the face of her husband's courage and fidelity, Pierre's love for her would remain locked behind closed doors. He would honor his com-mitment never to speak of love to her again.

Joost laid his head down on his saddle and was soon asleep. François and Pierre once more spent hours discussing the crucible that brought them together.

"Tomorrow we set out for Geneva. We should be able to get there in a few days. I cannot wait to hold my sweet Madeleine and my chil-dren in my arms once again." François straightened his posture and retied his stubborn, thick hair into his queue. "Do you think she will still find me attractive? Do I look too emaciated and poorly?"

Pierre smiled at the sudden vanity from a man who had endured so much. "She will find you as handsome as ever, I'm sure. Now go to sleep, so you will have some color in your cheeks."

The three men settled into sleep as the fire died down.

JOOST WOKE THEM UP, SINGING AND PUSHING THE BARN door open. "Get up, sleepyheads. I have something to discuss with you."

The others rose quickly, ready to get on the last leg of their journey.

"What is it, Joost?" Pierre splashed water from the bucket on his face.

"I've decided to take leave of you here."

François looked at Joost from the stall where he had quartered his horse. "What are you talking about?"

"You have no more need of me. Pierre knows the way through the mountains. You are faring better and better every day. Besides, I sense a strong compulsion to get back to my grandfather." Joost got his saddle. "But there's something I want to do first." He grinned at Pierre.

"And that would be?"

"I want to baptize you in the river." Joost chuckled. "Would that meet with your approval?"

"I-I guess so. Will it be 'legal'? What do you think, François?"

"Absolutely! After all, Joost, you *are* preparing for the ministry. And I am an elder in the church. We'll make it legal. Saddle your horses. We'll go do it right now."

"Let's eat a bite first, then we can head down to the river for the baptism. I'll take my leave of you there and will start for home. You two can head for Geneva."

They rode the brief distance to the river and tied their horses to trees lining the bank. Joost and Pierre removed their boots and hats and waded into the cold water.

Pierre shuddered. "Are you sure this is how you do this?"

Joost's countenance radiated his joy. "Our forefather, John Calvin, stated that the mode is not important, but the declaration that you are a new creature in Christ is." He placed one hand on Pierre's shoulder and dipped the other in the water, pouring it over Pierre's head. "Pierre Boveé, is it your desire to declare to all here present—"

He nodded to François, who smiled in acknowledgement and removed his hat.

"—that you have come to faith and will follow God all the rest of the days of your life?"

"It is."

"Then I baptize you, my brother, in the name of the Father, the Son, and the Holy Ghost."

Joost dipped Pierre in the cold, bubbling stream. And all three shouted, "Amen!"

Shivering and dripping wet, Joost held Pierre around the shoulders as they emerged from the river. "Good-bye, my new brother. I will remember you in my prayers."

"I am honored. I wish I could stay with you and learn from you. You have much wisdom for such a young man."

"I must go attend to my grandfather. But our house is always open to you."

François embraced Joost despite the dripping water. "How can I ever thank you and Isaac? You rescued me from certain death, nursed me back to health, and financed my excursion to find my family."

Joost shook his head as he attempted to dry himself off with a blanket. "Are you an elder in our faith and don't understand that God arranges these things? You should understand that."

"But I must say, I have learned that one views circumstances differently when one is the recipient of such generosity."

"Bow your head and say thank you. That's all you need to do."

All three men swung into their saddles.

François grabbed Joost's arm in farewell. "I shall never forget you and your family. Embrace your grandfather for me. God be with you."

Joost turned west and galloped away, waving as he went. "And with you. *Au revoir.*"

"*Au revoir!*" Pierre and François turned their horses north and started for Grenoble.

THIRTY-TWO

François turned in his saddle and took one last look at the manor. The sun was climbing high overhead, but the two were not in a hurry. François had told Pierre that they couldn't get much farther than Grenoble before nightfall even if they quickened their pace, so there seemed to be no sense in pushing the horses. François pointed out neighboring farms and landmarks to Pierre as the afternoon wore on.

Dusk began to settle on the rolling hills as the two guided their horses into a shallow ravine and set up camp for the night. François had gathered some cabbages that had survived under a heavy mulch of leaves from the overgrown garden at the estate. He coaxed the scrawny vegetables into a watery soup over the fire.

"Tell me what it is like to be Huguenot." Pierre's curiosity about

the religion of his new friends and his recently discovered faith propelled him into questioning this man for whom his admiration was
growing. "I can't imagine what it must be like to live in fear for your life
simply because of what you believe. How did all this come about? If
we all worship the same God, why all the animosity and cruelty?"

"It's a long story."

"We've got time."

"Surely you know the history of the Reformation."

"*Oui*, I know of the German monk, Martin Luther. But as a Catholic,
I'm beginning to think that I may not have been taught the whole
picture."

François smiled. "Wrongs and atrocities have occurred on both
sides."

Pierre tossed a flagon of wine to François, who took a swig.

"The Huguenots' beginnings date back to John Calvin—another
monk. He became a Protestant pastor in Paris and was forced to flee
to Geneva. Calvinist Huguenots came into being around 1550 when
preachers brought Bibles to France from Switzerland. We were a new
'reformed religion' that was practiced by many members of the French
nobility. But even so, we were viewed as protesters—*Protestants*."

"Like Madeleine's family?"

"Yes. Monsieur Vaudois teetered on the brink at times, balancing
his personal beliefs and catering to the whims of King Louis and his
governmental officials." François began to pace back and forth in front
of the fire. "We believe in salvation through individual faith, and the
right to interpret Scripture for oneself. That puts us in direct conflict
with both the Catholic Church and the king of France. May I ask you
something, Pierre?"

"*Oui*."

"In your recent experience with God, did you feel the birth of something new in your spirit?"

"Yes."

"Do you believe that quickening of your spirit to have been brought about by God himself?"

"Absolutely."

"And did that experience require the assistance of a priest?"

"N-no. Though I did need some explanation afterward, which you and Joost so graciously provided."

"To be sure. In order to mature in that new life, we all need instruction. But the initial experience of salvation did not require a priest to usher it in. True?"

"True."

"That is largely what we are fighting about. We do not believe a priest or even the pope has any special powers, including the forgiveness of sins."

Pierre let out a long sigh. "*Mon Dieu*, I didn't know. I understand now why the hatred of the Huguenots is so vicious. To be in opposition to the pope . . ."

"Yes, conflict was inevitable. The Church was concerned over its loss of control over souls. The government feared Protestant demands for a voice in the local rule. And Protestant nobles began to employ their strength for their own political advancement. It all erupted in the St. Bartholomew's Day Massacre in 1572, during the wedding celebration of the arranged marriage of Protestant Henry of Navarre and the Catholic daughter of Catherine de Medici. Thousands of Huguenots were slaughtered. Henry escaped only by agreeing to convert to Catholicism."

François threw a piece of wood on the fire, then continued, "But when Henry became king, he issued the Edict of Nantes, which gave

Huguenots basic civil and religious rights. And though the Edict offered relief for the past seventy or eighty years, it now seems that Louis is yielding to pressure from Catholic churchmen. Madeleine assures me that the king has little knowledge of the actual activities of the dragoons—but that's difficult for me to imagine."

Pierre shifted uncomfortably, shaking his head. "*Non*, I believe that could very possibly be the truth. Although the king keeps a tight rein on governmental decisions, the activities of the military are a different question, especially the dragoons. They have become quite the 'fashionable' segment of the military in the past few years—dashing and masculine. But they are also the basest element, a brutal group." Pierre poked at the fire with a stick. "The opinion among the officials at court is that most of the Huguenots have converted. Obviously that is in error."

"Whether Louis is ignorant of what is going on or whether he is personally issuing the orders, the persecution of the Huguenots is escalating. And for our family in particular . . . we will be hounded until . . ."

"Until when?"

"I don't know. Until we are out of Louis' reach. He will never willingly let Madeleine go. And his arm is long. Many of our brothers and sisters are fleeing to other countries. It's a difficult time for Huguenots."

Pierre stared into the fire. "I am so sorry. I am ashamed."

"No good will come by agonizing about circumstances over which you had no control. You have experienced a change of heart. God is merciful."

A heavy curtain of silence descended, and neither man spoke for a few moments.

Then Pierre asked cautiously, "Did you ever consider converting? Just saying the words in order to save your family, and then go on worshiping God as you please? Surely nobody would blame you."

"I almost did."

Shocked, Pierre said, "You did?"

François nodded. "When I was brought before Louis, I almost relented. What harm could it do? Surely God would understand and forgive me. I'd be protecting my family." A cough interrupted his narration.

François tried to coax a few more drops from the wine flagon. After catching his breath, he continued, "But something beyond my own strength filled my spirit, and I was able to withstand the pressure. If our faith is not worth living—or dying for—what is? God will take care of our families better than I, a mortal man, could ever do. We must trust him even in those perilous, frightening junctures."

"I have much to learn from you." Pierre stared at this battle-weary hero. "How did you survive the galleys?"

"The Bible says that God's grace is sufficient for us. I have found that to be so—whether in the face of cruelty or the threat of death, his grace sustained me. *La Fidelle* was initially a naval ship, and the conscription was grueling and cruel, but then the ship sailed to Brest and was converted back to a merchant ship. That's when Monsieur Fourié found me. God's hand was evident in all of this."

Pierre pushed leaves around in the dirt with a stick. "I don't know that I could have been as brave as you have proved to be. This new life in Jesus Christ has made me feel like a newborn baby in an adult body."

He looked at François through the thin smoke rising from the campfire, then stood and gave the reluctant hero a slight bow—not the exaggerated flourish of the French court, but a humble acknowledgement of an exceptional man.

"You have my utmost admiration, Monsieur Clavell."

THIRTY-THREE

Pierre awoke the next morning to the tortured heaving and coughing of his traveling companion. "That cough sounds serious." He pulled himself out of his sleeping gear and stretched. "Can I do anything for you?"

François sat next to the smoldering fire holding a piece of cloth over his mouth. He looked up at Pierre, his eyes red-rimmed from a sleepless night. "Water—I'd like some water."

When François removed the cloth from his mouth to speak, Pierre saw splotches of blood on the fabric. "I don't like the looks of this. I'll be right back."

Pierre returned quickly from the nearby stream with a container of cold water and poured the clear, cool liquid into a cup. "I thought you were doing better."

"I did too. But I'm afraid it's worse." He reached for his knapsack and pulled out another handkerchief. "Let's ride into Grenoble. I know an apothecary there, a wise woman who knows about medical remedies. She can tell me what to do."

Pierre frowned. "I've seen the work of the king's physicians—butchers, all of them. Spare me from any of those medical charlatans."

"I agree. But Madame Benoît is not like that. She is wise in the ways of the plants and herbs that God provides. I probably need some wild cherry leaves or simply some more honey and wine syrup. She taught Madeleine how to make all sorts of balms and remedies for our family."

"Hmmpff." Pierre didn't appear fully convinced. "If that's what you think we need to do, I'll submit to your wishes. But will you be safe if we venture into town? This was your district, wasn't it?"

"If the king's soldiers aren't about, we are as safe as if we were in our mother's arms. We treated our people justly, and they loved and respected us. I don't expect their feelings have changed."

Pierre began to gather up their gear. "Nevertheless, when we get to the outskirts of town, I will ride on ahead of you and scout it out. To meet a band of dragoons head-on is not what we want, especially some of my father's henchmen. It's possible they could recognize you."

"Very well. But I'm fairly certain we can slip in and out without notice." François looked at the rising sun. "We can make Grenoble easily by noon."

PIERRE RODE INTO GRENOBLE, DAUPHINÉ PROVINCE, WITH the name and memorized directions of how to get to the apothecary shop. The clip-clop of his horse down the streets soon became lost in the normal activity of the marketplace—women with children in tow, businesses open for trade, horses and buggies tied to hitching posts in front of stores, a few beggars here and there lifting their weary eyes to each passerby in hope of a handout.

He proceeded to the address that François had given him, but he saw no sign announcing the occupation of the resident. He tied his horse to a hitching rail out front and rang a small bell at the side of an open window. A ledge jutted out below it, obviously for the dispensing of wares.

A wizened old woman opened the window and peered out. She held a mortar and pestle in her hands and continued to grind with the pestle as she spoke. A fragrant mixture of lavender, thyme, sage, and an amalgamation of herbs drifted through the window.

"What can I do for you, young man?" The old woman set her equipment down on the ledge and wiped her hands on her apron. A long, gray braid hung down her back from under her close-fitting head covering. The strings on the cap hung loose on her shoulders. "I have a good selection of herbs for what ails you."

"Something for a cough."

"*Oui*, monsieur. What kind of cough? Dry? Congested? Lots of phlegm? Consistent? Hacking? From the throat or the chest?"

"So many varieties . . ." Pierre leaned on the ledge. "One that comes on with a vengeance and won't stop. One that is accompanied by . . ."

The old woman raised her eyebrows and waited for him to continue.

"One that ends with blood in the phlegm."

"I see. You look healthy enough to me. Is this for you?"

"No, for my traveling companion. I left him . . . I left him resting."

Pierre proceeded with caution. Should he tell her that the former lord of this area, François Clavell, was on the edge of town waiting for a concoction for his infirmity?

If she knew it was François for whom Pierre inquired, perhaps she would doctor him. But she might turn him over to the authorities. How could he be sure she wouldn't betray them?

"Come in, come in."

Pierre entered the foyer. The walls were lined with heavy, dark wooden shelves that housed hundreds of bottles, each one labeled, all stacked neatly in rows in alphabetical order. Bundles of odorous dried grasses and flowers hung suspended from hooks in the ceiling.

"I am not familiar with this area. Grenoble seems to be a thriving city. Is business good?"

"*Oui*. We have been very fortunate. The weather has been mild this year, and the plants of the fields have been abundant. We have no seigneur at the present, but in the past our governing lord was a good one."

"Where is he now?"

"Carried away by the king's dragoons. We don't know where he is—or his family. They burned the estate."

"Why were they taken away?"

"They are Huguenot and refused to convert. And . . ."

"Yes?"

"They say that Madame Clavell was once a lover of King Louis', and that he issued the invitation for her to return to be his mistress."

"And she refused?"

"*Oui*. How did you know?"

"Did you know the Clavells well?"

"Oh, *oui*, monsieur. They called on me many times through the years, for remedies of all kinds. And I treated the Vaudois family

345

as well, Madame Clavell's family who governed before she married François Clavell."

The woman moved back and forth between the counter and the shelves mixing crushed leaves, seeds, and flowers. "Such a shame. They were a wonderful family."

Pierre lowered his voice. "It is François Clavell who sent me here."

The woman gasped and ceased in her preparations. "You have seen him? He is alive?"

"Yes, but he is very ill. The cough remedy is for him." Pierre lowered his voice. "Monsieur Clavell is the traveling companion of whom I spoke. I am very concerned about his condition."

Madame Benoît took charge of the situation at once. "I will finish mixing the medicine, then you will take me to him. I shall tend to him myself." She untied her apron and threw it on the counter.

"*Oui*, madame." Pierre smiled at her sudden assumption of command.

The woman finished mixing her remedy quickly and locked the front door. She instructed Pierre to follow her to the back of the store. "My buggy is out back. Come."

The pair walked through a back room that obviously served as Madame Benoît's laboratory. A stool stood in front of a long counter where bowls and trays sat holding mixtures of seeds, leaves, and plants. Large jugs of water lined the wall, and basins of water and oil sat at various stages along the counter.

The woman pulled a rough, black woolen cloak, dotted with patches, off a peg on a wooden rack next to the door and hobbled down the steps to the little stable in back of her store.

Pierre helped hitch her horse to an old, rickety buggy. "I'll go around front and get my horse. Monsieur Clavell is anxiously awaiting our return. He will be glad to see you."

Pierre ran through the alley beside the store and mounted his horse. He heard the creaking buggy approaching, and Madame Benoît waved him on as she emerged from the alley onto the street.

Pierre led the old woman back the way he had come into town. *Lord, am I doing the right thing? Is this woman going to turn us into the authorities?* He heard not a sound in reply, but calmness settled about him. *Thank you, Lord. I will proceed.*

THE ODD PAIR, A COURTIER IN KING LOUIS' COURT AND an old woman driving a buggy, arrived at the location in apt time. She was surprisingly adept at keeping up with Pierre.

François sat huddled against a tree, shivering, with a blanket pulled around his shoulders. Pierre jumped from his horse and motioned to Madame Benoît to bring her buggy to a halt. He grabbed her horse's bridle and guided them to the small grove of trees where François rested.

"Madame Benoît!" François stood, the blanket falling to the ground. "I am so glad to see you, but you needn't have left your shop." He bowed slightly to her as she toddled toward her former seigneur.

The woman wasted no time on formalities or small talk. "From what Monsieur Boveé tells me, you need immediate attention." She began to unpack her satchel. "Young man, fetch my other bag for me."

Pierre finished tying up the horses and removed a large black bag from the rear of the buggy.

"And you don't need to be seen in Grenoble. The king's dragoons show up at odd times. We never know when they are in town."

"Thank you, madame. You have taken such good care of us through the years. I just have a cough I can't seem to shake. I'm sure some of your good remedies will fix me up right away." François smiled and patted her hand.

Madame Benoît noticed his bloodstained handkerchief on the rock from which François had arisen. "So, you've been coughing up blood? For how long?"

She motioned for him to sit back down.

"I'm afraid I've had it for several months. It began while I was in the galleys. King Louis sentenced me to the galleys for . . . for . . ."

"It doesn't matter why the king decided to put you there. I hear that it doesn't take much more than being a Huguenot these days to be sentenced to the galleys, hung, or thrown in the Bastille. It sounds as though you have experienced much of the king's wrath." The old woman touched François gently on his forehead. "Hmm. You have a fever."

"Probably so. I've gotten used to it, and I just go on with my days."

"Do you struggle to breathe? Does your chest feel heavy?"

François nodded. "You are correct."

"I can give you something to soothe the cough on a temporary basis, but . . ."

"Tell me what you perceive. I want to know."

Madame Benoît hesitated. "I fear you have contracted *consommation d'huile*. I'd imagine it runs rampant in the galleys."

"Tell me exactly what that means. What should I expect?"

"You may expect seasons of feeling more normal, and then seasons of ill health. As the months progress, however . . ." Madame Benoît lowered her head. She picked up her bag, settled it on the rock, and began to open jars.

"Go ahead, *s'il vous plaît*. I must know the whole truth."

"I am sorry, Monsieur Clavell, but aside from a miraculous intervention of God, you are dying."

None of the three spoke for what seemed an unending space of time. The only sounds to be heard were the sounds of the forest, birds chirping, the rustle of leaves in the breeze.

"How long?" In spite of his malady, François' voice was strong.

"It's hard to tell. And who knows what God, in his mercy, will grant you. You could have two or three more years, if you take care of yourself. Or it could be months, even weeks."

"I see. I suspected as much, although I have felt so much better on our journey back to my family. It's amazing what the prospects of reuniting with the woman he loves will do for a man."

"Love possesses tremendous power for healing."

Pierre watched the man who held the heart of the one woman whom he had ever loved, and felt surprising compassion for him. How strange life was. Pierre held in his care the well-being and safe passage of this man who stood in the way of his being able to claim the woman of his dreams. But take good care of him, Pierre would. He would fulfill his mission.

Madame Benoît dispensed a supply of cough remedies and herbs. "This should last you several weeks. Where are you headed?"

"Geneva. Madeleine awaits me outside of Geneva."

"C'est bon. You will have no trouble purchasing more herbs there. The bugle plant will give you the most relief, in my opinion." She stepped back and packaged the bottles in a leather pouch. "I must get back to my shop."

Pierre unhitched the old woman's horse and put her supplies into the buggy. François helped Madame Benoît into the rig, and Pierre moved to mount his horse.

The woman waved Pierre off. "No need for that. I know the way."

"But, madame, I am happy to escort you back."

"You take care of Monsieur Clavell."

François took Madame Benoît's hand. "Thank you for coming."

"I would not think of doing anything less for you. Take care of yourself. Get to your family and lavish them with love. Cherish your time with them. God be with you, Monsieur Clavell."

François kissed her wrinkled, rough hand. "God bless your healing hands."

François turned to Pierre as the old woman left. "Pierre, I ask of you a favor."

"Anything, my friend."

"You must give me your word." François' eyes pleaded with Pierre. "Madeleine must not know how ill I am."

"But . . ."

"Your word."

Pierre sighed, long and heavy, and nodded. "You have my word."

"Now take me to her—quickly. We have no time to waste."

THIRTY-FOUR

Madeleine climbed the stairs with an armload of heavy quilts that had been washed, dried, and folded to be put away for the approaching summer. She hummed a traditional Huguenot hymn as she raised the lid of a trunk and placed the blankets inside. "Let God arise, let his enemies be scattered . . ."

O, God, I am still trusting you to arise and come to our rescue. Scatter our enemies, confuse them, and bring our—

Madeleine couldn't finish her prayer. She prayed every day, several times a day, for François' safe return to the family. When was God going to answer?

You know my heart, Father. I'm tired, and I'm wondering if my prayers are doing any good, if they are even reaching you. God, have mercy on us. I'm not giving up. I will not give up. I will never give up!

The aroma of chickens and rabbits cooking over the fireplace in the kitchen below drifted up the stairs. Madeleine hurried to finish her chores before the evening meal. Vangie sat on the floor, playing with her doll and a miniature cradle that Henri had carved for her.

"Vangie, put your toys away and go call your brothers in. And all of you wash up for supper."

The little girl screwed up her face and began to complain. "But, Maman . . ."

"No excuses. Go."

Vangie gathered her toys and dumped them into a wooden box in the corner of the room, but held on to one doll. "May I take Lisbeth to supper with me? She's hungry too."

"That's fine."

Vangie skipped out of the room and down the stairs. Madeleine heard her calling to Charles and Philippe, who were helping Jean and Armond with the evening chores.

Suddenly, in a flurry of shouts and stamping of feet on the stairs, Philippe flew into the room, breathless, his eyes bulging. "*Ma-ma-man!* It's . . . it's . . ." He stopped to catch his breath.

"What is it? What's happened?"

"It's Papa! Look out the window—it's Papa!"

Madeleine ran to the window and looked down the road at two horsemen, and at Charles jumping up and down and running toward them. She bounded down the stairs, hardly feeling her feet beneath her. Philippe followed close behind. They pushed past Claudine, who stood in the doorway holding Vangie, bouncing her up and down in her excitement. Vangie stared at the two men. Henri ran as fast as his aged legs would take him, shouting to Jean and Armond, who were washing up outside at the well.

Suzanne appeared at the door of their cottage. She picked up the edge of her skirt and began to run to the main house. "Madame! Madame! Monsieur is here. He's alive. Oh, *mon Dieu*, he's alive!"

Madeleine and Philippe stopped in front of the doorway, nearly colliding with Suzanne as she flew up the porch steps. Pastor Du Puy and Madame Du Puy stood on the porch, clapping their hands and beaming. "Oh, praise God from whom all blessings flow!"

François jumped off his horse, gave the reins to Pierre, and ran toward Madeleine.

She stumbled down the steps into his arms, crying and laughing. "François, you're alive! You've come back to us!" She stood back and peered into his face. "Let me look at you."

"I'm afraid I'm a bit travel worn."

She took his hat off and pushed his hair away from the scar and touched it gently. "You look fine, my dear husband. Oh, I love you so much. I knew you were alive and would find us."

François took her face in his hands and kissed her. "Yes, I am very much alive. And I love you more than you will ever know."

Charles and Philippe crowded around their parents, and François gathered them all in his embrace, threw back his head, and laughed. Jean burst into the family circle and clasped his brother in a bear hug.

François looked around at his family and friends. Then he spotted Vangie, still in Claudine's arms. He walked toward the child. "Come here, Vangie. Don't you know your papa?"

Hesitant, she looked away with her fingers in her mouth, then stretched out her arms to him.

"Awww, that's right, my little one. It's your papa. You do remember, don't you?"

She continued to stare at him. Then she pointed to Pierre. "I remember him."

"Ah, yes. He was your rescuer from the convent, wasn't he? Your hero."

Vangie jumped down from François' arms and into Pierre's.

He laughed and swung her around. "Hello, Princess."

"Hello, Prince." Vangie squealed. "Do it again!"

François smiled. "Looks as if you have an admirer there."

"It's mutual, I assure you. After all, I'm going to marry her when she grows up—right, Vangie?"

Vangie grinned and bobbed her head up and down.

Putting Vangie down, Pierre bowed to Madeleine, sweeping his hat around and taking her hand.

"Nonsense, Pierre. We've been through too much for formalities. Come here." Madeleine embraced him. "*Merci, merci,* my loyal friend. How can I ever thank you? You risked everything you had to salvage our family."

"It was my pleasure, madame. I am ever at your service."

She looked into his eyes and discerned a new thing. His affection for her was still present in his gaze, but something else, something deep, glimmered through his eyes into hers. "You seem different, Pierre."

"*Oui,* madame. I am different."

François stepped in. "You have no idea how different. Pierre and I have talked for hours on our journey. God has proven himself mighty in all of our stories. We have much to talk about, much to tell."

François turned around to view the entourage around him. "Where are Elisabeth—and Thérèse?"

Henri shook his head, and Madeleine took François' arm. "They are both gone, my love. As you just said, we have much to talk about."

Pastor Du Puy joined the group. "What a glorious day! We must praise God for his faithfulness." With no introduction or preparation, he began, "Heavenly Father, our hearts are so full of thanksgiving we can hardly contain ourselves. You are good, and your mercy endures forever."

Madeleine stood beside François, grasping his arm and hand. The children gathered around their reunited parents. Jean pulled his cap off and bowed his head. Madame Du Puy raised her hands in praise to God, and Henri, Armond, and the others bowed their heads as Pastor Du Puy prayed.

Madeleine glanced at François and gripped his hand more tightly. Out of the corner of her eye, she could see Pierre kneeling in the dust. Tears streamed down his cheeks.

The pastor finished his prayer with a hearty *Amen!* "Now everybody, come in. Come in! This is a day the Lord has made. It's time to fellowship and rejoice."

Everybody began chattering at once and moved into the house. "Where did you find each other?" "Are you well, François?" "How did you survive the galleys?" "How did you get out of the galleys?"

François held up his hands. "It's a long, unbelievable story. A story of God's mercy and grace." He laughed again. "Let's sit down, and I will begin."

AFTER HIS MORNING LEVER, KING LOUIS MOVED QUICKLY through the Grande Entrée to his office to issue orders for the day before going to Mass. In the midst of instructing the Most Exalted of the Court, a courtier entered.

"Your Majesty, an emissary from Switzerland awaits an audience with you."

"Ah! Very good. Send him in."

An obviously road-weary courier was escorted into the private room and bowed before the king.

"Yes, my boy. What news do you have for me from Geneva?"

"We delivered your mandate, Your Majesty, to expel the Huguenots from their city. Then we stationed ourselves to watch their progress. They set about informing the French Protestants that they were no longer welcome, and in a few days, with great ceremony, they began escorting the refugees out of the front gates of the city."

Louis' face lit up. "Continue."

The courier hesitated.

"Go on, go on."

"Sire, I regret to tell you . . ." The young man seemed unable to continue. "They, well, they . . ."

"I command you to tell me what happened!" Louis thundered, pounding his cane on the floor.

The courier, visibly shaken, finally communicated his findings to the king. "The Swiss s-simply allowed the Huguenots to come back into the city by way of the back gates! Not-not only allowed them back in, but welcomed them with open arms." The lad seemed unable to look up.

Louis' voice began in a rumble and exploded in a roar. "What are you telling me? That the Swiss have refused my mandate to expel the Huguenots from their cities?"

"It seems incredible, b-but that is what we observed."

Louis whipped around and paced the floor, his officials backing up to give him plenty of room. He faced the courier. "You are dismissed. Please remain available at the chateau for further orders."

"Yes, Your Majesty." The cringing courier backed out in a bow and fairly ran from the private royal quarters.

"We shall see about this. The Swiss cannot defy the king of France that easily. There will be consequences." The king sat at his desk, muttering to himself. "We shall see . . ."

Later that day, King Louis watched his son, the heir to the throne of France, ride alongside him, chasing the hounds that were after a wolf. He was a perfect son. Louis was very proud of him, his only legitimate son, his firstborn.

Louis chuckled to himself at his son's aggression in the hunt. The Grand Dauphin liked nothing better than hunting wolves. They were after one particularly cunning old wolf that continued to elude the Dauphin. He had chased this one three times, and the clever canine always managed to escape. But the king was certain that one day the wolf's luck would run out, and they would capture him. Nothing could escape the seizure of the king forever.

The reunited Clavell family, their hosts, and friends talked throughout the meal, jumping from one subject to another, punctuated by questions from the children. After the meal, they sat around the fireplace chatting. Vangie fell asleep in her papa's lap. Henri, Armond, and Suzanne went to their cottages, and the Du Puys excused themselves. Charles drifted off to sleep on the floor, surrounded by the toy soldiers his father had salvaged from the ashes of the estate.

Madeleine sat next to François, her hand on his arm. She stroked his hair and squeezed his hand from time to time. She just wanted to be next to him, to touch him, to reassure herself that he was home. He was truly home.

François turned to Madeleine and motioned her to come outside with him. He pushed open the wooden door, and they stepped out onto the porch. A full moon sat on the crest of the mountaintops and painted the landscape with shadowy fingers.

François gathered his wife in his arms. His voice barely above a whisper, he asked a question that had been burning in his spirit. "Madeleine, when I was brought in front of Louis before he sent me to the galleys, he-he insinuated that Philippe could be his son. Please understand—after all we have suffered, it makes no difference in how I feel about either of you. I am just so grateful we are alive and together again. But I need to know. It would answer the question as to why the king has become so persistent in his vengeance upon our family."

He pulled back and looked at her with an intensity she had never seen in his eyes before. "I want all things to be clean and fresh as we begin the rest of our lives together. I feel I've been given the gift of life for a second time, reborn. I just need to know."

Madeleine brushed his hair out of his eyes. "I missed doing that. I love your stubborn, unruly hair." She smiled at him. "My sweet, gentle François. You are so good." She took his hands in hers. "When I was at court, Louis and I were very young, and I made some foolish choices. I was in love with him. He beguiled me and swept me off my feet. I thought he would be true to the pronouncements of love that he made to me."

She paused for a long while. François waited.

The sound of crickets chirping in the night air became deafening.

Finally she spoke. "When my parents realized what was happening between Louis and me, they took me away. I never told my parents the details of our relationship, but they suspected. I never saw Louis after we left court, although he sent couriers and messages begging me to come back. He married Marie Thérèse three months after that. In the meantime, you came into my life."

Madeleine laughed. "And, in your quiet way, you enchanted me. I realized then that what I had felt for Louis was mere infatuation. What young girl wouldn't be enamored with the attentions of a king? But what I felt for you was genuine love—love that would sustain a family and a life." She hesitated again. "*Non, mon amour,* I was not pregnant when we married. Philippe is not Louis' son. He is your son, François. He is a Clavell."

François looked up at the night sky, then closed his eyes and inhaled a long, deep breath. Looking at his wife in the moonlight, he cupped her face in his hands. "You are so beautiful." He kissed her on one cheek, and then on the other. "Thank you, *ma bien aimée.* Thank you for loving me, for believing in me, and . . . and for not giving up. Thank you for fighting to preserve our family."

The couple lingered for a bit on the porch in silence. Madeleine stood in front of François with her back to him, cradled in his arms, the freedom of truth washing the grime of the past two years from their souls. They gazed at the moon bathing the foothills and the meadow with its luminous glow.

François turned her around. "To merely say '*Je t'aime*' seems trite. But I can't think of any other words to tell you how I feel and what a treasure you are to me. We are indeed most blessed."

After a few more minutes, Madeleine and François went back inside and joined the small gathering. Pierre sat on the fringes of the circle of the Clavell family, joining in the conversation from time to time. Madeleine smiled at him from across the room, and then turned her attention to something François was saying. But not before she detected a flicker of emotion in the handsome courtier's gray eyes. He avoided her gaze the rest of the evening.

Madeleine watched her children and the men around the fire, and, for the first time in two years, felt safe within the embrace of her family. What would they do? Where would they go? She didn't know—perhaps they would go to Holland, or maybe even across the ocean to the New World. Wherever they went, she knew they would never again bear the terror of religious persecution. They were together. They were free. They had emerged from the shadow of the Sun King.

Author Note

An odor—stale, sour—filtered from the plastic bag and mingled with the musty air of the attic. Brown, brittle pieces of dry leather fluttered from the container as I gently removed the antique epistle from its protective covering—a published genealogy of my family, dating from the seventeenth century—what a treasure! A mere quirk landed the worn book in my possession when my elderly aunt passed away. It had not been willed to me. It simply ended up with me. I secretly hoped none of my cousins would remember it and show up one day, hand outstretched, to claim ownership of the journal.

I turned the delicate pages and began to read of the religious turmoil in France that fashioned forever the beliefs and destiny of the Clewell family. The French spelling differed—*Clavel*, sometimes *Clavell*. Why did that matter to my ancestors to change it? It seemed to me a minor point.

I stared at the journaling of the vibrant soul of my family, whittled to impersonal black notations on a yellowed antique page. I was humbled by the sacrifice my ancestors made for our faith. The words of the volume drew me into their world.

Thus began my journey in recreating, in my imagination, the journey of the Clavell family from Grenoble, Dauphiné Province, France.

I have attempted to keep the "bones" of the history of the persecution of the French Huguenots in seventeenth-century France accurate. The information surrounding King Louis and Versailles are factual, aside from the connection with the Clavell family. The sinew, muscle, and flesh of the story are fictitious.

Thank you for coming on this journey with me. I trust that as you read about the Clavell family's search for religious freedom that you, too, will find yourself grateful for those who have gone before us and were found faithful.

I would love to hear from you. E-mail me at GPar0719@aol.com or join my blog at www.goldenkeyesparsons.com.

Reading Group Guide

1. What, if anything, do you know about your family heritage? Before reading *In the Shadow of the Sun King*, had you ever considered that your ancestors may have had to pay a costly price for the freedom you enjoy?

2. Name two ways in which you can relate to Madeleine and François. Name two ways in which you cannot.

3. What do you think was the most difficult obstacle Madeleine had to face? List in order of difficulty, with 5 being the most challenging.

    ____ Her children's lives being in jeopardy

    ____ Not knowing whether her husband was dead or alive, perhaps having to endure tortuous, life-threatening conditions

    ____ Having to flee her country, lose her home, and begin a new life

    ____ Losing her mother

    ____ Confronting King Louis

4. How did you respond when Jean had to kill the dragoon in the barn? Were you shocked? What was your opinion of him after

that? What about after he led the attack on the soldiers in the forest? Do you think Jean was ever able to recover emotionally from these two incidents?

5. What were your feelings toward King Louis as the story developed? Did you empathize with him at all?

6. Did you find yourself hoping Pierre would express his feelings to Madeleine? Why or why not?

7. Did you hope Pierre and Madeleine would end up together, or did you want Madeleine to remain faithful and reunite with François? Why or why not?

8. How do you think you would react in the face of outright persecution of your faith? What if your family were in danger, and all you had to do to rescue them from that threat was to say, "I convert"?

9. Do you think King Louis truly cared for Madeleine? Why or why not?

10. Why do you think King Louis was so persistent in pursuing Madeleine?

11. Do you believe that Philippe was King Louis' son or François' son? Give reasons for your opinion.

12. Do you think King Louis was sincere in his desire to convert the Huguenots, or was he simply a tyrant?

13. What character traits in Madeleine do you most admire? With which character flaws do you identify?

14. Which scene was your favorite?

Acknowledgements

L ittle did I know as a first-time author how many people would be involved in the publication of the *Darkness to Light* novels. There are too many to acknowledge, but I must try to name a few.

First of all, I want to thank Marita Littauer of CLASS, who was the first one to say to me, "You need to be published." And then she put feet to that, forming a critique group consisting of Linda Jewell, Raelene Searle, Sherri Buerkle, Marita, and myself, who met every month in Albuquerque, New Mexico. Those women slashed my manuscripts with plenty of red marks, but always bound up the wounds with words of encouragement. Marita, who was the director of the Glorieta Christian Writers Conference at the time, offered me the opportunity to serve on staff, where I met my agent . . .

Mary Beth Chappell, Zachary Shuster Harmsworth Literary & Entertainment Agency, New York, New York, without whom I am certain I would still be seeking a publisher. She believed in the manuscript from the beginning and she believed in me, and was always ready to go to bat for both.

To my physical family: my husband, Blaine, and our three beautiful girls—Amber, Andra, and Amanda—who are now three beautiful grown women; to our grandsons, Evan and James, who served as the prototypes for Philippe and Charles; to the other grandsons, Cody, Cale, Casey, Collin, and Seth, who provided characteristics and mannerisms for the story; and especially to our granddaughter, Crysta, who thinks her "Go-Go" can do anything. They never ceased to believe in me.

To my spiritual family at Faith Mountain Fellowship Church, Red River, New Mexico, who genuinely inquired from time to time, "How's the book coming?" And to the board of our ministry, Matters of the Heart, Wayne and Marsha Kidd, who encouraged, supported, and prayed for this book and the right publisher.

To Thomas Nelson Publishing and especially my editors, Natalie Hanemann, who is so easy to work with and who fell in love with the story from the beginning, and LB Norton, under whose radar for perfection my novel emerged better than I could ever have written it on my own.

To my dad, Chester Arthur Keyes, Jr., long since deceased, who, as a newspaper editor/printer, developed in me at an early age a love and passion for the written word. A very troubled man in many ways, nevertheless, he would have been so proud of this book and of me.

And most of all, this whole process has been such a "God thing." Thank you, Jesus. To you belongs all the glory.

COMING FALL 2009

A Prisoner at Versailles

BOOK 2 IN THE
DARKNESS TO LIGHT SERIES